My Life
as an Indian

Fort Benton, from a photograph taken in the early eighties

My Life
as an Indian

The Story of a Red Woman and a White Man
in the Lodges of the Blackfeet

J. W. Schultz

Skyhorse Publishing

Skyhorse Publishing books may be purchased in bulk at special
discounts for sales promotion, corporate gifts, fund-raising, or
educational purposes. Special editions can also be created to
specifications. For details, contact the Special Sales Department,
Skyhorse Publishing, 307 West 36th Street, 11th Floor, New York,
NY 10018 or info@skyhorsepublishing.com.

Skyhorse® and Skyhorse Publishing® are registered trademarks of
Skyhorse Publishing, Inc.®, a Delaware corporation.

www.skyhorsepublishing.com

10 9 8 7 6 5 4

Library of Congress Cataloging-in-Publication Data

Schultz, James Willard, 1859-1947.
  My life as an Indian : the story of a Red woman and a White
man in the lodges of the Blackfeet / J.W. Schultz.
      p. cm.
  ISBN 978-1-60239-734-7 (pbk.)
  1. Schultz, James Willard, 1859-1947. 2. Schultz, James Willard,
1859-1947--Relations with Indians. 3. Siksika Indians--Social
life and customs. 4. Piegan Indians--Social life and customs.
5. Montana--Social life and customs. 6. Pioneers--Montana-
-Biography. 7. Whites--Montana--Biography. 8. Interracial
marriage--Montana. 9. Montana--Biography. 10. West (U.S.)--
Biography. I. Title.
  E99.S54S3 2009
  978'.00497--dc22
  [B]
                                              2009024936

Printed in the United States of America

PUBLISHER'S NOTE

Under the title of "In the Lodges of the Blackfeet," this story originally appeared as a serial in "Forest and Stream."

EDITORIAL NOTE

In this account of his long residence with the Blackfeet, Mr. Schultz has given us a remarkable story. It is an animated and vivid picture of Indian life. The scene is on the plains in the old days, in the picturesque period when the tribe lived in a primitive way, subsisting on the buffalo and at war with hostile neighbours. It is a true history and not romance, yet abounds in romantic incident. In its absolute truthfulness lies its value.

The book has extraordinary interest as a human document. It is a study of human nature in red. The author has penetrated the veil of racial indifference and misunderstanding and has got close to the heart of the people about whom he writes. Such an intimate revelation of the domestic life of the Indians has never before been written. The sympathetic insight everywhere evident is everywhere convincing. We feel that the men and the women portrayed are men and women of actual living existence. And while in the lodges on the Marias the elemental passions have fuller and franker sway, we recognise in the Blackfoot as here revealed a creature of common humanity like our own. His are the same loves and hates and hopes and fears. The motives which move him are those which move us. The Indian is the white man without the veneer of civilisation.

The chapters of this volume were published serially in "Forest and Stream" under the title "In the Lodges of the Blackfeet" and over the *pseudonym* W. B. Anderson. The title page now bears the author's real name. Not only is the story a true one, but many of the characters still live, though to-day under conditions as different as though centuries had intervened. FATHER PRANDO died in the year 1906.

GEO. BIRD GRINNELL.

CONTENTS

PRINCIPAL CHARACTERS

NÄT-AH'-KI—A Blackfoot Indian girl who becomes the wife of the AUTHOR; a cheerful and sweet-tempered woman about whom the interest of the story centres. The book's finest character.

THE CROW WOMAN—An Arickaree captured long ago by the Crows and later taken from them by the Bloods.

MRS. BERRY—A Mandan woman, wife of an old time Indian trader, mother of BERRY and friend of the CROW WOMAN; learned in the ancient lore of her tribe.

DIANA—An orphan Indian girl, educated by ASHTON; a noble and brilliant woman, who meets a tragic death.

THE AUTHOR—At the age of twenty goes west to Montana Territory in search of wild life and adventure, and finds both with the Piegan Blackfeet; he marries into the tribe and lives with them for many years; goes with them on the hunt, and on the warpath; joins in their religious ceremonies; and as a squawman lives the Indian life.

BERRY—A mixed-blood Indian trader, born on the upper Missouri River; speaks half a dozen Indian languages, and is very much at home in Indian camps; an adept at all the tricks of the Indian trade.

SORREL HORSE—White man, trapper, and Indian trader; has an Indian family.

ASHTON—A young white man from the East who carries about with him a secret sorrow but finds peace at last.

FATHER PRANDO—A devoted Jesuit Priest whose life is given to mission work among the Indians. The Blackfeet's friend, comforter, and helper during the terrible Famine Year.

RISING WOLF—Early Hudson Bay man, typical trapper, trader, and interpreter of the romantic days of the early fur-trading period.

HEAVY BREAST—A Blackfoot partisan, leader of war parties, the possessor of a medicine pipe.

WOLVERINE—A Blackfoot, brother-in-law of SORREL HORSE, whom the AUTHOR helped to steal his wife.

WEASEL TAIL
TALKS-WITH-THE-BUFFALO } Blackfeet, close friends and hunting and war companions of the AUTHOR.

LIST OF ILLUSTRATIONS

My Life
as an Indian

MY LIFE AS AN INDIAN

CHAPTER I

FORT BENTON

WIDE, brown plains, distant, slender, flat-topped buttes; still more distant giant mountains, blue-sided, sharp-peaked, snow-capped; odour of sage and smoke of camp fire; thunder of ten thousand buffalo hoofs over the hard, dry ground; long-drawn, melancholy howl of wolves breaking the silence of night, how I loved you all!

I am in the sere and yellow leaf, dried and shrivelled, about to fall and become one with my millions of predecessors. Here I sit, by the fireplace in winter, and out on the veranda when the days are warm, unable to do anything except live over in memory the stirring years I passed upon the frontier. My thoughts are always of those days; days before the accursed railroads and the hordes of settlers they brought swept us all, Indians and frontiersmen and buffalo, from the face of the earth, so to speak.

The love of wild life and adventure was born in me, yet I must have inherited it from some remote ancestor, for all my near ones were staid, devout people. How I hated the amenities and conventions of society; from my earliest youth I was happy only when out in the great forest which lay to the north of my home, far beyond the sound of church and school bell, and the whistling locomotives. My visits to those grand old woods were necessarily brief, only during summer and winter vacations. But a day came when I could go where and when I chose, and one warm April morning long ago I left St. Louis on a Missouri River steamboat, bound for the Far West.

The Far West! Land of my dreams and aspirations! I had read and re-read Lewis and Clark's "Journal," Catlin's "Eight Years," "The Oregon Trail," Fremont's expeditions; at last I was to see some of the land and the tribes of which they told. The sturdy flatbottom, shallow-draft, stern-wheel boat was tied to the shore every evening at dusk, resuming her way at daylight in the morning, so I saw every foot of the Missouri's shores, 2,600 miles, which lay between the Mississippi and our destination, Fort Benton, at the head of navigation. I saw the beautiful groves and rolling green slopes of the lower river, the weird "bad lands" above them, and the picturesque cliffs and walls of sandstone, carved into all sorts of fantastic shapes and form by wind and storm, which are the features of the upper portion of the navigable part of the river. Also I saw various tribes of Indians encamped upon the banks of the stream, and I saw more game than I had thought ever existed. Great herds of buffalo swimming the river often impeded the progress of the boat. Numberless elk and deer inhabited the groves and slopes of the valley. On the open bottoms grazed bands of antelope, and there were bighorn on nearly every butte and cliff of the upper river. We saw many grizzly bears, and wolves, and coyotes; and in the evenings, when all was still aboard, the beavers played and splashed alongside the boat. What seemed to me most remarkable of all, was the vast number of buffalo we passed. All through Dakota, and through Montana clear to Fort Benton, they were daily in evidence on the hills, in the bottoms, swimming the river. Hundreds and hundreds of them, drowned, swollen, in all stages of decomposition, lay on the shallow bars where the current had cast them, or drifted by us down the stream. I believe that the treacherous river, its quicksands, and its unevenly frozen surface in winter, played as great havoc with the herds as did the Indian tribes living along its course. We passed many and many a luckless animal, sometimes a dozen or more in a place, standing under some steep bluff which they had vainly endeavoured to climb, and there they were, slowly but surely sinking down, down into the tenacious black mud or sands, until finally the turbid water would flow smoothly on over their lifeless forms. One would naturally think that animals crossing a stream and finding themselves under a high cut bank would turn out again into the stream and swim down until they found a good landing place; but this is just what the buffalo, in many cases, did not do. Having once determined to go to a certain place, they made a bee-line for it; and, as in the case of those we saw dead and dying under the cut banks, it seemed as if they chose to die rather than to make a detour in order to reach their destination.

After we entered the buffalo country there were many places which I passed with regret; I wanted to stop off and explore them. But the captain of the boat would say: "Don't get impatient; you must keep on to Fort Benton; that's the place for you, for there you'll meet traders and trappers from all over the Northwest, men you can rely upon and travel with, and be reasonably safe. Good God, boy, suppose I should set you ashore

here? Why, in all likelihood you wouldn't keep your
scalp two days. These here breaks and groves shelter
many a prowlin' war party. Oh, of course, you don't
see 'em, but they're here all the same."

Foolish "tenderfoot," innocent "pilgrim" that I was,
I could not bring myself to believe that I, I who thought
so much of the Indians, would live with them, would
learn their ways, would be a friend to them, could possibly receive any harm at their hands. But one day,
somewhere between the Round Butte and the mouth of
the Musselshell River, we came upon a ghastly sight.
On a shelving, sandy slope of shore, by a still smouldering
fire of which their half-burned skiff formed a part, lay
the remains of three white men. I say remains ad-
visedly, for they had been scalped and literally cut to
pieces, their heads crushed and frightfully battered,
hands and feet severed and thrown promiscuously about.
We stopped and buried them, and it is needless to say
that I did not again ask to be set ashore.

Ours was the first boat to arrive at Fort Benton that
spring. Long before we came in sight of the place the
inhabitants had seen the smoke of our craft and made
preparations to receive us. When we turned the bend
and neared the levee, cannon boomed, flags waved, and
the entire population assembled on the shore to greet us.
Foremost in the throng were the two traders who had
sometime before bought out the American Fur Company, fort and all. They wore suits of blue broadcloth,
their long-tailed, high-collared coats bright with brass
buttons; they wore white shirts and stocks, and black
cravats; their long hair, neatly combed, hung down to
their shoulders. Beside them were their skilled employees—clerks, tailor, carpenter—and they wore suits
of black fustian, also brass-buttoned, and their hair was

likewise long, and they wore parfleche-soled moccasins, gay with intricate and flowery designs of cut beads. Behind these prominent personages the group was most picturesque; here were the French employees, mostly creoles from St. Louis and the lower Mississippi, men who had passed their lives in the employ of the American Fur Company, and had cordelled many a boat up the vast distances of the winding Missouri. These men wore the black fustian capotes, or hooded coats, fustian or buckskin trousers held in place by a bright-hued sash. Then there were bull-whackers, and mule-skinners, and independent traders and trappers, most of them attired in suits of plain or fringed and beaded buckskin, and nearly all of them had knives and Colt's powder and ball six-shooters stuck in their belts; and their headgear, especially that of the traders and trappers, was home-made, being generally the skin of a kit fox roughly sewn in circular form, head in front and tail hanging down behind. Back of the whites were a number of Indians, men and youths from a near by camp, and women married to the resident and visiting whites. I had already learned from what I had seen of the various tribes on our way up the river, that the everyday Indian of the plains is not the gorgeously attired, eagle plume bedecked creature various prints and written descriptions had led me to believe he was. Of course, all of them possessed such fancy attire, but it was worn only on state occasions. Those I now saw wore blanket or cow (buffalo) leather leggings, plain or beaded moccasins, calico shirts, and either blanket or cow-leather toga. Most of them were bareheaded, their hair neatly braided, and their faces were painted with reddish-brown ochre or Chinese vermilion. Some carried a bow and quiver of arrows; some had flint-lock fukes, a few the more

modern cap-lock rifle. The women wore dresses of calico;
a few "wives" of the traders and clerks and skilled
labourers even wore silk, and gold chains and watches,
and all had the inevitable gorgeously hued and fringed
shawl thrown over their shoulders.

At one glance the eye could take in the whole town,
as it was at that time.   There was the great rectangular
adobe fort, with bastions mounting cannon at each corner.   A short distance above it were a few cabins, built
of logs or adobe.   Back of these, scattered out in the
long, wide flat-bottom, was camp after camp of trader
and trapper, string after string of canvas-covered
freighters' wagons, and down at the lower end of the
flat were several hundred lodges of Piegans. All this
motley crowd had been assembling for days and weeks,
impatiently awaiting the arrival of the steamboats. The
supply of provisions and things brought up by the boats
the previous year had fallen far short of the demand.
There was no tobacco to be had at any price.   Keno
Bill, who ran a saloon and gambling house, was the only
one who had any liquor, and that was alcohol diluted
with water, four to one.   He sold it for a dollar a drink.
There was no flour, no sugar, no bacon in the town, but
that did not matter, for there was plenty of buffalo and
antelope meat.   What all craved, Indians and whites,
was the fragrant weed and the flowing bowl.   And
here it was, a whole steamboat load, together with a
certain amount of groceries; no wonder cannon boomed
and flags waved, and the population cheered when the
boat hove in sight.

I went ashore and put up at the Overland Hotel,
which was a fair-sized log cabin with a number of log-
walled additions.   For dinner we had boiled buffalo
boss ribs, bacon and beans, "yeast powder" biscuit,

coffee with sugar, molasses, and stewed dried apples. The regular guests scarcely touched the meat, but the quantities of bread, syrup, and dried apples they stowed away was surprising.

That was a day to me, a pilgrim fresh from the East, from the "States," as these frontiersmen called it, full of interest. After dinner I went back to the boat to see about my luggage. There was a gray-bearded, long-haired old trapper standing on the shore looking absently out over the water. His buckskin trousers were so bagged at the knees that he seemed to be in the attitude of one about to jump out into the stream. To him approached a fellow passenger, a hair-brained, windy, conceited young fellow bound for the mining country, and said, looking intently at the aforesaid baggy knees, "Well, old man, if you're going to jump, why don't you jump, instead of meditating over it so long?"

He of the buckskins did not at first comprehend, but following the questioner's intent stare he quickly saw what was meant. "Why, you pilgrim," he replied, "jump yourself." And instantly grasping the youth by the legs below the knees he heaved him out into about three feet of water. What a shout of laughter and derision arose from the bystanders when the ducked one reappeared and came gasping, spluttering, dripping ashore. He looked neither to the right nor the left, but hurried on board to the seclusion of his cabin, and we saw him no more until he pulled out on the stage the next morning.

I had letters of introduction to the firm which had bought out the American Fur Company. They received me kindly and one of them took me around introducing me to the various employees, residents of the town, and to several visiting traders and trappers.

Of the latter I met one, a man only a few years older than myself, who I was told was the most successful and daring of all the traders of the plains. He spoke a number of Indian languages perfectly, and was at home in the camps of any of the surrounding tribes. We somehow took to each other at once, and I passed the balance of the afternoon in his company. Eventually we became great friends. He still lives; and as I may in the course of this story tell some of the things we did together, for which we are now both truly sorry, I will not give his right name. The Indians called him the Berry; and as Berry he shall be known in these chronicles of the old plains life. Tall, lean, long-armed and slightly stoop-shouldered, he was not a fine looking man, but what splendidly clear, fearless dark brown eyes he had; eyes that could beam with the kindly good nature of those of a child, or fairly flash fire when he was aroused to anger.

It was not half an hour after the arrival of the steamboat, before whisky dropped to the normal price of "two bits" per drink, and tobacco to $2 per pound. The white men, with few exceptions, hied to the saloons to drink, and smoke, and gamble. Some hurried to load their wagons with sundry kegs and make for the Indian camp at the lower end of the bottom, and others after loading ran out on the Teton as fast as their horses could go. The Indians had hundreds and hundreds of prime buffalo robes, and they wanted whisky. They got it. By the time night closed in, the single street was full of them charging up and down on their pinto ponies, singing, yelling, recklessly firing their guns, and vociferously calling, so I was told, for more liquor. There was a brisk trade that night at the rear doors of the saloons. An Indian would pass in a good head and tail buffalo robe and receive for it two and even three bottles of liquor. He might just as well have walked boldly in at the front door and traded for it over the bar, I thought, but I learned that there was a United States marshal somewhere in the Territory, and that there was no telling when he would turn up.

In the brightly lighted saloons the tables were crowded by the resident and temporary population, playing stud and draw poker, and the more popular game of faro. I will say for the games as played in those wide open and lawless days that they were perfectly fair. Many and many a time I have seen the faro bank broken, cleaned out of its last dollar by lucky players. You never hear of that being done in the "clubs," the exclusive gambling dens of to-day. The men who ran games on the frontier were satisfied with their legitimate percentage, and they did well. The professionals of to-day, be it in any town or city where gambling is prohibited, with marked cards, false-bottom faro boxes, and various other devices take the players' all.

I never gambled; not that I was too good to do so, but somehow I never could see any fun in games of chance. Fairly as they were conducted there was always more or less quarreling over them. Men a half or two-thirds full of liquor are prone to imagine things and do what they would recoil from when sober; and, if you take notice, you will find that, as a rule, those who gamble are generally pretty heavy drinkers. Somehow the two run together. The professional may drink also, but seldom when he is playing. That is why he wears broadcloth and diamonds and massive gold watch chains; he keeps cool and rakes in the drunken plunger's coin. In Keno Bill's place that evening I was looking on at a game of faro. One of those bucking it was a tall, rough, bewhiskered bull-whacker, full of whisky and quarrelsome, and he was steadily losing. He placed a blue chip, $2.50, on the nine spot, and coppered it; that is, he placed a small marker upon it to signify that it would lose; but when the card came it won, and the dealer flicked off the marker and took in the chip.

"Here, you," cried the bull-whacker. "What you doin'? Give me back that chip and another one with it. Don't you see that the nine won?"

"Of course it won," the dealer replied, "but you had your bet coppered."

"You're a liar!" shouted the bull-whacker, reaching for his revolver and starting to rise from his seat.

I saw the dealer raising his weapon, and at the same instant Berry, crying out, "Down! Down!" dragged me with him to the floor; everyone else in the room who could not immediately get out of the door also dropped prone to the floor. There were some shots, fired so quickly that one could not count them; then there was a short dense silence, broken by a gasping, gurgling groan. Men shuffled to their feet and hurried over to the smoke-enveloped corner. The bull-whacker, with three bullet holes in his bosom, lay back in the chair from which he had attempted to arise, quite dead; the faro dealer, white, but apparently calm, stood on the opposite side of the table stanching with his handkerchief the blood from the nasty furrow a bullet had ploughed in his right cheek.

"Close call for you, Tom," said some one.

"He sure branded me," the dealer grimly replied.

"Who was he? What outfit was he with?" was asked.

"Don't know what his name was," said Keno Bill "but I believe he rolled in with Missouri Jeff's bull-train

Let's pack him into the back room, boys, and I'll get word to his friends to come an' plant him."

This was done; the blood-stained chair was also removed, ashes were scattered on some dark spots staining the floor, and after all hands had taken a drink on the house the games were resumed. Berry and I strolled out of the place. I felt queer; rather shaky in the legs and sick at the stomach. I had never before seen a man killed; for that matter, I had never even seen two men in a fist fight. I could not forget that terrible death gurgle, nor the sight of the dead man's distorted face and staring eyes.

"Awful, wasn't it?" I remarked.

"Oh, I don't know," Berry replied, "the fish got what he was looking for; these bad men always do, sooner or later. He started first to pull his gun, but he was a little too slow."

"And what next?" I asked. "Will not the dealer be arrested? Will not we be subpœnaed as witnesses in the case?"

"Who will arrest him?" my friend queried in turn. "There are no police, nor officers of the law here of any description."

"Why—why, how, then, with so many desperate characters as you evidently have here, how do you manage to preserve any form of law and order?"

"Seven—eleven—seventy-seven," Berry sententiously replied.

"Seven—eleven—seventy-seven," I mechanically repeated. "What is that?"

"That means the Vigilance Committee. You don't know exactly who they are, but you may be sure that they are representative men who stand for law and order; they are more feared by criminals than are the courts and prisons of the East, for they always hang a murderer or robber. Another thing; do not think that the men you saw sitting at the tables in Keno Bill's place are, as you termed them, desperate characters. True, they gamble some, and drink some, but on the whole they are honest, fearless, kind-hearted fellows, ready to stay with a friend to the end in a just cause, and to give their last dollar to one in need. But come, I see this little shooting affair has sort of unnerved you. I'll show you something a little more cheerful."

We went on up the street to a fair-sized adobe cabin. Through the open doors and windows came the strains of a violin and concertina, and the air was as lively a one as I ever had heard. Many and many a time I heard it in after years, that and its companion dance pieces, music that had crossed the seas in the ships of Louis XV., and, taught by father to son for generations, by ear, had been played by the voyageurs up the immense length of the Mississippi and the Missouri, to become at last the popular music of the American in the Far Northwest.

We arrived at the open doorway and looked in. "Hello, Berry; come in, old boy," and "Bon soir, Mons. Berri, bon soir; entrez! entrez!" some of the dancers shouted; we went in and took seats on a bench against the wall. All of the females in the place were Indians, and for that matter they were the only women at that time in all Montana, barring a few white hurdy-gurdy girls at the mines of Helena and Virginia City, and of the latter the less said the better.

These Indian women, as I had remarked in the morning when I saw some of them on the levee, were comely, of good figure and height, and neatly dressed, even if they were corsetless and wore moccasins; far different

"They were of much pride and dignity; that one could see at a glance"

indeed from the squat, broad, dark natives of the Eastern forests I had seen. And they were of much pride and dignity; that one could see at a glance. And yet they were what might be termed jolly, chattering and laughing like so many white women. That surprised me. I had read that Indians were a taciturn, a gloomy, silent people, seldom smiling, to say nothing of laughing and joking with the freedom and abandon of so many children.

"This," Berry told me, "is a traders' and trappers' dance. The owner of the house is not at home, or I would introduce you to him. As to the others"—with a sweep of his hand—"they're too busy just now for any introduction ceremony. I can't introduce you to the women, for they do not speak English. However, you must dance with some of them."

"But, if they do not speak our language, how am I to ask them to dance with me?"

"You will walk up to one of them, the one you choose, and say: 'Ki-tak-stai pes-ka'—will you dance?"

I never was what you may call bashful or diffident. A quadrille had just ended. I boldly walked up to the nearest woman, repeating the words over and over that I might not forget them, bowed politely, and said, "Ki-tak-stai pes-ka?"

The woman laughed, nodded her head, replied, "Ah," which I later learned was yes, and extended her hand; I took it and led her to a place for another quadrille just forming. While we were waiting she spoke to me several times, but I could only shake my head and say: "I do not understand." Whereupon she would laugh merrily and say a lot more in her language to her neighbour, another comely young woman, who would also laugh and look at me with amusement in her eyes. I began to feel embarrassed; I'm not sure that I did not blush.

The music struck up and I found that my partner was a light and graceful dancer. I forgot my embarrassment and enjoyed the quadrille, my strange partner, the strange music, and strange surroundings immensely. And how those long-haired, buckskin-clad, moccasined plainsmen did caper and cut pigeon wings, and double shuffle, and leap and swing in the air! I wondered if I could ever, since that seemed to be the style, learn to do likewise. I determined to try it anyhow, but privately at first.

The quadrille ended, I started to lead my partner to a seat, but instead she led me over to Berry, who had also been dancing, and spoke rapidly to him for a moment.

"This," said he to me, "is Mrs. Sorrel Horse. (Her husband's Indian name.) She invites us to accompany her and her husband home and have a little feast."

Of course we accepted and after a few more dances departed. I had been introduced to Sorrel Horse. He was a very tall, slender man, sorrel haired, sorrel whiskered, blue eyed; a man, as I afterward learned, of extremely happy temperament under the most adverse conditions, a sincere and self-sacrificing friend to those he liked, but a terror to those who attempted to wrong him.

Sorrel Horse's home was a fine large Indian lodge of eighteen skins, set up beside his two canvas-covered wagons near the river's bank. His wife built a little fire, made some tea, and presently set before us the steaming beverage with some Dutch oven baked biscuits, broiled buffalo tongue, and stewed bull berries. We heartily enjoyed the meal, and I was especially taken with the luxurious comfort of the lodge; the soft buffalo robe couch upon which we sat, the sloping willow back rests at each end of it, the cheerful little fire in the centre, the oddly shaped, fringed and painted parfleches in which Madam Sorrel Horse kept her provisions and her various belongings. It was all very new and very delightful to me, and when after a smoke and a chat, Sorrel Horse said: "You had better camp here for the night, boys," my happiness was complete. We went to sleep on the soft couch covered with soft blankets and listening to the soft murmur of the river's current. This, my first day on the plains, had been, I thought, truly eventful.

CHAPTER II

IT WAS agreed that I should join Berry in the autumn, when he would begin the season's trade with the Indians. He owned a large bull-train, with which he hauled freight from Fort Benton to the mining camps in summer, finding in that much more profit than in trading for the deer, elk, and antelope skins, which were about the only things of value that the Indians had to barter at that season. Buffalo robes were valuable only from animals killed from November to February inclusive. I did not wish to remain in Fort Benton; I wanted to hunt and travel about in this land of glorious sunshine and dry, clear air; so I bought a roll of bedding, large quantities of tobacco, and .44 rim-fire cartridges for my Henry rifle, a trained buffalo horse and saddle, and pulled out of the town with Sorrel Horse and his outfit. Perhaps if I had gone to the mines instead I would have done better in a financial way. More steamboats had arrived, the place was full of people bound for the gold fields, and there were many just from there with heavy sacks of gold-dust in their battered grips and greasy bags. They had made their stake, they were bound for the States; for "God's country," they said. God's country! If there was a more beautiful land than that of the great sunlit plains and mountains, grand and soul-inspiring in their immensity, I never saw it. I am glad I did not get the mining fever, for then I would probably never have learned to know them intimately. There are some things of far more value than gold. For instance, a life free from cares or duties of any kind; a life in which every day and every hour brings its share of pleasure and satisfaction, of excitement, of happily earned and well-enjoyed fatigue. Had I, too, gone to the placer fields I might have made a fortune, and returned to the States, and settled down in some deadly monotonous village, where the most exciting things that ever happened were church festivals and funerals!

Sorrel Horse's wagons, a lead and a trail, drawn by an eight-horse team, were heavily loaded with provisions and trade-goods, for he was going with a band of the Piegans, the Small Robes, on their summer hunt. And this was what had made me at once accept his invitation to accompany him; I would have an opportunity to study the people. Much has been written about the Piegan Blackfeet, and those who are interested in the subject should read Mr. Grinnell's books, "Blackfoot Lodge Tales" and "The Story of the Indian."

Sorrel Horse's brother-in-law, Lis'-sis-tsi, Wolverine, and I became great friends. I soon learned to use the sign language, and he helped me in my studies of the Blackfoot language, so difficult that few white men ever did become proficient in it. I may say that by diligently committing my studies of it to writing and by paying especial attention to pronunciation and accent, I learned to speak it as well as any white man ever did, with perhaps one or two exceptions.

How I enjoyed that summer, part of which we passed at the foot of the Belt Mountains and part on Warm Spring Creek and the Judith River. I joined in the frequent buffalo runs, and on my swift and well-trained horse managed to kill my share of the great animals. I hunted antelope, elk, deer, bighorn, and bear with Wolverine. I would sit for hours on a mountain slope or the summit of some lone butte, and watch the herds and bands of game about me, gaze at the grand mountains and the vast and silent plain, and pinch myself to realise that I was really I, and that it was all real and not a dream. Wolverine apparently never tired of all this any more than I; he would sit by my side, a dreamy look in his eyes as he gazed about him, and frequently exclaim "i-tam-ap-i," which is the word for happiness or perfect content.

Yet Wolverine was not always happy; there were days when he went about with a long face and a preoccupied air, never speaking except to answer some question. One day in August when he was in this mood I asked what was troubling him.

"There is nothing troubling me," he replied. Then after a long silence; "I lied, I am in great trouble. I love Piks-ah'-ki and she loves me, but I cannot have her; her father will not give her to me."

Another long silence: "Yes, well?" I urged, since he had forgotten or did not feel inclined to enlighten me further.

"Yes," he went on, "her father is a Gros Ventre, but her mother is Piegan. Long ago my people protected the Gros Ventres, fought their battles, helped them to hold their country against all enemies. And then the two tribes quarrelled, and for many years were at war with each other. This last winter they made peace. It was then I first saw Piks-ah'-ki. She is very beautiful; tall, long hair, eyes like an antelope, small hands and feet. I went much to her father's lodge, and we would look at each other when the others there were not noticing. One night I was standing by the doorway

" 'She came out for an armful of wood' "

of the lodge when she came out for an armful of wood from the big pile lying there. I took hold of her and kissed her, and she put her arms around my neck and kissed me back. That is how I know she loves me. Do you think"—anxiously—"that she would have done that if she did not love me?"

"No, I do not think she would."

His face brightened and he continued: "At that time I had only twelve horses, but I sent them to her father with a message that I would marry his daughter. He sent the horses back and these words: 'My daughter shall not marry a poor man!'

"I went with a war party against the Crows and drove home myself eight head of their best horses. I traded for others until I had thirty-two in all. Not long ago I sent a friend with them to the Gros Ventre camp to ask once more for this girl I love; he soon returned, driving back the horses and this is what her father said: 'My daughter shall never marry Wolverine, for the Piegans killed my son and my brother.' "

I had no comment to make. He looked at me hesitatingly two or three times and finally said: "The Gros Ventres are encamped on the Missouri, at the mouth of this little (Judith) river. I am going to steal the girl from her people; will you go with me?"

"Yes," I quickly replied. "I'll go with you, but why me? Why don't you ask some of the Raven Carriers to go with you, as you belong to that society?"

"Because," he replied, laughing a little constrainedly, "because I might fail to get the girl; she might even refuse to go with me, and then my good friends would tell about it, and people would always be joking me. But you, if I fail, I know you will never tell about it."

One evening about dusk we quietly left the camp.

No one except Sorrel Horse—not even his wife—knew of our departure. Naturally, she would be alarmed about her brother's absence, and he was to tell her that the youth had gone in to Fort Benton with me for a day or two. But how genial old Sorrel Horse did laugh when I told him where we were going and for what purpose.

"Haw, haw, haw! That's pretty good! A pilgrim, only three months in the country and going to help an Indian steal a girl!"

"When does one cease to be a pilgrim?" I asked.

"When he has learned all about things and ceases to ask fool questions. I should say, in your case, that people will quit calling you 'pilgrim' in about five years. It takes most of 'em about fifteen to become acclimated, as you may say. But joking aside, young man, this is a pretty serious thing you are going in for; don't get into any trouble; always keep close to your horse and remember that it is better to run than to fight; you can live longer by doing so as a general rule."

We left the camp at dusk, for in those days it was not safe for a couple of men to ride over the great plains in the daytime; too many war parties of various tribes were abroad, seeking glory and wealth in the scalps and chattels of unwary travellers. We rode out of the Judith valley eastward on to the plain, and when we were far enough out to avoid the deep coulées running into it, turned and paralleled the course of the river. Wolverine led a lively but gentle pinto pony on which we had packed some bedding, and a large bundle done up in a fine buffalo robe and bound with many a thong. These things he had taken out of camp the night before and hidden in the brush. There was a glorious full moon, and we were able to trot and lope along at a good pace. We had not travelled many miles from camp before we began to hear the bellowing of the buffalo; it was their mating season and the bulls kept up a continuous deep, monotoned bellow or roar as they charged and fought about from band to band of the great herds. Several times during the night we rode close to a band and startled them, and they ran off thundering over the hard ground and rattling their hoofs, away, away in the soft moonlight; we could hear them still running long after they had disappeared from view. It seemed as if all the wolves in the country were abroad that night, for they could be heard in all directions, near and far, mournfully howling. What a sad, solemn cry theirs was; so different from the falsetto, impish yelping of the coyotes.

On, on Wolverine went, urging his horse and never looking back, and I kept close up and said nothing, although I thought the pace too fast on a plain honey-combed with badger and prairie-dog holes. When at last day began to break we found ourselves in a country of high pine-clad buttes and ridges, and two or three miles from the Judith valley. Wolverine stopped and looked all around, trying to pierce the distance still shrouded in the dusk of early morning.

"So far as I can see," he said, "everything looks well. The buffalo and the prairie runners (antelope) feed quietly. But that is not a sure sign that an enemy is not near; even now some of them may be sitting in the pines of those buttes looking down upon us. Let us hurry to the river—we must have water—and hide in the timber in the valley."

We unsaddled in a grove of cottonwoods and willows and led our horses to water. On a wet sand bar where we came to the stream there were a number of human footprints so recently made that they seemed to be as fresh as our own tracks. The sight startled us and we looked about anxiously, holding our rifles in readiness for a quick aim. There was no timber on the opposite side of the stream at that point, and we had just come through the grove above us, so we realised that the makers of the tracks were not in our immediate vicinity.

"Crees or men from across the mountains," said Wolverine, again examining the tracks. "No matter which; they are all our enemies. We must be careful and keep a good watch, as they may be nearby."

We drank our fill and went back into the grove, tying our horses so that they could eat a little of the grass and wild peas growing luxuriantly beneath the trees.

"How could you know," I asked, "that those whose tracks we saw are not Crows, or Sioux, or other people of the plains?"

"You noticed," Wolverine replied, "that the footprints were wide, rounding, that even the prints of their toes could be seen; that was because they wore soft-bottom moccasins, the sole, as well as the upper part, of tanned deer or buffalo skin. Only those people use such footwear; all those of the plains here wearing moccasins with hard parfleche soles."

I had been very hungry until I saw the footprints in the sand, after that I was too busy watching, and listening for a possible enemy to think of anything else; and I fervently wished that I had remained in camp and left the young Indian to do his own girl stealing.

"I will go around the inner edge of the grove and have a look at the country and then we will eat," said Wolverine.

I wondered what we would eat, well knowing that we dared not kill anything, nor build a fire, even if we had

meat. But I said nothing, and while he was gone I re-
saddled my horse, remembering my friend's advice to
stay close to it. Presently Wolverine returned.

"The war party passed through the grove," he said,
"and went on down the valley. About two nights
from now they will be trying to steal the Gros Ventre
horses. Well, we will eat."

He undid the buffalo robe bundle and spread out a
number of articles; heavy red and blue cloth, enough
for two dresses. The stuff was made in England and
the traders sold it for about $10 a yard. Then there
were strings of beads, brass rings, silk handkerchiefs,
Chinese vermilion, needles, thread, ear-rings—an assort-
ment of things dear to the Indian women.

"For her," he said, laying them carefully aside and
producing some eatables; dry stale bread, sugar, dried
meat, and a string of dried apples.

"I stole them from my sister," he said. "I thought
that we might not be able to shoot any game or build
a fire."

That was a long day. By turns we slept a little, that
is, Wolverine slept. I am sure I scarcely dozed, for I
was always expecting the war party to jump us. Yes,
I was pretty young at the business then, and so was the
Indian. What we ought to have done, after getting
water, was to have ridden to the top of some butte and
remained there during the day. From such a point we
could have seen the approach of an enemy a long way
off, and our swift horses could have easily taken us
beyond his reach. It was mere luck that we were not
seen to enter the valley and the cottonwood grove, for
there a war party could have surrounded us and ren-
dered our escape difficult, if not impossible.

Up to this time Wolverine had made no definite plan

to get the girl away. Sometimes he would say that he would steal into the camp and to her lodge at night, but that was certainly risky, for if he did succeed in getting to the lodge without being taken for an enemy come to steal horses he might awaken the wrong woman and then there would be a terrible outcry. On the other hand, if he boldy went into the camp on a friendly visit, no doubt old Bull's Head, the girl's father, would· suspect his purpose and closely watch her. But this discovery of a war party moving down the river toward the Gros Ventre camp gave him a plain opening.

"I knew that my medicine would not desert me," he suddenly said that afternoon, laughing happily; "and see, the way is clear before us. We will ride boldly into camp, to the lodge of the great chief, Three Bears. I will say that our chief sent me to warn him of a war party working this way. I will say that we ourselves have seen their tracks along the bars of the river. Then the Gros Ventres will guard their horses; they will ambush the enemy; there will be a big fight, big excitement. All the men will rush to the fight, and that will be my time. I will call Piks-ah'-ki, we will mount our horses and fly."

Again we rode hard all night, and at daylight came in sight of the wide dark gash in the great plain which marked the course of the Missouri. We had crossed the Judith the evening before, and were now on a broad trail worn in deep furrows by the travois and lodge poles of many a camp of Piegans and Gros Ventres, travelling between the great river and the mountains to the south. The sun was not high when at last we came to the pine-clad rim of the valley and looked down into the wide, long bottom at the mouth of the Judith; there, whitely gleaming against the dark foliage of a cottonwood grove, were the lodges of the Gros Ventres, some 300 and more. Hundreds and hundreds of horses were feeding on the sage brush flat; riders were galloping here and there, driving their several bands to water, or catching up fresh animals for the daily hunt. Although still a couple of miles away we could hear the confused noise of the camps, shouts, childish laughter, singing, the beating of drums.

"Ah!" Wolverine exclaimed. "There is the camp. Now for the big lie." Then, more seriously, "Pity me, great Sun! pity me, you under-water creature of my dream! Help me to obtain that which I seek here."

Oh, yes, the youth was in love. Cupid plays havoc with the hearts of red as well as white people. And—dare I say it?—the love of the red, as a rule, is more lasting, more faithful than the love of the superior race.

We rode into the camp stared at by all as we passed along. The chief's lodge was pointed out to us. We dismounted at the doorway, a youth took charge of our horses, and we entered. There were three or four guests present enjoying an early feast and smoke. The chief motioned us to the seat of honour on his own couch at the back of the lodge. He was a heavy, corpulent man, a typical Gros Ventre, Big Belly.

The pipe was being passed and we smoked a few whiffs from it in our turn. A guest was telling a story, when he finished it the chief turned to us, and asked, in good Blackfoot, whence we had come. Nearly all the older Gros Ventres at that time spoke Blackfoot fluently, but the Blackfoot never could speak Gros Ventre; it was too difficult for anyone not born and reared with them to learn.

"We come," Wolverine replied, "from up the Yellow (Judith) river, above the mouth of the Warm Spring.

My chief, the Big Lake, gives you this—producing and handing him a long coil of rope tobacco—and asks you to smoke with him in friendship."

"Ah!" said Three Bears, smiling, and laying the tobacco to one side. "Big Lake is my good friend. We will smoke with him."

"My chief also sends word with me that you are to keep close watch of your horses, for some of our hunters have found signs of a war party travelling this way. We ourselves, this white man here, who is my friend, and I, we also have come across their trail. We saw it yesterday morning up the river. There are twenty, maybe thirty of them, and they are on foot. Perhaps to-night, surely by to-morrow night, they will raid your herd."

The old chief asked many questions as to what tribe the war party might be, just where we had seen their tracks, and so on, which Wolverine answered as best he could. Then some boiled meat, some dried buffalo back fat, and some pemmican were set before us, and we had our breakfast. While we were eating the chief conferred with his other guests, and they soon went away, as I presumed, to tell the news and prepare to surprise the expected raiders. Three Bears informed us that his lodge was ours; that our horses would be cared for; our saddles and bridles were brought in and piled near the doorway. I forgot to mention that Wolverine had cached his precious bundle away back on the trail soon after daylight.

After our breakfast and another smoke, during which the chief asked all manner of questions about the Piegans, Wolverine and I strolled through the camp and down to the banks of the river. On the way he pointed out the lodge of his prospective father-in-law. Old

Bull's Head was a medicine man, and the outside of his abode was painted with the symbols of his particular dream-given power, two huge grizzly bears in black, below which were circles of moons in red.   We sat by the river a while, watching a lot of boys and young men swim; I noticed, however, that my companion kept an eye on the women continually coming for water.   Evidently the particular one he longed to see did not appear, and we turned back toward the chief's lodge after a time.   Just back of it a couple of women were killing a fat pup of three or four months by strangulation.

"Why are they killing that dog?"   I asked.

"Ugh," Wolverine replied, making a wry face, "it is for a feast for us."

"A feast for us!"   I repeated in astonishment.   "Do you mean that they will cook the dog, will expect us to eat it?"

"Yes, these Gros Ventres eat dog; they think it better than buffalo meat, or other meat of any kind.   Yes, they will stew it and set it before us, great bowls of it, and we must eat of it or they will be displeased."

"I will not touch it," I cried.   "No, I will never touch it."

"But you will, you must, unless you wish to make enemies of our friends; and"—despondently—"perhaps spoil my chance of getting that which I have come for."

Well, in due time the meat of the dog was set before us; very white it looked, and certainly the odour of it was far from disagreeable.   But—it was dog.   Never in my life had I dreaded to do anything more than to taste of it, yet I felt that I must.   I grasped a rib, set my muscles determinedly, and bolted the meat upon it, blinking and swallowing and swallowing to keep it down. And it stayed down; I made it stay, although for a moment it was a toss-up which would win—the nausea or my will. In this manner I managed to eat a small part of that set before me, partaking liberally of some berry pemmican, which was a sort of side dish. I was glad when the meal was over. Oh yes, I was very glad; and it was many an hour after before my stomach became normal.

It was thought that the expected enemy would possibly arrive that night; so as soon as it was dark nearly all the men of the camp picked up their weapons and crept out through the sage bush to the foot of the hills, stringing out far above and below and back of their feeding herds. Wolverine and I had our horses up and saddled, he telling the chief that in case a fight began we would ride out and join his men. My comrade went out early in the evening, I sat up for an hour or more, and as he did not return, I lay down on the couch, covered myself with a blanket and was soon sound asleep, not waking until morning. Wolverine was just getting up. After breakfast we went out and walked around and he told me that he had found a chance to whisper to Piksah'-ki the night before, when she had come outside for wood, and that she had agreed to go with him whenever the time came. He was in great spirits, and as we strolled along the shore of the river could not help breaking out in the war songs which the Blackfeet always sing when they are happy.

Along near noon, after we had returned to the lodge, among other visitors a tall, heavy, evil-featured man came in; by the nudge Wolverine gave me as he sat down opposite and scowled at us I knew that he was Bull's Head. He had a heavy growth of hair which he wore coiled on his head like a pyramid. He talked for some time with Three Bears and the other guests, and then, to my surprise, began to address them in Black-foot, talking at us, and there was real and undisguised hatred in his tone.

"This story of an approaching war party," he said, "is all a lie. Look at it; the Big Lake sends word that his people have seen their trail; now, I know that the Piegans are cowards; still, where there are so many of them they would be sure to follow such a trail and at-tack the enemy. No, they never saw any such trail, never sent any such word; but I believe an enemy has come, and is in our camp now, not after our herds but our women. Last night I was a fool. I went out and watched for horse-stealers; I watched all night, but none came. To-night I shall stay in my lodge and watch for women-stealers, and my gun will be loaded. I advise you all to do the same."

And having had his say, he got up and flounced out of the lodge, muttering to himself, undoubtedly cursing all the Piegans, and one in particular. Old Three Bears watched him depart with a grim smile, and said to Wol-verine:

"Do not remember his words; he is old, and cannot forget that your people killed his son and his brother. Others of us"—with a deep sigh—"others of us also lost brothers and sons in the war with your people, yet we made the great peace. What is past is past; the dead cannot be brought to life, but the living will live longer and be happier now that we have ceased to fight and rob one another."

"You speak the truth," said Wolverine. "Peace between we two people is good. I forget the old man's words. Do you also forget them and guard your horses, for this night surely the enemy will come."

Again at dusk we saddled our horses and picketed

them close to the lodge. Wolverine putting his saddle
on the pinto pony and shortening the stirrups. He
intended to ride his own animal bareback. He told me
that Piks-ah'-ki had been under guard of her father's
Gros Ventre wives all day; the old man not trusting
her Piegan mother to accompany her after wood and
water for the lodge. I again went to sleep early, my
companion going out as usual. But this time I did not
rest until morning, for I was awakened by the firing of
guns out on the flat, and a great commotion in camp,
men shouting and running toward the scene of the fight,
women calling and talking excitedly, children crying and
shrieking. I hurried out to where our horses were
picketed, carrying my own rifle and Wolverine's. He
owned a fine Hawkins, 32 balls to the pound, which
Sorrel Horse had given him. I learned afterward that
old Bull's Head was one of the first to rush to the rescue
of his horses when the firing began. As soon as he had
left the lodge Wolverine, who was lying nearby in the
sage brush, ran to it and called his sweetheart's name.
Out she came, followed by her mother, carrying several
little bags. A minute later they came to where I stood,
both women crying. Wolverine and I unfastened the
horses.

"Hurry," he cried, "hurry."

He gently took the girl from where she was crying
in the embrace of her mother and lifted her into the
saddle, handing her the bridle reins.

"Listen," cried the mother, "you will be good to her,
I call the Sun to treat you as you do her."

"I love her, and I will be good to her," Wolverine
answered, and then to us: "Follow me, hurry."

Away we went over the flat, straight for the trail upon
which we had entered the valley, and straight toward

the fight raging at the foot of the hill. We could hear the shots and shouts; see the flash of the guns. This was more than I had bargained for; again I was sorry I had started out on this girl-stealing trip; I didn't want to charge in where the bullets of a fight that didn't interest me were flying. But Wolverine was leading, his sweetheart riding close behind him, and there was nothing for me to do but follow them. As we neared the scene my comrade began to shout:

"Where is the enemy? Let us kill all of them. Where are they? Where do they hide?"

I saw his point. He didn't intend that the Gros Ventres should mistake us for some of the raiders. But the latter; suppose we ran on to any of them?

The firing had ceased and the shouting; all was quiet ahead of us, but we knew that there in the moonlit sage brush both parties were lying, the one trying to sneak away, the other trying, without too much risk, to get sight of them. We had but a hundred yards or more now between us and the foot of the hill, and I was thinking that we were past the danger points when, with a sputter of fire from the pan and a burst of flame from the muzzle, a flint-lock gun was discharged right in front of Wolverine, and down went his horse and he with it. Our own animals suddenly stopped. The girl shrieked and cried out:

"They have killed him! Help, white man, they have killed him!"

But before we could dismount we saw Wolverine extricate himself from the fallen animal, spring to his feet and shoot at something concealed from us by the sage brush. We heard a deep groan, a rustling of the brush and then Wolverine bounded to the place and struck something three or four hard blows with the barrel of

his rifle. Stooping over he picked up the gun which had
been fired at him.

"I count a coup," he laughed, and running over to me
and fastening the old fuke in the gun sling on the horn
of my saddle, said, "Carry it a ways until we get out of
the valley."

I was about to tell him that I thought he was foolish
to delay us for an old fuke, when right beside of us, old
Bull's Head appeared, seeming to have sprung all at
once out of the brush, and with a torrent or angry words
he grasped the girl's horse by the bridle and attempted to
drag her from the saddle. She shrieked and held on
firmly, and then Wolverine sprang upon the old man,
hurled him to the ground, wrenched his gun from him,
and flung it far; then he sprang lightly up behind Piks-
ah'-ki, dug his heels into the pony's flanks, and we were
off once more, the irate father running after us and
shouting, no doubt for assistance to stop the runaways.
We saw other Gros Ventres approaching, but they did
not seem to be hurrying, nor did they attempt in any
way to stop us. No doubt the angry old man's words
had given them the key to the situation, and, of course,
it was beneath their dignity to mix up in a quarrel about
a woman. We went on as fast as we could up the steep,
long hill, and soon ceased to hear the old man's com-
plainings.

We were four nights getting back to the Piegan camp,
Wolverine riding part of the time behind me and part of
the time behind the girl, when we were on the trail. We
picked up, en route, the precious bundle which Wolverine
had cached, and it was good, the next morning, to see
the girl's delight when she opened it and saw what it
contained. That very day while we rested she made
herself a dress from the red cloth, and I can truthfully

say that when she had arrayed herself in it, and put on her beads and rings and ear-rings, and a lot of other pretty things, she certainly looked fine. She was a very comely young woman anyway, and, as I afterward learned, as good as she was handsome. She made Wolverine a faithful and loving wife.

Fearing that we would be followed we had taken a circuitous route homeward, and made as blind a trail as possible, and upon our arrival at camp learned that old Bull's Head had got in there two days ahead of us. He was very different now from the haughty and malevolent man he had been at home. He fairly cringed before Wolverine, descanted upon his daughter's beauty and virtues, and said that he was very poor. Wolverine gave him ten horses and the fuke he had taken from the Indian he killed the night of our flight from the Gros Ventre camp. Old Bull's Head informed us that the war party were Crees, and that his people had killed seven of them, and that they had not succeeded in stealing a single horse, so completely were they surprised when attacked.

Well, I went on no more girl-stealing raids, but I believe I did other things just as foolish on the plains in my youthful days.

CHAPTER III

ACCORDING to arrangement, I joined Berry at the end of August, and prepared to accompany him on his winter's trading expedition. He offered me a share in the venture, but I was not yet ready to accept it; I wanted to be absolutely free and independent for a few months more to go and come as I chose, to hunt, to roam about with the Indians and study their ways.

We left Fort Benton early in September with the bull train, creeping slowly up the hill out of the bottom, and scarcely any faster over the level of the now brown and dry plains. Bulls are slow travellers, and these had a heavy load to haul. The quantity and weight of merchandise that could be stowed away in those old-time "prairie schooners" were astonishing. Berry's train now consisted of four eight-yoke teams, drawing twelve wagons in all, loaded with fifty thousand pounds of provisions, alcohol, whisky, and trade goods. There were four bull-whackers, a night-herder who drove the "cavayard"—extra bulls and some saddle horses—a cook, three men who were to build the cabins and help with the trade, with Berry and his wife, and I. Not a very strong party to venture out on the plains in those times, but we were well armed, and, hitched to one of the trail wagons, was a six-pound cannon, the mere sight or sound of which was calculated to strike terror to any hostiles.

Our destination was a point on the Marias River,

some forty-five miles north of Fort Benton. Between that stream and the Missouri, and north of the Marias to the Sweetgrass Hills and beyond, the country was simply dark with buffalo, and, moreover, the Marias was a favourite stream with the Blackfeet for their winter encampments, for its wide and by no means deep valley was well timbered. In the shelter of the cotton-wood groves their lodges were protected from the occasional north blizzards, there was an ample supply of fuel and fine grass for the horses. There were also great numbers of deer, elk, and mountain sheep in the valley and its breaks, and the skins of these animals were in constant demand; buckskin was largely used for the summer clothing and the footwear of the people.

September on the plains! It was the most perfect month of all the year in that region. The nights were cool, often frosty; but the days were warm, and the clear air was so sweet and bracing that one seemed never to get enough of it. Nor could one tire of the grand, the wondrous, extent of plain and mountains, stretching out, looming up in every direction. To the west were the dark Rockies, their sharp peaks standing out sharply against the pale blue sky; northward were the three buttes of the Sweetgrass Hills; eastward dimly loomed the Bear Paws; south, away across the Missouri, the pine-clad Highwood Mountains were in plain sight; and between all these, around, beyond them, was the brown and silent plain, dotted with peculiar flat-topped buttes, deeply scamed with stream valleys and their numerous coulées. Some men love the forest; the deep woods where lone lakes sparkle and dark streams flow slow and silent; and it is true that they have a charm of their own. But not for me, not for me. My choice is the illimitable plain with its distant mountains, its lone buttes, its cañons fantastically rock-walled, its lovely valleys beckoning one to the shelter of shady groves by the side of limpid streams. In the forest one is ever confined to a view of a few yards or rods round about; but on the plains—often I used to climb to the top of a butte, or ridge, and sit by the hour gazing at the immense scope of country extending far, far to the level horizon in all directions except the west, where the Rockies rise so abruptly from the general level of the prairie. And how good one felt to see the buffalo, and the antelope, and the wolves, scattered everywhere about, feeding, resting, playing, roaming about, apparently in as great numbers as they had been centuries before. Little did any of us dream that they were all so soon to disappear.

We were nearly three days travelling the forty-five miles to our destination. We saw no Indians en route, nor any signs of them. On all sides the buffalo and antelope grazed quietly, and those in our path did not run far to one side before they stopped, and began to crop the short but nutritious grasses. We encamped the second night by a spring at the foot of the Goose Bill, a peculiarly shaped butte not far from the Marias. The wagons were drawn up in the form of a corral, as usual, and in the centre of it our lodge was put up, a fine new one of sixteen skins. Berry and his wife, a couple of the men and I slept in it, the others making their beds in the wagons, on the merchandise. We had a good supper, cooked over a fire of buffalo chips, and retired early. The night was very dark. Some time after midnight we were awakened by a heavy tramping in the corral; something crashed against a wagon on one side of us, and then against another one on the other side. The men in the wagons began to call out, asking

"Where the Rockies rise so abruptly from the general level of the prairie"

one another what was up; Berry told us in the lodge to take our rifles and pile out. But before we could get out of bed something struck our lodge and over it went, the poles snapping and breaking, the lodge skin going on and undulatingly careering about the corral as if it were endowed with life; in the intense darkness we could just see it, dancing round and round, a fiendish dance to a step of its own. At once all was excitement. Mrs. Berry shrieked; we men shouted to one another, and with one accord we all fled to the shelter of the wagons and hurriedly crept under them. Some one fired a shot at the gyrating lodge skin; Berry, who was beside me, followed suit, and then we all began to shoot, rifles cracking on all sides of the corral. For a minute, perhaps, the lodge skin whirled about, and dashed from one end of the corral to the other more madly than ever; and then it stopped and settled down upon the ground in a shapeless heap; from under it we heard several deep, rasping gasps, and then all was still. Berry and I crawled out, walked cautiously over to the dim, white heap and struck a match; and what did we see but the body of a huge buffalo bull, still almost completely enveloped in the now tattered and torn lodge covering. We could never understand how and why the old fellow wandered into the corral, nor why, when he charged the lodge, some of us were not trampled upon. Berry and his wife occupied the back side of the lodge, and he went right over them in his mad career, apparently without even putting a hoof on their bed.

We arrived at the Marias about noon the next day, and went into camp on a finely timbered point. After dinner the men began to cut logs for the cabins, and Berry and I, mounting our horses, rode up the river in quest of meat. We had plenty of fat buffalo cow ribs on hand, but thought that a deer or elk would be good for a change. On our hunt that day we rode up to a point where the "Baker battle" afterward occurred. That is what it is called, "Baker's battle," and the place, "Baker's battlefield." But that was no battle; 'twas a dreadful massacre. The way of it was this: The Piegan Blackfeet had been waylaying miners on the trail between Fort Benton and the mines, and they had also killed a man named Malcolm Clark, an old employee of the American Fur Co., who was living with his Indian family near the Bird Tail Divide. This man Clark, by the way, was a man of fierce and ungovernable temper, and in a fit of anger had severely beaten a young Piegan who was living with him and herding his horses. Now if you have anything against an Indian, never try to obtain satisfaction by beating him; either get your gun and kill him, or leave him alone, for if you strike him blood alone will wipe out the disgrace, and sometime or other, when you are least expecting it, he will surely kill you. This is what happened to Clark. The young man got a passing war party to back him, and he murdered Clark. The War Department then concluded that it was time to put a stop to the Piegan depredations, and Colonel Baker, stationed at Fort Shaw, was ordered to seek Black Weasel's band and give them a lesson. It was January 23, 1870, at daylight, that the command arrived at the bluff overlooking a wooded bottom of the Marias, and there among the trees were pitched eighty lodges of the Piegans, not, however, Black Weasel's band; these were under Chief Bear's Head; but Colonel Baker did not know that. Bear's Head's people were, in the main, friendly to the whites.

In a low tone Colonel Baker spoke a few words to his men, telling them to keep cool, aim to kill, to spare none of the enemy, and then he gave the command to fire. A terrible scene ensued. On the day previous many of the men of the camp had gone out toward the Sweetgrass Hills on a grand buffalo hunt, so, save for Chief Bear's Head and a few old men, none were there to return the soldiers' fire. Their first volley was aimed low down into the lodges, and many of the sleeping people were killed or wounded in their beds. The rest rushed out, men, children, women, many of the latter with babes in their arms, only to be shot down at the doorways of their lodges. Bear's Head, frantically waving a paper which bore testimony to his good character and friendliness to the white men, ran toward the command on the bluff, shouting to them to cease firing, entreating them to save the women and children; down he also went with several bullet holes in his body. Of the more than four hundred souls in camp at the time, very few escaped. And when it was all over, when the last wounded woman and child had been put out of misery, the soldiers piled the corpses on overturned lodges, firewood, and household property, and set fire to it all.

Several years afterward I was on the ground. Everywhere scattered about in the long grass and brush, just where the wolves and foxes had left them, gleamed the skulls and bones of those who had been so ruthlessly slaughtered. "How could they have done it?" I asked myself, time and time again. "What manner of men were those soldiers who deliberately shot down defenceless women and innocent children?" They had not even the excuse of being drunk; nor was their commanding officer intoxicated; nor were they excited, or in any danger whatever. Deliberately, coolly, with steady and deadly aim, they shot them down, killed the wounded, and then tried to burn the bodies of their victims.   But I will say no more about it; think it over yourself and try to find a fit name for men who did this.*

On our way up the river we saw many doe and fawn deer, a bunch of cow and calf elk, but not a buck nor bull of either species.   On our way homeward, however, along toward sunset, the male deer were coming in from the breaks and coulées to water, and we got a large, fat, buck mule deer.   Madame Berry hung a whole forequarter of it over the lodge fire, and there it turned and slowly roasted for hours; about 11 o'clock she pronounced it done, and although we had eaten heartily at dusk, we could not resist cutting into it, and it was so good that in a short time nothing was left of the feast but the bones.   I know of no way of roasting meat equal to this.   You must have a lodge—to prevent draughts —a small fire; suspend the roast from a tripod above the blaze, and as it cooks give it an occasional twirl; hours are required to thoroughly roast it, but the result more than repays the labour involved.

The men soon cut and dragged out the required logs,

---

* The Baker massacre, which took place Jan. 23, 1870, on the Marias River, was in its day a well-known event.   The official reports declare that 173 Indians were killed and 100 women and children captured.   Later and more accurate reports led to the belief that 176 people were killed.   Of the killed, fifteen men were reported as fighting men between the ages of fifteen and thirty-seven, eighteen were middle-aged and old men between thirty-seven and seventy.   The women killed numbered ninety, and the children under twelve years of age— many of them infants in arms—fifty-five.   When the news of the massacre reached the East, the newspapers took it up, and there was much excitement about it. General Sheridan was bitterly assailed for his action.   There never was any question but that the camp which Colonel Baker attacked was one of friendly Indians; people who had committed no depredations.   The village to which the murderers belonged was that of Mountain Chief, which at the time was camped on Belly River in British America.   Details of this destruction of life will be found in Manypenny's "Our Indian Wards."

EDITOR.

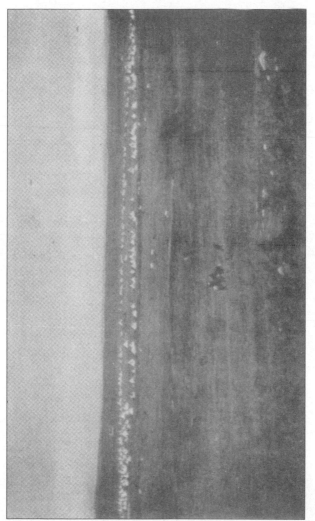

"That great camp of seven hundred lodges"

put up the walls of our "fort," and laid on the roof of poles, which was covered with a thick layer of earth. When finished, it formed three sides of a square and contained eight rooms, each about sixteen feet square. There was a trade room, two living rooms, each of which had a rude but serviceable fireplace and chimney, built of mud-mortared stones. The other rooms were for storing merchandise and furs and robes. In the partitions of the trade room were numerous small holes, through which rifles could be thrust; at the back end of the square stood the six-pounder. With all these precautions for defence and offence, it was thought that even the most reckless party of braves would think twice before making an attack upon the traders. But, of course, liquor was to be the staple article of trade, and even the most experienced man could never foretell what a crowd of drink-crazed Indians would do.

The fort was barely completed when the Piegan Blackfeet arrived, and pitched their lodges in a long, wide bottom about a mile below us. I passed the greater part of my time down in their camp with a young married man named Weasel Tail, and another who bore a singular name: Talks-with-the-buffalo. These two were inseparable companions, and somehow they took a great liking to me, and I to them. Each one had a fine new lodge, and a pretty young wife. I said to them once: "Since you think so much of each other, I do not understand why you do not live together in one lodge. It would save much packing, much wear of horses when travelling, much labour of gathering fire-wood, of setting up and breaking camp."

Talks-with-the-buffalo laughed heartily. "It is easy to see," he replied, "that you have never been married. Know this, my good friend: Two men will live together in quiet and lasting friendship, but two women never; they will be quarrelling about nothing in less than three nights, and will even try to drag their husbands into the row. That is the reason we live separately; to be at peace with our wives. As it is, they love each other, even as my friend here and I love each other, and thus, for the good of us all, we have two lodges, two fires, two pack outfits, and enduring peace."

Thinking the matter over, I realised that they were right. I knew two sisters once, white women—but that is another story. And after I married, and my wife and I took up our home with a friend and his wife for a time—but that is still another story. Oh, yes, the Indian knew whereof he spoke; neither white nor Indian married women can manage a common household in peace and friendship.

I enjoyed myself hugely in that great camp of seven hundred lodges—some thirty-five hundred people. I learned to gamble with the wheel and arrows, and with the bit of bone concealed in one or the other of the player's hands, and I even mastered the gambling song, which is sung when the latter game is being played around the evening lodge fire. Also, I attended the dances, and even participated in the one that was called "As-sin-ah-pes-ka"—Assiniboin dance. Remember that I was less than twenty years of age, just a boy, but perhaps more foolish—more reckless than most youths.

In this Assiniboin dance, only young unmarried men and women participate. Their elders, their parents and relatives, beat the drums and sing the dance song, which is certainly a lively one, and of rather an abandoned nature. The women sit on one side of the lodge, the men on the other. The song begins, every one joining in. The dancers arise, facing each other,

rising on their tip toes, and them sinking so as to bend the
knees. Thus they advance and meet, then retreat,
again advance and retreat a number of times, all singing,
all smiling and looking coquettishly into each others'
eyes. Thus the dance continues, perhaps for several
hours, with frequent pauses for rest, or maybe to feast
and smoke. But all the fun comes in toward the close
of the festivities; the lines of men and women have
advanced; suddenly a girl raises her robe or toga, casts
it over her own and the head of the youth of her choice,
and gives him a hearty kiss. The spectators shout with
laughter, the drums are beaten louder than ever, the
song increases in intensity. The lines retreat, the
favoured youth looking very much embarrassed, and
all take their seats. For this kiss payment must be
made on the morrow. If the young man thinks a great
deal of the girl, he may present her with one or two
horses; he must give her something, if only a copper
bracelet or string of beads. I believe that I was an
"easy mark" for those lively and, I fear, mercenary
maidens, for I was captured with the toga, and kissed
more often than any one else. And the next morning
there would be three or four of them at the trading post
with their mothers; and one must have numerous yards
of bright prints; another some red trade cloth and beads;
still another a blanket. They broke me, but still I
would join in when another dance was given.

But if I danced, and gambled, and raced horses, my
life in the camp was by no means a continual round of
foolishness. I spent hours and hours with the medicine
men and old warriors, learning their beliefs and traditions, listening to their stories of the gods, their tales
of war and the hunt. Also I attended the various religious ceremonies; listened to the pathetic appeals of

the medicine men to the Sun as they prayed for health, long life, and happiness for the people. It was all exceedingly interesting.

Alas! Alas! why could not this simple life have continued? Why must the railroads, and the swarms of settlers have invaded that wonderful land, and robbed its lords of all that made life worth living? They knew not care, nor hunger, nor want of any kind. From my window here I hear the roar of the great city, and see the crowds hurrying by. The day is bitterly cold, yet the majority of the passers by, women as well as men, are thinly clad, and their faces are thin, and their eyes express sad thoughts. Many of them have no warm shelter from the storm, know not where they can get a little food, although they would gladly work for it with all their strength. They are "bound to the wheel," and there is no escape from it except by death. And this is civilisation! I, for one, maintain that there is no satisfaction, no happiness in it. The Indians of the plains back in those days of which I write, alone knew what was perfect content and happiness, and that, we are told, is the chief end and aim of men—to be free from want, and worry, and care. Civilisation will never furnish it, except to the very, very few.

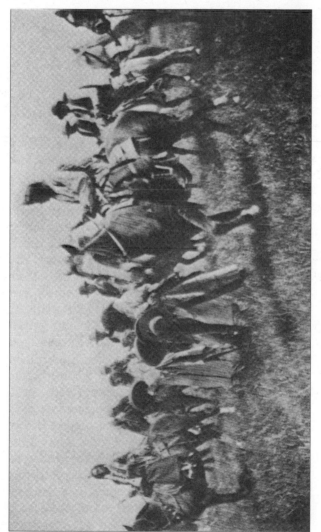

"I attended various religious ceremonies"

CHAPTER IV

A WAR TRIP FOR HORSES

THE young and middle-aged men of the tribe were constantly setting out for, or returning from war, in parties of from a dozen to fifty or more. That was their recreation, to raid the surrounding tribes who preyed upon their vast hunting ground, drive off their horses, and take scalps if they could. It was an inspiring sight to witness the return of a party which had been successful. A few miles back from camp they would don their picturesque war clothes, paint their faces, decorate their horses with eagle plumes and paint, and then ride quietly to the brow of the hill overlooking the village. There they would begin the war song, whip their horses into a mad run, and, firing guns and driving before them the animals they had taken, charge swiftly down the hill into the bottom. Long before they arrived the camp would be in an uproar of excitement, and the women, dropping whatever work they had in hand, would rush to meet them, followed more slowly and sedately by the men. How the women would embrace and hang on to their loved ones safely returned; and presently they could be heard chanting the praises of husband, or son, or brother. "Fox Head has returned!" one would cry. "Oh, Ai! Fox Head, the brave one, has returned, driving before him ten of the enemy's herd. Also, he brings the scalp of an enemy whom he killed in battle. Oh, the brave

47

one! He brings the weapons of this enemy he killed; brave Fox Head!"

And so it would go on, each woman praising the valour of her particular relative; and then the returned warriors, tired, hungry, thirsty, but proud of their success and glad to be once more at home, would retire to their lodges, and their faithful women folk, mother, and wife, and sister, would hasten to prepare for them a soft couch, and bring cool water, and set out a feast of the choicest meat and pemmican and dried berries. They were so happy and so proud, that they could not sit still; and every now and then one of them would go out and walk about among the lodges, again chanting praise of the loved one.

No sooner did one of these parties return than others, incited by their success and anxious to emulate it, would form a party and start out against the Crows, or the Assiniboins, or perhaps the Crees, or some of the tribes on the far side of the Back-bone-of-the-world, as the Rockies were called. Therefore I was not surprised one morning to be told that they were about to start on a raid against the Assiniboins. "And you can go with us if you wish to," Talks-with-the-buffalo concluded. "You helped your friend to steal a girl, and you might as well try your hand at stealing horses."

"I will," I replied, "I'll go with you; it is just what I have been longing to do."

When I told Berry of my intention, both he and his wife protested strongly against it. "You have no right to risk your life," he said, "for a few cayuses." "Think how your people would mourn," said his wife, "if anything should happen to you."

But my mind was made up; I was determined to go, and I did; but not for the intrinsic value of any horses

Framework of a sweat lodge

or other plunder that I might obtain; it was the excitement and the novelty of the thing which attracted me. There were to be thirty of us, and Heavy Breast, a grim and experienced warrior of some forty years, was to be our partisan, or leader. He himself was the owner of a medicine pipe, which was considered to have great power. He had carried it on many an expedition, and it had always brought him and his parties good luck; taken them through various conflicts unharmed. But for all this, we had to get an old medicine man to pray with us in the sacred sweat lodge before we started, and to pray for us daily during our absence.   Old Lone Elk was chosen for this responsible position; his medicine was of great power and had found favour with the Sun these many years. The sweat lodge was not large enough to accommodate us all, so half of the party went in at a time, I remaining with my two friends and going in with the last division.   At the entrance of the sweat lodge we dropped our robes or blankets, our only covering, and creeping in at the low doorway, sat around the interior in silence while the red-hot stones were passed in and dropped in a hole in the centre. Lone Elk began to sprinkle them with a buffalo tail dipped in water and as the stifling hot steam enveloped us he started a song of supplication to the Sun, in which all joined. After that the old man prayed long and earnestly, beseeching the Sun to pity us; to carry us safely through the dangers which would beset our way, and to give us success in our undertaking. Then the medicine pipe was filled, lighted with a coal which was passed in, and as it was passed around, each one, after blowing a whiff of smoke toward the heavens and the earth, made a short prayer to the Sun, to Old Man and Mother Earth. And when my turn came, I also made the prayer, audibly like the rest, and to the best of my ability. No one smiled; my companions believed that I was sincere in my avowal to be one of them in word, thought, and deed. I wanted to know these people; to know them thoroughly; and I considered that the only way to do so was for a time to live their life in every particular in order to win their entire confidence. And so I made an earnest prayer to the Sun, and I thought of something I had learned in other days in a far away country: "Thou shalt have no other gods before me," etc. I believed all that once, and listened to a Presbyterian preacher of a Sunday threatening us with hell's fire and brimstone and the terrible anger of a vengeful God. Why, after hearing one of those sermons I was afraid to go to bed, lest in my sleep I should be snatched into perdition. But all that was now past; I had no more faith, nor fear, nor hope, having concluded that one can only say, "I do not know." So I prayed to the Sun with right good will in the furtherance of my plan.

It was getting late in the season, and the Assiniboins were thought to be a long way from us, somewhere near the mouth of the Little River, as the Blackfeet name the stream we call Milk River. So it was decided that we should set out on horseback instead of afoot. The latter was the favourite way of making a raid, for a party travelling in that manner left no trail, and could effectually conceal themselves during the daytime.

So one evening, led by our partisan, we set forth and travelled southeastward over the dark plain, paralleling the river. My companions were not the befringed and beaded and painted and eagle plume decked warriors one reads about and sees pictured. They wore their plain, every-day leggings and shirt and moccasins and either the blanket or the cowskin toga. But tied to their saddles were their beautiful war clothes, and in a small parfleche cylinder their eagle plume or horn and weasel-skin head dresses. When going into battle, if there was time, these would be donned; if not, they would be carried into the fray, for they were considered to be great medicine, the shirt especially, upon which was painted its owner's dream, some animal or star or bird, which had appeared to him during the long fast he made ere he changed from careless youth to responsible warrior.

We rode hard that night, and morning found us within a short distance of the mouth of Marias River. In all directions buffalo and antelope were to be seen quietly resting or grazing; evidently there were no other persons than us anywhere in the vicinity. "It will not be necessary to hide ourselves this day," said Heavy Breast, and detailing one of the party to remain on the edge of the bluff for a lookout, he led us down into the valley, where we unsaddled and turned our horses out by the stream—all but Weasel Tail and I; we were told to get some meat. A charge of powder and a ball meant much to an Indian, and as I had plenty of cartridges for my Henry rifle, and could get plenty more, it fell to me to furnish the meat—a pleasant task. We had not far to go to find it. Less than half a mile away we saw a fine band of antelope coming into the valley for water, and by keeping behind various clumps of sarvis and cherry brush, I managed to get within a hundred yards of them, and shot two, both bucks, in good order. We took the meat, the tongues, liver, and tripe and returned to camp, and every one was soon busily roasting his favourite portion over the

fire, every one except Heavy Breast., To him fell
always the best meat, or a tongue if he wanted it, and
a youth who was taking his first lesson on the war trail
cooked it for him, brought him water, cared for his
horse, was, in fact, his servant. A partisan was a man
of dignity, and about as unapproachable as an army
general. While the rest chatted and joked, and told
yarns around the camp fire, he sat apart by himself,
and by a separate fire if he wished it. He passed much
time in prayer, and in speculating regarding the por-
tent of his dreams. It often happened that when far
from home and almost upon the point of entering an
enemy's village, a partisan's dream would turn the
party back without their making any attempt to accomplish their object.

After leaving the Marias, we were careful to conceal
ourselves and our horses as well as possible during the
daytime. We skirted the eastern slope of the Bear's
Paw Mountains, the eastern edge of the Little Rockies
—in Blackfoot, Mah-kwi-is-stuk-iz: Wolf Mountains.
We expected to find the Gros Ventres encamped somewhere along here—it will be remembered that they
were at this time at peace with the Blackfeet—but we
saw no signs of them less than four or five months old,
and we concluded that they were still down on the
Missouri River. Wherever we camped, one or more
sentinels were kept posted in a position overlooking
the plains and mountains roundabout, and every evening they would report that the game was quiet, and that
there was no sign of any persons except ourselves in
all that vast region.

One morning at daylight we found ourselves at the
foot of a very high butte just east of the Little Rockies,
which I was told was the Hairy Cap, and well was it

"When going into battle, if there was time, the war clothes would be donned"

named, for its entire upper portion was covered with a
dense growth of pine. We went into camp at the foot
of it, close to a spring and in a fine grassy glade entirely
surrounded by brush. Talks-with-the-buffalo and I
were told to ascend to the summit of the butte and
remain there until the middle of the day, when others
would take our place. We had both saved a large
piece of roast buffalo ribs from the meal of the previous
evening, so, drinking all the water we could hold and
lugging our roast, we climbed upward on a broad game
trail running through the pines, and finally reached the
summit. We found several war houses here, lodges
made of poles, brush, pieces of rotten logs; so closely laid
that not a glimmer of a fire could shine through them.
It was the way war parties of all tribes had of building a fire for cooking or to warm themselves without
betraying their presence to any passing enemy.
We saw six of these shelters, some of them quite recently built, and there were probably more in the vicinity. My companion pointed out one which he had
helped build two summers before, and he said that the
butte was frequented by war parties from all the tribes
of the plains, because it commanded such an extended
view of the country. Indeed it did. Northward we
could see the course of Milk River and the plains beyond it. To the south was visible all the plain lying
between us and the Missouri, and beyond the river
there was still more plain, the distant Snowy and
Moccasin mountains and the dark breaks of the Musselshell. Eastward was a succession of rolling hills and
ridges clear to the horizon.

We sat down and ate our roast meat, and then Talks-
with-the-buffalo filled and lighted his black stone pipe
and we smoked. After a little I became very drowsy.

"You sleep," said Talks-with-the-buffalo, "and I will keep watch." So I lay down under a tree and was soon in dreamland.

It was about ten o'clock when he awoke me. "Look! Look!" he cried excitedly, pointing toward the Missouri. "A war party coming this way."

Rubbing my eyes, I gazed in the direction indicated, and saw bands of buffalo skurrying to the east, the west, and northward toward us, and then I saw a compact herd of horses coming swiftly toward the butte, driven by a number of riders. "They are either Crees or Assiniboins," said my companion; "they have raided the Crows or the Gros Ventres, and, fearing pursuit, are hurrying homeward as fast as they can ride."

Running, leaping, how we did speed down the side of that butte. It seemed but a moment ere we were among our companions, giving our news. Then what a rush there was to saddle horses, don war clothes and head dresses, and strip off shield coverings. And now Heavy Breast himself ascended the side of the butte until he could get a view of the oncoming party, while we waited for him at its base. He stood there, perhaps a hundred yards from us, looking, looking out over the plain, and we began to get nervous; at least I did. I thought that he never would come down and give us his plan. I must confess that, now the time was at hand when I was to engage in an assault, I dreaded it, and would have been mightily glad at that moment to be safely with Berry away up on the Marias. But there could be no retreat; I must go with the rest and do my share, and I longed to have it all over with.

After a wait of five or ten minutes, Heavy Breast joined us. "They will pass some distance east of here," he said. "We will ride down this coulée and meet

them." It wasn't much of a coulée, just a low, wide
depression in the plain, but deep enough to conceal us.
Every little way our leader would cautiously ride up to
the edge of it and look out southward, and finally he
called a halt. "We are now right in their path," he
said. "As soon as we can hear the beat of their horses'
hoofs we will dash up out of here at them."

How my heart did thump; my throat felt dry; I was
certainly scared. Like one in a daze, I heard Heavy
Breast give the command, and up we went out of the
coulée, our leader shouting, "Take courage; take courage! Let us wipe them out!"

The enemy and the herd they were driving were not
more than a hundred yards distant when we got upon a
level with them, and our appearance was so sudden that
their horses were stampeded, some running off to the
east and some to the west. For a moment they tried
to round them in again, and then we were among them,
and they did their best to check our advances, firing
their guns and arrows. Some were armed only with
the bow. One after another I saw four of them tumble
from their horses to the ground, and the rest turned and
fled in all directions, our party close after them. They
outnumbered us, but they seemed to have little courage.
Perhaps our sudden and unexpected onslaught had demoralised them at the start. Somehow, the moment
I rode out of the coulée and saw them, I felt no more
fear, but instead became excited and anxious to be right
at the front. I fired at several of them, but of course
could not tell if they fell to my shots or those of our
party. When they turned and fled I singled out one
of them, a fellow riding a big strawberry pinto, and
took after him. He made straight for Hairy Cap and
its sheltering pines, and I saw at once that he had the

better horse and would get away unless I could stop him with a bullet; and how I did try to do so, firing shot after shot, each time thinking, "This time I must certainly hit him." But I didn't. Three times he loaded his flint lock and shot back at me. His aim must have been as bad as mine, for I never even heard the whiz of the bullets, nor saw them strike. On, on he went, putting more distance between us all the time. He had now reached the foot of the butte, and urged the horse up its steep side, soon reaching a point where it was so nearly perpendicular that the animal could carry him no farther. He jumped off and scrambled on up, leaving the horse. I also dismounted, kneeled down, and taking deliberate aim, fired three shots before he reached the pines. I saw the bullets strike, and not one of them was within ten feet of the fleeing mark. It was about the worst shooting I ever did.

Of course, I was not foolish enough to try to hunt the Indian in those thick pines, where he would have every advantage of me. His horse had run down the hill and out on the plain. I rode after it, and soon captured it. Riding back to the place where we had charged out of the coulée, I could see members of our party coming in from all directions, driving horses before them, and soon we were all together again. We had not lost a man, and only one was wounded, a youth named Tail-feathers; an arrow had fearfully lacerated his right cheek, and he was puffed up with pride. Nine of the enemy had fallen, and sixty-three of their horses had been taken. Every one was jubilant over the result. Every one was talking at once, telling in detail what he had done. I managed to attract Heavy Breast's attention. "Who were they?" I asked.

"They were Crees."

"How could you tell that they were?"

"Why, I understood some of the words they shouted," he replied. "But even if they had not uttered a sound, I would still have recognised them by their mean faces and by their dress."

I rode over to one of them lying on the ground nearby. He had been scalped, but I could see that his countenance was quite different from a Blackfoot's face. Besides, there were three blue tattooed marks on his chin, and his moccasins and garments were unlike anything I had seen before.

We changed horses and turned homeward, plodding along steadily all that afternoon. The excitement was over, and the more I thought of it, the more pleased I was that I had not killed the Cree I chased into the pines. But the others; those I had fired at and seen drop; I succeeded in convincing myself that they were not my bullets that had caused them to fall. Had I not fired as many as twenty shots at the man I chased and each one had sped wide of the mark? Of course, it was not I who laid them low. I had captured a fine horse, one stronger and more swift than my own good mount, and I was satisfied.

We got home in the course of four or five days, and you may well believe that there was great excitement over our arrival, and many a dance with the scalps by those who had at one time or another lost dear ones at the hands of the Crees. Hands and faces and moccasins painted black, bearing the scalps on a willow stick, little parties would go from one part of the village to another, sing the sad song of the dead, and dance in step to its slow time. I thought it a very impressive ceremony, and wish I could remember the song, just for the sake of old times.

Dear old Berry and his wife killed the fatted calf over my safe return; at least we had, besides choice meats and bread and beans, three dried apple pies and a plum (raisin) duff for dinner. And I will remark that the two latter courses were a rare treat in those days in that country. I was glad to get back to the fort. How cheerful was the blaze in the wide fireplace of my sleeping room; how soft my couch of buffalo robes and blankets! I stayed pretty close to them for a time, and did nothing but sleep and eat and smoke; it seemed as if I would never get enough sleep.

CHAPTER V

W HO should roll in one day but Sorrel Horse and his
wife, with whom I had passed the summer, and
with them came young Bear Head—once the Wolverine—and his Gros Ventre wife, whom I had helped
him steal from her people. That is, I went with him
on that expedition to the Gros Ventre camp, and gave
him very good will in his undertaking if nothing more.
Berry and his wife were as glad to meet them all again
as I was, and gave them one of the rooms in the fort
until such time as Sorrel Horse should have a cabin of
his own. He had decided to winter with us, trap
beaver and poison wolves, and perhaps do a little trading with the Indians. With Bear Head to help him,
he soon built a comfortable two-room cabin just back of
our place, and put in two good fireplaces like ours. I
was glad of the fireplaces, for I counted on spending
some little time by them in the long winter evenings to
come. Nothing on earth gives one such a sense of rest
and abiding peace as a cheerful blaze in a wide fireplace
when cold weather comes, and blizzards from the north
sweep down over the land.

Among other things, I had brought west with me a
shotgun, and, now that the geese and ducks were moving south, I had some very good shooting. Whenever
I went out for a few birds a number of Indians always
followed me to see the sport; they took as much delight

in seeing a bird fall at the crack of the gun as I did in
making the shot.   Once I dropped eleven widgeons from
a flock passing by, and the onlookers went wild with
enthusiasm over it.   But I could never induce them to
accept any of the fowl I killed; birds and fish they would
not eat, regarding the latter especially as unclean.   All
they cared for was ni-tap-i wak-sin: real food, by which
was meant the meat of buffalo and the various other
ruminants.

In November many of the Blackfeet proper came
down from the north, where they had been summering
along the Saskatchewan and its tributaries, and following them came the Kai-na, or Bloods, another tribe
of the Blackfeet.   The latter went into camp a mile
below the Piegans, and the former pitched their lodges
about half a mile above our fort.   We now had, including women and children, something like 9,000 or
10,000 Indians about us, and the traders were kept busy
all day long.   Buffalo robes were not yet prime—the
fur did not get its full growth until about the first of
November—but a fair trade was done in beaver, elk, deer,
and antelope skins.   About the only groceries the Indians
bought were tea, sugar, and coffee, and they cost them,
on an average, one dollar per pint cupful.   Blankets—
three-point—were twenty dollars; or four prime head-
and-tail buffalo robes, each; a rifle, costing fifteen dollars,
sold for one hundred dollars; whisky—very weak—was
five dollars per quart, and even a package of Chinese vermilion sold for two dollars.   There was certainly profit
in the trade.   As a matter of fact, there was not
a single thing in the trader's stock that was not an
unnecessary article of luxury to the Indian.   The
trader's argument was something like this: The
Indians don't need these things, but if they will have

them, they must pay my price for them. I'm not risking my life in this business for anything but big profits.

Of course Berry did not expect to get all the trade of the three great camps. Parties were continually going into Fort Benton with robes and furs, indeed, the larger part of the trade went there; nevertheless, the little fort on the Marias did a fine business.

Winter came early that year, in the fore part of November. The lakes and streams froze over, there were several falls of snow, which the northwest winds gathered up and piled in coulées and on the lee side of the hills. It was not long before the buffalo began to keep away from the river, where the big camps were. A few, of course, were always straggling in, but the great herds stayed out on the plains to the north and south of us. After the snow fell they went no more to water anyhow, as they got enough of it in the form of snow, eaten with the grass. So long as they took water in this way they remained fat, no matter how long and severe the winter was; but as soon as the snow began to melt and water stood everywhere on the plains in little pools, they drank it and lost flesh rapidly. Since the buffalo came no more near the stream the Indians were obliged to go out on a two or three days' camping trip, in order to get what meat and skins they needed, and several times during the season I went with them, accompanying my friends, Weasel Tail and Talks-with-the-buffalo. On these short hunts few lodges were taken, fifteen or twenty people arranging to camp together, so we were somewhat crowded for room. Only enough women to do the cooking accompanied the outfit.

As a rule, the hunters started out together every morning, and sighting a large herd of buffalo, approached them as cautiously as possible, until finally the animals

became alarmed and started to run, and then a grand
chase took place, and if everything was favourable
many fat cows were killed.   Nearly all the Piegans had
guns of one kind or another; either flint-lock or per-
cussion-cap, smooth-bore or rifle; but in the chase many
of them, especially if riding swift, trained horses, preferred to use the bow and arrow, as two or three arrows
could be discharged at as many different animals while
one was reloading a gun.   And yet those old smooth-
bores were quickly loaded.   The hunter carried a number of balls in his mouth; as soon as his piece was discharged he poured a quantity of powder from the horn
or flask into his hand and thence down the barrel;
then taking a ball from his mouth he dropped it down
on top of the powder, gave the stock a couple of sharp
blows to settle the charge, and primed the pan or put
on the cap, as the case might be.   When loaded in this
manner the piece had to be held muzzle up else the ball
would roll out; and when ready to shoot the hunter
fired the instant he brought the gun down to the level
of the mark.   Some of the hunters—fine shots and
astride exceptionally swift and long-winded horses—
often killed twenty and even more buffalo on a single
run, but I think the average number to the man was not
more than three.   After one of these hunts the main
camp was a sanguinary sight.   There were string atfer
string of pack horses loaded down with meat and hides,
and some hunters even slung a hide or two or a lot of
meat across their saddles and perched themselves on top
of that.   There was blood everywhere; on the horses,
along the trail, on the clothing, and even on the faces
of the hunters.

I went on several of these hunts when the weather was
so cold that a buffalo hide froze stiff as it dropped away

from the cut of the knife; yet, the Indians skinned their quarry bare-handed. I wore the heaviest of underclothing, a thick flannel shirt, a buckskin shirt, coat, and waistcoat, a short buffalo robe overcoat. and buffalo robe "shaps," and even then there were times when I was uncomfortably cold, and my cheeks and nose became sore from frequent nippings of frost. The Indians wore only a couple of shirts, a pair of blankets or cowskin leggins, fur cap, buffalo robe gloves and moccasins—no socks. Yet they never froze, nor even shivered from the cold. They attributed their indifference to exposure to the beneficial effect of their daily baths, which were always taken, even if a hole had to be cut in the ice for the purpose. And they forced their children to accompany them, little fellows from three years of age up, dragging the unwilling ones from their beds and carrying them under their arms to the icy plunge.

When on these short hunts there was no gambling nor dancing. Some medicine man always accompanied a party, and the evenings were passed in praying to the Sun for success in the hunt, and in singing what I may term songs of the hunt, especially the song of the wolf, the most successful of hunters. Everyone retired early, for there was little cheer in a fire of buffalo chips.

You have perhaps noticed on the northwestern plains, circles of stones or small boulders, varying in size from twelve to twenty and more feet in diameter. They were used to weight the lower edge of lodge skins, to prevent the structure being blown over by a hard wind, and when camp was moved they were simply rolled off the leather. Many of these circles are found miles and miles from any water, and you may have wondered how the people there encamped managed to assuage their thirst;

they melted snow; their horses ate snow with the grass; buffalo chips were used for fuel. The stone circles mark the place of an encampment of winter hunters in the long ago. Some of them are so ancient that the tops of the stones are barely visible above the turf, having gradually sunk into the ground of their own weight during successive wet seasons.

By the latter end of November the trade for robes was in full swing, thousands of buffalo had been killed, and the women were busily engaged in tanning the hides, a task of no little labour. I have often heard and read that Indian women received no consideration from their husbands, and led a life of exceedingly hard and thankless work. That is very wide of the truth so far as the natives of the northern plains were concerned. It is true, that the women gathered fuel for the lodge—bundles of dry willow, or limbs from a fallen cottonwood. They also did the cooking, and besides tanning robes, converted the skins of deer, elk, antelope, and mountain sheep into soft buckskin for family use. But never a one of them suffered from overwork; when they felt like it they rested; they realised that there were other days coming, and they took their time about anything they had to do. Their husbands never interfered with them, any more than they did with him in his task of providing the hides and skins and meat, the staff of life. The majority—nearly all of them—were naturally industrious and took pride in their work; they joyed in putting away parfleche after parfleche of choice dried meats and pemmican, in tanning soft robes and buckskins for home use or sale, in embroidering wonderful patterns of beads or coloured porcupine quills upon moccasin tops, dresses, leggings, and saddle trappings. When robes were to be traded they got their share of the proceeds; if the husband chose to buy liquor, well and good, they bought blankets and red and blue trade cloth, vermilion, beads, bright prints, and various other articles of use and adornment.

Berry and some of his men made several flying trips to Fort Benton during the winter, and on one of them brought out his mother, who had been living there with her companion, the Crow Woman. Mrs. Berry, Sr., was a full-blooded Mandan, but very light-coloured, and brown-haired. She was tall and slender, good-looking, very proud and dignified, but of great kindness of heart. She was very good to me, nursing me when ill and giving me strange and bitter medicines, always picking up and putting away with care the things I scattered about, washing and mending my clothes, making for me beautiful moccasins and warm gloves. She could not have done more had she been my own mother; I was under obligations to her which nothing could ever repay. When I contracted mountain fever, and one evening became delirious, it was she who tended me, and brought me safely out of it. Her companion, the Crow Woman, was equally kind to me. She was a woman with a romance, and one evening, after I became well acquainted with her, she told me the story of her life as we sat before the fire.

CHAPTER VI

THE STORY OF THE CROW WOMAN

IS-SÄP-AH'-KI—Crow Woman—as the Blackfeet named her, was an Arickaree, of a tribe which, in the days of Catlin, who visited the tribes in 1832, lived some distance below the Mandans, on the banks of the Missouri. Like the Mandans, they lived in a village of mound-like earth-covered lodges, surrounded by a strong and high palisade of cottonwood logs stuck endwise into the ground. They were members of the widely scattered Pawnee, or Caddoan family, but they had been long separated from the parent stock. They could converse with the Crows, who are related to the Gros Ventres of the village. Their own language—like the Mandan—was an extremely difficult one for an outlander to learn. The Crows and Arickarees were at times on terms of friendship, and again there were long periods when they were at war with each other.

The Crow Woman married early. She must have been a very handsome girl, for even in her old age, when I knew her, although wrinkled and gray-haired, she was still good-looking. She had lovely eyes, sparkling and mischievous, and her temperament was a most happy one. After many and bitter experiences she had at last found, with her good friend Mrs. Berry, a haven of peace and plenty which was assured to her so long as she lived. This is the story she told me as we sat before the fireplace, that winter night so many years ago:

"We were very happy, my young husband and I, for

66

we truly loved each other.   He was a good hunter, always keeping our lodge well supplied with meat and skins, and I, too, worked hard in the summer planting, and watering as they grew, a nice patch of beans and corn and pumpkins; in the winter I tanned many robes and many buckskins for our use.   We had been married two winters; summer came, and for some reason the buffalo left the river, all except a few old bulls, and remained away out on the plains.   My people did not like to hunt out there, for we were only a small tribe; our men were brave, but what could a few of them do against a great band of our many enemies?   So some were content to remain safely at home and eat the tough meat of the straggling bulls; but others, more brave, made up a party to go out where the great herds were.   My husband and I went with them; he did not want me to go, but I insisted upon it.   Since we had been married we had not been separated even for one night; where he went I had sworn to go also.   Our party travelled southward all day over the green-grassed plain; along toward evening we saw many bands of buffalo, so many that the country was dark with them; we rode down into a little valley, and made camp by a stream bordered by cottonwoods and willows.

"Our horses were not very strong, for always at night they were driven inside the stockade of our village, and, feeding daily over the same ground outside, they soon tramped and ate off the grass; they had no chance to become fat.   Some enemy or other was always prowling around our village at night, and we could not let them remain outside and wander to where the feed was good.

From our camp by the creek we started out every morning, the women following the men, who carefully looked over the country and then went after that band of

buffalo which could be most surely approached. Then,
when they had made the run, we rode out to where the
great animals lay and helped skin and cut up the meat.
When we got back to camp we were busy until evening
cutting the meat into thin sheets and hanging it up to
dry in the wind and the sun. Thus for three mornings
we went out, and our camp began to look red; you could
see the red from afar, the red meat drying. We were
very happy.

"I was proud of my husband. He was always in
the lead; the first to reach the buffalo, the last one to
quit the chase, and he killed more of them—always fine
fat animals —than any other one of the party. And he
was so generous; did anyone fail to make a kill he would
call to him and give him one, sometimes two, of his own
kill.

"On the fourth morning we went out soon after sunrise, and only a little way from camp the men made a
run and killed many buffalo. My husband shot down
nine. We were all hard at work skinning them and
getting the meat in shape to pack home, when we saw
those who were at the far end of the running ground
hurriedly mount their horses and ride swiftly toward
us with cries of 'The enemy! the enemy!' Then we
also saw them, many men on swift horses riding down
upon us, their long war bonnets fluttering in the wind;
and they were singing the war song; it sounded terrible
in our ears. They were so many, our men so few, there
was no use in trying to make a stand against them. We
all mounted our horses, our leader shouting: 'Ride
for the timber at the camp; it is our only chance. Take
courage; ride, ride fast.'

"I whipped my horse as hard as I could and pounded
his sides with my heels; my husband rode close beside

me also whipping him, but the poor thing could go only
so fast, the enemy were getting nearer and nearer all the
time.   And then, suddenly, my husband gave a little
cry of pain, threw up his hands, and tumbled off on to
the ground.   When I saw that I stopped my horse, got
down, and ran to him and lifted his head and shoulders
into my lap.   He was dying; blood was running from
his mouth in a stream; yet he made out to say: 'Take
my horse; go quick; you can outride them.'

"I would not do that.   If he died I wanted to die also;
the enemy could kill me there beside him.   I heard the
thunder of their horses' feet as they came on, and covering my head with my robe I bent over my husband, who
was now dead.   I expected to be shot or struck with a
war club, and I was glad for whither my dear one's
shadow went, there I would follow.   But no; they passed
swiftly by us and I could hear shots and cries and the
singing of the war song as they rode on into the distance.
Then in a little while I heard again the trampling of a
horse, and looking up I saw a tall man, a man full of
years, looking down at me.   'Ah,' he said, 'I made a
good shot; it was a long way, but my gun held straight.'

"He was a Crow, and I could talk with him.   'Yes,
you have killed my poor husband; now have pity and
kill me, too.'

"He laughed.   'What?' he said, 'kill such a pretty
young woman as you?   Oh, no.   I will take you home
with me and you shall be my wife.'

" 'I will not be your wife.   I will kill myself,' I began, but he stopped me.   'You will go with me and do
as I say,' he continued, 'but first I must take the scalp
of this, my enemy.'

" 'Oh, no,' I cried, springing up as he dismounted.
'Oh, do not scalp him.   Let me bury him, and I will do

anything you say. I will work for you, I will be your
slave, only let me bury this poor body where the wolves
and the birds cannot touch it.'

"He laughed again, and got up into the saddle. 'I
take your word,' he said. 'I go to catch a horse for you
and then you can take the body down to the timber by
your camp.'

"And so it was done. I wrapped my dear one in robes
and lashed the body on a platform which I built in a
tree by the little stream, and I was very sad. It was a
long, long time, many winters, before I took courage
and found life worth living.

"The man who had captured me was a chief, owning
a great herd of horses, a fine lodge, many rich things;
and he had six wives. These women stared very hard
at me when we came to the camp, and the head wife
pointed to a place beside the doorway and said: 'Put
your robe and things there.' She did not smile, nor
did any of the others; they all looked very cross, and
they never became friendly to me. I was given all of
the hardest work; worst of all, they made me chip hides
for them, and they would tan them into robes; every
day this was my work when I was not gathering wood or
bringing water to the lodge. One day the chief asked
me whose robe it was I was chipping, and I told him.
The next day, and the next, he asked me the same
question, and I told him that this hide belonged to one
of his wives, that to another, and so on. Then he became angry, and scolded his wives. 'You will give her
no more of your work to do,' he said. 'Chip your own
hides, gather your share of wood; mind what I say, for
I shall not tell you this again.'

"This Crow chief was a kind man, and very good to
me; but I could not like him. I turned cold at his

touch.   How could I like him when I was always mourning so for the one who was gone?

"We travelled about a great deal.   The Crows owned so many horses that after camp was all packed and lodge poles trailed, hundreds and hundreds of fat, strong animals were left without a burden of any kind.   Once there was talk of making peace with my people, and I was very glad, for I longed to be with them again.   A council was held, and it was decided to send two young men with tobacco to the chief of the Arickaree and ask that peace be declared.   The messengers went, but they never returned.   After waiting three moons (months) for them, it was thought that they had been killed by those whom they went to visit.   Then we left the Elk River (Yellowstone) and moved to the upper part of Dried Meat River (Musselshell).   This was the fifth summer after my capture.   It was berry time and the bushes were loaded with ripe fruit, which we women gathered in large quantities and dried for winter use. We went out one day to some thickets on the north slope of the valley, some distance from camp, where there were more berries than at any other place we had found.   There had been trouble in our lodge that morning; while my captor—I never could call him my husband—was eating, he asked to see the amount of berries we had gathered; his wives brought out their stores, the head woman five sacks of them, the others two and three each.   I had but one sack, and another partly full, to show.   'How is this?' the chief asked.   'Has my little Arickaree wife become lazy?'

" 'I am not lazy,' I answered, angrily.   'I have picked a great quantity of berries; and every evening I have spread them out to dry, covering them well after sunset so that the night dew would not injure them;

but in the morning, when I have removed the covers and exposed them to the sun's heat, I have found many, very many less than I had placed there. This has happened every night since we came to camp here.'

" 'That is strange,' he said. 'Who could have taken them? Do you women know anything about it?' he asked his wives.

"They said that they did not.

" 'You lie,' he cried, angrily, rising from his seat and pushing his head wife back out of his way. 'Here, little woman, are your berries; I saw them stealing them'; and from the head wife he took two sacks, from the others one each, and threw them over to me.

"Oh, those women were angry. They did not speak to me all that morning, but if looks could have killed me, then I would have died, for they scowled at me all the time. When the chief drove in the horses each caught the one she wanted and rode out to the berry patch.

"The five kept close together that day, leaving me to go by myself; and if I went near them they would move away to some distant bushes. Some time after midday they began to move toward me, and in a little time they were at work all around close by. Still they did not speak, nor did I. My little sack was again full; I stooped over to empty the berries into a larger sack; something struck me a terrible blow on the head; I knew no more.

"When I came back to life the sun was setting. I was alone, my horse was gone, and my large berry sack was missing; the small one, empty, lay by my side. I was very dizzy, very sick. I felt of my head; there was a great swelling on it, and much dried blood in my hair. I sat up to better look around and heard some one calling me, the tramp of a horse, and then the chief rode

up beside me and dismounted. He didn't say anything at first, just felt of my head carefully, and of my
arms, and then: 'They said that they could not find
you when they were ready to return to camp; that you
had run away. I knew better. I knew that I would
find you here, but I thought to find you dead.'

" 'I wish I were,' I said, and then for the first time I
cried. Oh, how lonely I felt. The chief lifted me up
into his saddle and got on the horse behind me, and we
rode home to the lodge. When we went inside the wives
just glanced at me quickly, and then looked away. I
was about to lie down on my couch by the doorway
when the chief said: 'Come here, here by my side is
now your place. And you,' to his head wife, giving her
a hard push, 'you will take her couch by the doorway.'

"That was all. He never accused his wives of attempting to kill me but from that time he treated them
coldly, never jesting nor laughing with them as he had
been used to doing. And whenever he left camp to
hunt, or to look for stray horses from his herd, I had to
accompany him. He would never leave me alone for
a day with the others. Thus it came about that when
he prepared to go with some of his friends on a raid
against the northern tribes I was told to get ready also.
It did not take me long; I packed my awl, needles, and
sinew thread in a little pouch, made some pemmican
and was ready.

"We were a small party, fifteen men, and one other
woman, newly married to a great war leader. It was not
proposed to make any attack upon our enemy, but to
travel cautiously through the country and raid the herds
of the first camp we found. We went on foot, travelling
by night and sleeping during a part of the long, hot
days. After many nights we arrived at the Big River

(Missouri) above the falls, right opposite where the Point-of-Rocks River (Sun River) joins it.   Daylight had come; looking up the valley of the little river we could see the lodges of a great camp, and band after band of horses striking out into the hills to graze.   Near us was a coulée where grew thick clumps of willows, we hurried to hide in them before we should be seen by any early risers of the strange camp.

"The men held a long talk, planning just what to do. They finally decided that it would be best for us to all cross the river and then, after taking some of the best horses in the camp, strike out eastward instead of re-crossing right there.   By going east for some distance before crossing back, it was thought that the enemy, should they follow us, would think us Crees or Assina-boins.   On some high, dry, well-grassed place we were to turn and head for home.   There the enemy would lose our trail, and keep on in the direction we had been travelling, while we could go homeward by easy rides, without fear of being overtaken.

"Soon after nightfall we crossed the river, going up the shore until we found a couple of big logs left by the high water. The men rolled them into the stream, lashed them together, placed their weapons and clothes and us two women on the raft and then, hanging on with one hand, and paddling with the other and kicking hard, they soon got it safely across.   As soon as we were landed they took off the lashings, pushed the logs out into the current, and carefully washed out our foot-prints on the muddy shore. We had landed just be-low the mouth of Point-of-Rocks River, at the edge of a choke-cherry thicket, and there we two women were told to remain until the men returned.   Each of them was to enter the camp for himself, cut loose such horses

as he could, and all were to meet as soon as possible at
the thicket there.   They started off right away, and we
two sat down to await their return.   We talked a little
while and then fell asleep, for we were both very tired
from our long journey, and at no time had we slept as
long as we wished to.   After a time I was awakened by
the howling of some wolves nearby; I looked up at the
Seven Persons (the Great Dipper) and saw by their
position that it was past the middle of the night.   I
aroused my companion and we talked again for a time,
wondering why none of the men had returned, saying
that perhaps there was some late dancing, or gambling,
or feasting in the strange camp, and that they were
waiting until all should be quiet before entering it.
Then we slept again.

"The sun was shining when we awoke, and we sprang
up and looked about us; none of our party had returned;
we became frightened.   We went to the edge of the brush
and looked out; away up the valley we could see the
horse herds again, and riders here and there travelling
on the hills.   I felt certain that the men had been discovered and killed, or had been chased so hard that they
could not return to us.   So, also, thought my companion.   We believed that as soon as night fell again
some of them would come for us.   There was nothing
for us to do but remain where we were.   It was a long,
long day.   We had no food, but that did not matter.
My companion was terribly worried.   'Perhaps my
husband has been killed,' she kept saying.   'Oh, if he
has what shall I do?'

"'I know how you feel,' I said, 'I, too, once had a
dear husband and I lost him.'

"'But don't you love your Crow husband?' she
asked.

"'He is not my husband,' I replied. 'I am his slave.'

"We went to the river, washed ourselves, and then returned to the edge of the brush, where we could look out, and sat down. My companion began to cry. 'Oh,' she said, 'if they do not return here, if they have been killed, what shall we do?'

"I had already thought of that, and I told her that far to the east on the banks of the Big River my people lived, and I would follow it until I found them. There were plenty of berries; I could snare the brush rabbits; I had flint and steel and could make a fire. I was sure I could make the long journey unless some accident happened. But I was not to attempt it. Some time after middle day we saw two riders coming along down the edge of Point-of-Rocks River, stopping here and there to get off their horses and look at the shore; they were trapping beaver. We crawled back into the centre of the brush and lay down, terribly scared, scarcely daring to breathe. The thicket was all criss-crossed by wide buffalo trails, there was no good place to hide; if the trappers should enter it? They did, and they found us; and one seized me and the other took my companion. They made us get up on their horses and brought us to their lodges. All the people crowded around to look at us. This was not new to me, and I just looked back at them, but my friend covered her head with her robe and wept loudly.

"This was the Blood tribe of the Blackfeet. I could not understand their language, but I could hand talk (the sign language). The man who had captured me began to ask questions. Who was I, where was I from, what was I doing down there in the brush? I told him. Then he told me that his people had surprised a war party sneaking into camp in the night, had killed four of them, and pursued the others to the breaks of the river below, where they managed to get away in the deep, dark cut coulées.

"'Was one of those you killed,' I asked, 'a tall man who wore a real bear's (grizzly) claw necklace?'

"He made the sign for yes.

"Then my Crow chief was dead! I cannot tell you just how I felt. He had been good to me, very kind. But he, or those with him, had killed my young husband; that I could not forget. I thought of his five wives; they would not miss him, all the great horse herd would be theirs; they would be glad when I, too, did not return.

"You have seen Deaf Man, the Blood who was here talking with me to-day. I lived in his lodge many years, and he and his wives were very kind to me. After a time I could think of my own people without crying, and made up my mind that I would never see them again. I was no longer called a slave, and made to do the work of others. Deaf Man would say that I was his youngest wife, and we would joke about the time he captured me. I was his wife and happy.

"So the winters went and we grew old, and then one summer when we were trading in Fort Benton, whom should I meet but my good friend here, who had come up on a fire-boat (steamer) to join her son. That was a happy day, for we had played together when we were children. She went at once to Deaf Man and pleaded with him to let me live with her, and he consented. And here I am, happy and contented in my old age. Deaf Man comes often to talk with us and smoke his pipe. We were glad of his visit to-day, and when he went home he carried much tobacco, and a new blanket for his old wife.

"There, I have told you a long story, my son, and night

fell long, long since. Go to bed, for you must be up early for your hunt to-morrow. The Crow Woman will awake you. Yes, these Blackfeet gave me that name. I hated it once, but have got used to it. We get used to anything in time."

"But wait," I said. "You did not tell me all. What became of the others of ycur party when you were attacked by the Crows?"

"I did not mention that," she replied, "for even to this day I do not like to think nor speak about it. There were many, many bodies scattered along the way of flight, scalped, naked, bloody, and dreadfully hacked up. Few escaped."

CHAPTER VII

A WHITE BUFFALO

ONE evening in the latter part of January there was much excitement in the three great camps. Some Piegan hunters, just returned from a few days' buffalo chase out on the plains to the north of the river had seen a white buffalo. The news quickly spread, and from all quarters Indians came in to the post for powder and balls, flints, percussion caps, tobacco, and various other articles. There was to be an exodus of hunting parties from the three villages in the morning and men were betting with each other as to which of the tribes would secure the skin of the white animal; each one, of course, betting on his own tribe. By nearly all the tribes of the plains an albino buffalo was considered a sacred thing, the especial property of the Sun. When one was killed the hide was always beautifully tanned, and at the next medicine lodge was given to the Sun with great ceremony, hung above all the other offerings on the centre post of the structure, and there left to shrivel gradually and fall to pieces. War parties of other tribes, passing the deserted place, would not touch it for fear of calling down upon themselves the wrath of the Sun. The man who killed such an animal was thought to have received the especial favour of the Sun, and not only he, but the whole tribe of which he was a member. A white robe was one thing which was never offered for sale; none who secured one might keep it any longer than until the time of the next medicine

lodge, the great annual religious ceremony. Medicine men, however, were permitted to take the strips
of trimming, cut to make even the border of the finished
robe, and to use them for wrapping their sacred pipes,
or for a bandage around the head, only to be worn,
however, on great occasions.

Of course I began to make inquiries about albino
buffalo.   My friend Berry said that in all his life he had
seen but four.   One very old Piegan told me that he had
seen seven, the last one, a very large cow robe, having
been purchased by his people from the Mandans for one
hundred and twenty horses, and, like all the others,
given to the Sun.   I further learned from Berry that
these albinos were not snow white, as is a white black-
bird or a crow, but cream coloured.   Well, if possible,
I wanted to see the much talked of animal, see it in life
skurry away over the plains with its dusky mates, so
I joined one of the hunting parties the next morning,
going, as usual, with my friends, Talks-with-the-buffalo
and Weasel Tail.   We planned the hunt in the lodge
of the latter, and as it was thought that we might be
some time away, it was decided to take one lodge and all
its contents, and to allow no others to crowd in upon
us.   "That is," Weasel Tail added, "that is, we'll do
this, and take our wives along, too, if you think they
will not get to quarrelling about the right way to boil
water, or as to the proper place to set an empty kettle."

His wife threw a moccasin at him, Madame Talks-
with-the-buffalo pouted and exclaimed "K'yä!" and
we all laughed.

We did not get a very early start; the days were short,
and after covering about twenty miles made camp in
a low, wide coulée.   There were fifteen lodges of our
party, all but ours crowded with hunters.   We had

many visitors of an evening who dropped in to smoke
and talk and feast, but at bedtime we had ample room
to spread our robes and blankets. We started early
the next morning and never stopped until we arrived
at a willow-bordered stream running out from the west
butte of the Sweetgrass Hills and eventually disappear-
ing in the dry plain. It was an ideal camping place,
plenty of shelter, plenty of wood and water. The big
herd in which the albino buffalo had been seen was met
with some fifteen or more miles southeast of our camp,
and had run westward when pursued. Our party
thought that we had selected the best location possible
in order to scour the country in search of it. Those
who had seen it reported that it was a fair-sized animal,
and so swift that it had run up to the head of the herd
at once and remained there—so far from their horses' best
speed, that they never got to determine whether it was
bull or cow. We were the extreme western camp of
hunters. Other parties, Piegans, Blackfeet, and Bloods
were encamped east of us along the hills, and southeast
of us out on the plain. We had agreed to do no running,
to frighten the buffalo as little as possible until the albino
had been found, or it became time to return to the river.
Then, or course, a big run or two would be made in
order to load the pack animals with meat and hides.

The weather was unfavourable. To say nothing of the
intense cold, a thick haze of glittering frost flakes filled
the air, through which the sun shone dimly. Objects
half a mile or less out on the plain could not be discerned.
We were almost at the foot of the west butte, but it and
its pine forest had vanished in the shining frost fog.
Nevertheless, we rode out daily on our quest, south,
west, or northward by one side or the other of the butte
toward the Little (Milk) River. We saw many buffalo;

thousands of them, in bands of from twenty or thirty to four or five hundred, but we did not find the white one. Other parties often dropped in at our camp for a bite and a smoke, or were met out on the plain, and they had the same report to make: plenty of buffalo, but no albino. I must repeat that the weather was intensely cold. Antelope stood humped up, heads down in the coulées; on the south slope of the butte, as we rode by its foot, we could see deer, and elk, and even big-horn in the same position. The latter would get out of our way, but the others hardly noticed our passing. Only the buffalo, the wolves, coyotes, and swifts were, as one may say, happy; the buffalo grazed about as usual, the others trotted around and feasted on the quarry they had hamstrung and pulled down, and howled and yelped throughout the long nights. No cold could find its way through their thick, warm coats.

I cannot remember how many days that cold time lasted, during which we vainly hunted for the albino buffalo. The change came about ten o'clock one morning as we were riding slowly around the west side of the butte. We felt suddenly an intermittent tremor of warm air in our faces; the frost haze vanished instantly and we could see the Rockies, partially enveloped in dense, dark clouds. "Hah!" exclaimed a medicine-pipe man. "Did I not pray for a black wind last night? And see, here it is; my Sun power is strong."

Even as he spoke the Chinook came on in strong, warm gusts and settled into a roaring, snapping blast. The thin coat of snow on the grass disappeared. One felt as if summer had come.

We were several hundred feet above the plain, on the lower slope of the butte, and in every direction, as far as we could see, there were buffalo, buffalo, and still more buffalo. They were a grand sight. Nature had been good to these Indians in providing for them such vast herds for their sustenance. Had it not been for the white man with his liquor, and trinkets, and his lust for land, the herds would be there to this day; and so would the red men, leading their simple and happy life.

It seemed about as useless as looking for the proverbial needle, to attempt to locate a single white animal among all those dark ones. We all dismounted, and, adjusting my long telescope, I searched herd after herd until my vision became blinded, and then I passed the instrument to some one beside me. Nearly all of the party tried it, but the result was the same; no white buffalo could be found. It was pleasant sitting there in the warm wind, with the sun shining brightly upon us once more. Pipes were filled and lighted and we smoked and talked about the animal we were after, of course; each one had his opinion as to where it was at that moment, and they varied in locality from the Missouri River to the Saskatchewan, from the Rockies to the Bear's Paw Mountains. While we were talking there appeared a commotion among the buffalo south-east of us. I got the telescope to bear upon the place and saw that a number of Indians were chasing a herd of a hundred or more due westward. They were far behind them, more than a mile, and the buffalo were widening that distance rapidly, but still the riders kept on, doggedly, persistently, in a long, straggling line. I passed the glass to Weasel Tail and told what I had seen. Everyone sprang to his feet.

"It must be," said my friend, "that they have found the white one, else they would give up the chase. They are far behind and their horses are tired; they 'lope very weakly. Yes, it is the white one they follow. I see it! I see it!"

We were mounted in a moment and riding out to intercept the herd; riding at a trot, occasionally broken by a short 'lope, for the horses must be kept fresh for the final run. In less than half an hour we arrived at a low, long, mound-like elevation, near which it seemed the herd must pass. We could see them coming straight toward it. So we got behind it and waited, my companions, as usual, removing their saddles and piling them in a heap. It was realised, of course, that the buffalo might get wind of us and turn long before they were near enough for us to make a dash at them, but we had to take that chance. After what seemed to me a very long time, our leader, peering over the top of the mound, told us to be ready; we all mounted. Then he called out for us to come on, and we dashed over the rise; the herd was yet over 500 yards distant, had winded us, and turned south. How the whips were plied; short-handled quirts of rawhide which stung and maddened the horses. At first we gained rapidly on the herd, then for a time kept at about their speed, and finally began to lose distance. Still we kept on, for we could all see the coveted prize, the albino, running at the head of the herd. I felt sure that none of us were able overtake it, but because the others did, I kept my horse going, too, shamefully quirting him when he was doing his very best.

It is a trite but true saying that "it is the unexpected that always happens." Out from a coulée right in front of the flying herd dashed a lone horseman, right in among them, scattering the animals in all directions. In much less time than it takes to tell it, he rode up right beside the albino, we could see him lean over and sink arrow after arrow into its ribs, and presently it stopped, wobbled, and fell over on its side. When we rode up to the place the hunter was standing over it, hands raised, fervently praying, promising the Sun the robe and the tongue of the animal. It was a three-year-old cow, yellowish-white in colour, but with normal coloured eyes. I had believed that the eyes of all albinos were of pinkish hue. The successful hunter was a Piegan, Medicine Weasel by name. He was so excited, he trembled so, that he could not use his knife, and some of our party took off the hide for him, and cut out the tongue, he standing over them all the time and begging them to be careful, to make no gashes, for they were doing the work for the Sun. None of the meat was taken. It was considered a sacrilege to eat it; the tongue was to be dried and given to the Sun with the robe. While the animal was being skinned, the party we had seen chasing the herd came up; they were Black-feet of the north, and did not seem to be very well pleased that the Piegans had captured the prize; they soon rode away to their camp, and we went to ours, accompanied by Medicine Weasel, who had left his camp to the eastward in the morning to hunt up some stray horses, and had wound up the day in a most unexpected manner. So ended that particular hunt.

Before the buffalo finally disappeared I saw one more —not a pure albino. In fact, Berry and I purchased the tanned robe, which, for want of a better term, we named the "spotted robe." Singularly enough, this animal was killed in 1881, when the last of the great herds were in the country lying between the Yellow-stone and Missouri rivers, and where in two more years they were practically exterminated. This animal was also a cow, a large five-year-old. The hair on its head, belly, legs, and tail was snow white, and there was a white spot on each flank about eight inches in diameter. When the hide was taken off, by ripping it in the usual mnnner, there was an eight or ten-inch border all around it of pure white, contrasting vividly with the beautiful, glossy, dark brown of the body of the robe. The animal was killed by a young North Blackfoot between Big Crooked Creek and Flat Willow Creek, both emptying into the lower Musselshell. We had at the time a large post on the Missouri, a couple of hundred miles below Fort Benton, and a branch post over on Flat Willow. Berry was on his way to visit the latter place when he came upon a party of Blackfeet just as they had concluded a run, and saw the spotted animal before it was skinned. He went no farther that day, but accompanied the young hunter to his father's lodge where the old man made him welcome. If there was ever a man on earth who could coax an Indian to do whatever he wished that man was Berry. He pleaded hard for that hide all the afternoon and far into the night. It was against all precedent and tradition to barter such a skin, belonging as it did to the Sun. It would be a sacrilege to sell it. The young hunter got out of the deal by giving it to his father, and, finally, as the old man knocked the ashes out of the last pipe before retiring, he sighed, and said wearily to Berry: "Well, my son, you shall have your way; my wife will tan the robe, and some day I will give it to you."

It was a beautifully tanned robe, and on the clean, white leather side the old man painted the record of his life; the enemies he had killed, the horses he had taken, the combats he had waged against the grizzly tribe, and

the animals and stars of his medicine. There were
other traders in the same bottom with us on the Missouri. One day, with his ancient wife, the old man
rode in and duly exhibited to them all the wonderful
robe, and, of course, they all wanted it. "I am not
ready to sell it," the crafty old man said to each one.
"After a while—well, we'll see; we'll see."

Then the traders vied with each other in being good
to the old man. During the balance of the winter they
kept him supplied with all the whisky, and tobacco,
and tea, and sugar and various other things that he could
use. Two or three times a week he and the old wife
would come down to our place loaded with bottles of
whisky and sit before the fireplace in our living room
and get comfortably full. I loved to watch and listen
to them, they were so happy, so loving, so given to
recalling the pleasant days of their youth and vigour.
And so it went on for several months, and finally one
spring day, when by chance our rivals happened to be
lounging in our trade room, the old couple sauntered
in and tossed the robe over the counter, the old man
saying to Berry: "There it is, my son. I fulfil my
promise. But put it away clear out of sight, lest I be
tempted to take it back."

Maybe we didn't enjoy the chagrin of our rivals!
Each one of them had been so sure that he was going
to get the odd robe. But then they were "pilgrims";
they didn't "savvy" the Indians. We got our 4,000
robes that winter, more than all the rest of them together. We finally sold the robe. The fame of it
spread up and down the river, and finally a Montreal,
Canada, gentleman, making a tour of the country,
heard of it; and when the steamboat he was on stopped
at our place he came in and bought it before we knew

where we were at. We did not wish to sell it, and named a price that we deemed prohibitive. To our amazement he laid down two large bills, threw the robe over his shoulder, and hurried back to the boat. Berry and I looked at each other and said things.

CHAPTER VIII

THERE was a little town in northern Montana, where upon certain days things would run along as smoothly and monotonously as in a village of this effete East. But at certain other times you would enter the place to find everyone on a high old tear. It seemed to be epidemic; if one man started to get gloriously full every one promptly joined in—doctor, lawyer, merchant, cattleman, sheepman and all. Well do I remember the last affair of that kind I witnessed there. By about 2 P. M. they got to the champagne stage— 'twas really sparkling cider or something of that kind— five dollars a bottle, and about fifty men were going from saloon to store and from store to hotel treating in turn— sixty dollars a round. I mention this as a prelude to what I have to say about drinking among the Indians in the old days. They were no worse than the whites in that way, and with them it seemed to be also epidemic.

Quietly and orderly a camp would be for days and days, and then suddenly all the men would start in on a drinking bout. Really, I believe that the Indians at such times, free as they were from any restraint, to whom law was an unknown term, were better behaved than would be a like number of our working-men in the same condition. True, they frequently quarrelled with each other when in liquor, and a quarrel was something to be settled only by blood. But let a thousand white men get drunk together, would there not ensue some fearful scenes? One reads of the ferocity of Indians when drinking, but my own experience was that on the whole they were exceedingly good-natured and jovial at such times, and often infinitely amusing. One night that winter on the Marias I was wending my way homeward from a visit at Sorrel Horse's place, when a man and woman came out of the trade room and staggered along the trail toward me. I slipped behind a cottonwood tree. The man was very unsteady on his feet and the woman, trying to help him along, at the same time was giving him a thorough scolding. I heard her say: "——, and you didn't look out for me a bit; there you were in that crowd, just drinking with one and then another, and never looking to see how I was getting along. You don't protect me at all; you don't care for me, or you would not have let me stay in there to be insulted."

The man stopped short and, swaying this way and that, gave a roar like a wounded grizzly: "Don't care for you; don't protect you; let you get insulted," he spluttered and foamed. "Who insulted you? Who? I say. Let me at him! Let me at him! I'll fix him with this."

Right there by the trail was lying a large, green, cottonwood log which would have weighed at least a ton. He bent over it and tried again and again to lift it, shouting: "Protect you! Insulted! Who did it? Where is he? Wait until I pick up this club and let me at him."

But the club wouldn't be picked up, and he became perfectly frantic in his efforts to lift it up and place it on his shoulder. He danced from one end to the other of it with increasing ardour and anger, until he finally fell over it exhausted, and then the patient woman picked him up—he was a little, light fellow—and carried him home.

I knew a young man who always became very mis-chievous when he drank. He had three wives and at such times he would steal their little stores of fine pem-mican, fancy bead-work, their needles and awls, and give them to other women. He was up to his pranks one morning as I happened along, and the women deter-mined to catch and bind him until he became sober. But he would not be caught; they chased him through the camp, out toward the hills, by the river, back to camp, when, by means of a travois leaning against it, he climbed to the top of his lodge, seated himself in the V-shaped crotch of the lodge poles, and jibed the women for their poor running qualities, enumerated the articles he had stolen from them, and so on. He was exceedingly hilarious. The wives held a whispered consultation, and one of them went inside. Their tormentor ceased jibing and began a drinking song:

"Bear Chief, he gave me a drink,
Bear Chief, he gave me a —— "

That was as far as he got. The wife had thrown a huge armful of rye grass from her couch upon the smouldering fire, it blazed up with a sudden roar and burst of flame which reached the tenderest part of his anatomy; he gave a loud yell of surprise and pain and leaped from his perch. When he struck the ground the women were upon him and I know not how many lariats they coiled about him before they bore him inside, amid the jeers and jests of a throng of laughing spectators, and laid him upon his couch.

But there was another side, and by no means a pleas-ant one to this drinking business. One night, when there were few Indians about, Berry, one of his traders named T. and I were lingering by the fireplace in the trade room.   There had been a crowd there earlier in the evening, and two remained, both sleeping off the effects of their carouse in a corner opposite us.   Suddenly Berry shouted: "Look out, T.!" at the same time giving him a fierce shove against me which sent us both to the floor.   And he was none too soon, for even as it was, an arrow grazed the skin of T.'s right side.   One of the drunken Indians had awakened, deliberately fitted an arrow to his bow, and was just about to let fly at T., when Berry saw him.   Before he could draw another arrow from his quiver we pounced on him and threw him outside.   Why he did it, if for some fancied wrong, or if he was still dreaming, we never knew.   He was a Blood, and they were a very treacherous tribe.

Another evening Berry unbarred the door to go out when it suddenly flew open and a tall Indian, frozen stiff, with an arrow sticking in his bosom, fell inside. Some one with grim humour had leaned the frozen body against the door with a view of giving us a surprise. The dead man was also a Blood, and it was never known who killed him.

Out on a hunt one day down on the Missouri, I killed a buffalo which had what the traders called a "beaver robe," because the hair was so exceedingly fine, thick, and of a glossy, silky nature.   Beaver robes were rare, and I had skinned this with horns and hoofs intact.   I wished to have it especially well tanned, as I intended it for a present to an Eastern friend.   The Crow Woman, good old soul, declared that she would do the work herself, and promptly stretched the hide on a frame.   The next morning it was frozen stiff as a board, and she was standing on it busily chipping it, when a half-drunk

Cree came along. I happened in sight just as he was
about to pull her off of the hide, and hurrying over
there I struck him with all my power square in the forehead with my fist. The blow did not stagger him. It
has often been said that it is nearly impossible to knock
an Indian down, and I believe it. Well, the Cree picked
up a broken lodge pole, the longest and heaviest end
of it, and came for me, and as I was unarmed I had to
turn and ignominiously run; I was not so swift as my
pursuer, either. It is hard to say what would have
happened—probably I would have been killed had
Berry not seen the performance and hurried to my assistance. The Cree was just on the point of giving me a
blow on the head when Berry fired, and the Indian fell
with a bullet through his shoulder. Some of his people
came along and packed him home. Then the Cree
chief and his council came over and we had a fine pow-
wow about the matter. It ended by our paying damages. We did our best always to get along with as
little friction as possible, but I did hate to pay that
Cree for a wound he richly deserved.

We traded several seasons with the Crees and North
Blackfeet down on the Missouri, they having followed
the last of the Saskatchewan buffalo herds south into
Montana. There was a certain young Blackfoot with
whom I was especially friendly, but one day he came
in very drunk and I refused to give him any liquor. He
became very angry and walked out making dire threats.
I had forgotten all about the incident when several
hours later his wife came running in and said that Took-
a-gun-under-the-water (It-su'-yi-na-mak-an) was coming to kill me. The woman was terribly frightened
and begged me to pity her and not kill her husband,
whom she dearly loved and who, when sober, would be

terribly ashamed of himself for attempting to hurt me.
I went to the door and saw my quondam friend coming, He had on no wearing apparel whatever except
his moccasins, and had painted his face, body, and limbs
with fantastic stripes of green, yellow, and red; he was
brandishing a .44 Winchester and calling upon the Sun
to witness how he would kill me, his worst enemy. Of
course I didn't want to kill him any more than his wife
wished to see him killed. Terror-stricken, she ran and
hid in a pile of robes, and I took my stand behind the
open door with a Winchester. On came he of the long
name, singing, shouting the war song, and saying repeatedly, "Where is that bad white man? Show him
to me that I may give him one bullet, just this one
little bullet?"

With carbine full cocked he strode in, looking eagerly
ahead for a sight of me, and just as he passed I gave him
a smart blow on top of the head with the barrel of my
rifle; down he dropped senseless to the floor, his carbine going off and sending the missile intended for me
through a case of tinned tomatoes on a shelf. The
woman ran out from her hiding place at the sound of the
shot, thinking that I had surely killed him; but her joy
was great when she learned her mistake. Together we
bound him tightly and got him home to his lodge.

Now, one often reads that an Indian never forgives a
blow nor an injury of any kind, no matter how much at
fault he may have been. That is all wrong. The next
morning Took-a-gun-under-the-water sent me a fine
buffalo robe. At dusk he came in and begged me to
forgive him. Ever after we were the best of friends.
Whenever I had time for a short hunt back in the breaks,
or out on the plains, I chose him for my companion,
and a more faithful and considerate one I never had.

I cannot say that all traders got along so well with the Indians as did Berry and I. There were some bad men among them, men who delighted in inflicting pain, in seeing blood flow. I have known such to kill Indians just for fun, but never in a fair, open fight. They were great cowards, and utterly unprincipled. These men sold "whisky" which contained tobacco juice, cayenne pepper, and various other vile things. Berry and I sold weak liquor, it is true, but the weakness consisted of nothing but pure water—which was all the better for the consumer. I make no excuse for the whisky trade. It was wrong, all wrong, and none realised it better than we when we were dispensing the stuff. It caused untold suffering, many deaths, great demoralisation among those people of the plains. There was but one redeeming feature about it: The trade was at a time when it did not deprive them of the necessities of life; there was always more meat, more fur to be had for the killing of it. In comparison with various Government officials and rings, who robbed and starved the Indians to death on their reservations after the buffalo disappeared, we were saints.

All in all, that was a pleasant winter we passed on the Marias. Hunting with the Indians, lounging around a lodge fire, or before our own or Sorrel Horse's fireplace of an evening, the days fairly flew. Sometimes I would go with Sorrel Horse to visit his "baits," and it was a great sight to see the huge wolves lying stiff and stark about, and even on them. To make a good bait a buffalo was killed and cut open on the back, and into the meat, blood, and entrails three vials of strychnine —three-eighths of an ounce—were stirred. It seemed as if the merest bite of this deadly mixture was enough to kill, a victim seldom getting more than 200 yards away before the terrible convulsions seized him. Of course, great numbers of coyotes and kit foxes were also posioned, but they didn't count. The large, heavy-furred wolf skins were in great demand in the East for sleigh and carriage robes, and sold right at Fort Benton for from three dollars to five dollars each. I had a fancy to take some of these stiffly-frozen animals home, and stand them up around Sorrel Horse's house. They were an odd and interesting sight, standing there, heads and tails up, as if guarding the place; but one day there came a chinook wind and they soon toppled over and were skinned.

So the days went, and then came spring. The river cleared itself of ice in one grand, grinding rush of massive cakes; green grass darkened the valley slopes; geese and ducks honked and quacked in every slough. We all, Indians and whites, wished to do nothing but lie out on the ground in the warm sunshine, and smoke and dream in quiet contentment.

CHAPTER IX

I HAVE A LODGE OF MY OWN

WHY don't you get a woman?" Weasel Tail abruptly asked one evening as Talks-with-the-buffalo and I sat smoking with him in his lodge.

"Yes," my other friend put in. "Why not? You have the right to do so, for you can count a coup; yes, two of them. You killed a Cree, and you took a Cree horse in the fight at the Hairy Cap."

"I took a horse," I replied, "and a good one he is; but you are mistaken about the Cree; you will remember that he escaped by running into the pines on Hairy Cap."

"Oh!" said Talks-with-the-buffalo, "I don't mean that one; we all know he got away, I mean one of those who first fell when we all fired into them. That tall one, the man who wore a badger-skin cap; you killed him. I saw the bullet wound in his body; no ball from any of our rifles could have made such a small hole."

This was news to me; I remembered well having shot several times at that particular warrior, but I never had thought that 'twas my bullet that ended his career. I did not know whether to feel glad or sorry about it, but finally concluded that it was best to feel glad, for he would have killed me if he could have done so. I was turning the matter over in my mind, recalling every little incident of that memorable day, when my host aroused me from my reverie: "I said, Why don't you take a woman? Answer."

97

"Oh!" I replied. "No one would have me. Isn't that a good reason?"

"Kyai-yo'!" exclaimed Madame Weasel Tail, clapping her hand to her mouth, the Blackfoot way of expressing surprise or wonder. "Kyai-yo'! What a reason! I well know that there isn't a girl in this camp but would like to be his woman. Why, if it wasn't for this lazy one here"—giving Weasel Tail's hand an affectionate squeeze—"if he would only go away somewhere and never come back, I'd make you take me. I'd follow you around until you would have to do so."

"Mah'-kah-kan-is-tsi!" I exclaimed, which is a flippant and slangy term, expressing doubt of the speaker's truthfulness.

"Mah'-kah-kan-is-tsi yourself," she rejoined. "Why do you think you are asked to all these Assiniboin dances, where all the young women wear their best clothes, and try to catch you with their robes? Why do you think they put on their best things and go to the trading post with their mothers or other relatives every chance they get? What, you don't know? Well, I'll tell you: they go, each one, hoping that you will notice her, and send a friend to her parents to make a proposal."

"It is the truth," said Weasel Tail.

"Yes, the truth," Talks-with-the-buffalo and his woman joined in.

Well, I laughed, a little affectedly, perhaps, and turned the conversation by asking about the destination of a war party which was to start out in the morning. Nevertheless, I thought over the matter a good deal. All the long winter I had rather envied my good friends Berry and Sorrel Horse, who seemed to be so happy with their women, Never a cross word, always the best

"A plainsman always said 'my woman' when speaking of
his Indian better-half"

of good fellowship and open affection for each other.
Seeing all this, I had several times said to myself: "It is
not good that the man should be alone." That quota-
tion is from the Bible, is it not, or is it from Shakespeare?
Anyhow, it is true. The Blackfeet have much the same
expression: "Mat'-ah-kwi täm-äp-i-ni-po-ke-mi-o-sin—
not found (is) happiness without woman."

After that evening I looked more closely at the various young women I met in the camp or at the trading
post, saying to myself: "Now, I wonder what kind of a
woman that would make? Is she neat, good-tempered,
moral?" All the time, however, I knew that I had no
right to take one of them. I did not intend to remain
long in the West; my people would never forgive me for
making an alliance with one. They were of old, proud
Puritan stock, and I could imagine them holding up
their hands in horror at the mere hint of such a thing.

You will notice that thus far in this part of my story
I have substituted the word woman for wife. A
plainsman always said "my woman" when speaking of
his Indian better half; the Blackfoot said the same:
"Nit-o-ké-man," my woman. None of the plainsmen
were legally married, unless the Indian manner in which
they took a woman, by giving so many horses, or so
much merchandise for one, could be considered legal.
In the first place there was no one in the country to
perform the marriage service except occasionally a
wandering Jesuit priest, and again, these men, almost
without exception, didn't care a snap what the law said
in regard to the matter. There was no law. Neither
did they believe in religion; the commands of the
church were nothing to them. They took unto themselves Indian women; if the woman proved good and
true, well and good; if otherwise, there was a separation.

In it all there was never a thought of future complications and responsibilities; their creed was: "Eat, drink, and be merry, for to-day we live and to-morow we die."

"No," I said to myself time and again; "no, it will not do; hunt, go to war, do anything but take a woman, and in the fall go home to your people." This is the line of conduct I laid out for myself and meant to follow. But——

One morning the Crow Woman and I were sitting out under a shade she had constructed of a couple of travois and a robe or two. She was busy as usual, embroidering a moccasin with coloured quills, and I was thoroughly cleaning my rifle, preparatory to an antelope hunt. A couple of women came by on their way to the trade room with three or four robes. One of them was a girl of perhaps sixteen or seventeen years, not what one might call beautiful, still she was good-looking, fairly tall, and well-formed, and she had fine large, candid, expressive eyes, perfect white, even teeth and heavy braided hair which hung almost to the ground. All in all, there was something very attractive about her. "Who is that?" I asked the Crow Woman. "That girl, I mean."

"Don't you know? She comes here often; she is a cousin of Berry's woman."

I went away on my hunt, but it didn't prove to be very interesting. I was thinking all the time about the cousin. That evening I spoke to Berry about her, learned that her father was dead; that her mother was a medicine lodge woman, and noted for her unswerving uprightness and goodness of character. "I'd like to have the girl," I said. "What do you think about it?"

"We'll see," Berry replied. "I'll talk with my old woman."

A couple of days went by and nothing was said by either of us about the matter, and then one afternoon Mrs. Berry told me that I was to have the girl, providing I would promise to be always good and kind to her. I readily agreed to that.

"Very well, then," said Mrs. Berry; "go into the trade room and select a shawl, some dress goods, some bleached muslin—no, I'll select the outfit and make her some white women's dresses like mine."

"But, hold on!" I exclaimed. "What am I to pay? How many horses, or whatever is wanted?"

"Her mother says there is to be no pay, only that you are to keep your promise to be good to her daughter."

This was quite unusual, to request that nothing be given over for a daughter. Usually a lot of horses were sent to the parents, sometimes fifty or more. Sometimes the father demanded so many head, but if no number was specified, the suitor gave as many as he could. Again, it was not unusual for a father to request some promising youth, good hunter and bold raider, to become his son-in-law. In that case he was the one to give horses, and even a lodge and household goods, with the girl.

Well, I got the girl. It was an embarrassing time for us both when she came in one evening, shawl over her face, while we were eating supper. Sorrel Horse and his woman were there, and with Berry and his madame they made things interesting for us with their jokes, until Berry's mother put a stop to it. We were a pretty shy couple for a long time, she especially. "Yes" and "no" were about all that I could get her to say. But my room underwent a wonderful transformation; everything was kept so neat and clean, my clothes were so nicely washed, and my "medicine" was

carefully taken out every day and hung on a tripod. I
had purchased a war bonnet, shield, and various other
things which the Blackfeet regard as sacred, and I did
not say to any one that I thought they were not so. I
had them handled with due pomp and ceremony.

As time passed this young woman became more and
more of a mystery to me. I wondered what she thought
of me, and if she speculated upon what I might think
of her. I had no fault to find, she was always neat,
always industrious about our little household affairs,
quick to supply my wants. But that wasn't enough.
I wanted to know her, her thoughts and beliefs. I
wanted her to talk and laugh with me, and tell stories,
as I could often hear her doing in Madame Berry's
domicile. Instead of that, when I came around, the
laugh died on her lips, and she seemed to freeze, to
shrink within herself. The change came when I least
expected it. I was down in the Piegan camp one afternoon and learned that a war party was being made up
to raid the Crows. Talks-with-the-buffalo and Weasel
Tail were going, and asked me to go with them. I
readily agreed, and returned to the post to prepare for
the trip. "Năt-ah'-ki," I said, bursting into our room,
"give me all the moccasins I have, some clean socks,
some pemmican. Where is my little brown canvas
bag? Where have you put my gun case? Where——"

"What are you going to do?"

It was the first question she had ever asked me.

"Do? I'm going to war; my friends are going, they
asked me to join them——"

I stopped, for she suddenly arose and faced me, and
her eyes were very bright. "You are going to war!"
she exclaimed. "You, a white man, are going with a
lot of Indians sneaking over the plains at night to steal

horses, and perhaps kill some poor prairie people. You
have no shame!"

"Why," I said, rather faintly, I presume, "I thought
you would be glad. Are not the Crows your enemies?
I have promised, I must go."

"It is well for the Indians to do this," she went on,
"but not for a white man. You, you are rich; you have
everything you want; those papers, that yellow hard
rock (gold) you carry will buy anything you want; you
should be ashamed to go sneaking over the plains like a
coyote. None of your people ever did that."

"I must go." I reiterated. "I have given my promise to go."

Then Nät-ah'-ki began to cry, and she came nearer
and grasped my sleeve. "Don't go," she pleaded, "for
if you do, I know you will be killed, and I love you so
much."

I was never so surprised, so taken aback, as it were.
All these weeks of silence, then, had been nothing but
her natural shyness, a veil to cover her feelings. I was
pleased and proud to know that she did care for me, but
underlying that thought was another one: I had done
wrong in taking this girl, in getting her to care for me,
when in a short time I must return her to her mother
and leave for my own country.

I readily promised not to accompany the war party,
and then, her point gained, Nät-ah'-ki suddenly felt
that she had been over-bold and tried to assume her
reserve again. But I would not have it that way. I
grasped her hand and made her sit down by my side,
and pointed out to her that she was wrong; that to
laugh, to joke, to be good friends and companions was
better than to pass our days in silence, repressing all
natural feeling. After that, the sun always shone.

I don't know that I have done right in putting all

this on paper, yet I think that if Năt-ah'-ki could know what I have written she would smile and say: "Oh, yes, tell it all; tell it just as it was."

For as you shall learn, it all came right in the end, all except the last, the very end.

You who have read the book "Blackfoot Lodge Tales" will remember that it was not allowable for a Blackfoot to meet his mother-in-law. I fancy that there are many white men who would rejoice if such a custom prevailed in civilised society. Among the Blackfeet a man could never visit the lodge of his mother-in-law, she could not enter his lodge when he was at home, both were obliged to go far out of the way, to endure any discomfort, in order to avoid meeting at any time and place. This queer custom caused not a few ludicrous scenes. I once saw a tall and dignified chief fall backward behind a high counter as his mother-in-law appeared in the doorway of the store. I have seen a man drop by the side of a trail and cover himself with his robe; and once I saw one jump off a high cut bank, clothes, robe, and all, into deep water, as the mother-in-law suddenly appeared nearby. In the case of a white man, however, this custom was somewhat modified. Knowing that he paid no attention to it, the mother-in-law would come into a room or lodge where he was, but would not speak to him. I had taken a fancy to my mother-in-law, and I was glad to have her come around. After a time I even succeeded in getting her to talk to me. She was a good woman, a woman of great firmness of character and rectitude, and she had brought up her daughter to be like her. The two thought everything of each other, and Năt-ah'-ki never tired of telling how much the good mother had done for her, what advice she had given, how many sacrifices she had made for her child's sake.

CHAPTER X

THE KILLING OF A BEAR

TOWARD the end of April we abandoned the trading post. Berry intended to resume freighting to the mines as soon as the steamboats began to arrive, and moved his family into Fort Benton. Thither also went Sorrel Horse and his outfit. The Bloods and Blackfeet moved north to summer on the Belly and Saskatchewan rivers. Most of the Piegans trailed over to Milk River and the Sweetgrass Hills country. The band with which I was connected, the Small Robes, pulled out for the foot of the Rockies, and I went with them. I had purchased a lodge and a half dozen pack and train animals to transport our outfit. We had a Dutch oven, two fry pans, a couple of small kettles, and some tin and iron tableware, of which Nät-ah′-ki was very proud. Our commissary consisted of one sack of flour, some sugar, salt, beans, coffee, bacon, and dried apples. I had plenty of tobacco and cartridges. We were rich; the world was before us. When the time came to move, I attempted to help pack our outfit, but Nät-ah′-ki stopped me at once.

"Aren't you ashamed?" she said. "This is my work; go up in front there and ride with the chiefs. I'll attend to this."

I did as I was ordered to do. After that I rode ahead with the big men, or hunted along by the way, and at evening on arriving at camp there was our lodge set up, a pile of fuel beside it, a bright fire within, over which the evening meal was being prepared. The girl and her mother had done it all, and when everything was in order the latter went away to the lodge of her brother, with whom she lived. We had many visitors, and I was constantly being asked to go and feast and smoke with this one and that one. Our store of provisions did not last long, and we soon were reduced to a diet of meat straight. Every one was contented with that but I; how I did long at times for an apple pie, for some potatoes even. I often dreamed that I was the happy possessor of some candy.

Leaving the abandoned fort we followed up the Marias, then its most northern tributary, the Cutbank River, until we came to the pines at the foot of the Rockies. Here was game in vast numbers; not many buffalo nor antelope just there, but elk, deer, mountain sheep, and moose were even more plentiful than I had seen them south of the Missouri. As for bears, the whole country was torn up by them. None of the women would venture out after fuel or poles for lodge or travois without an escort. Many of the hunters never molested a grizzly, the bear being regarded as a sort of medicine or sacred animal, many believing that it was really a human being. It was commonly called Kyai'-yo, but the medicine-pipe men were obliged when speaking of it to call it Pah'-ksi-kwo-yi, sticky mouth. They, too, were the only ones who could take any of the skin of a bear, and then merely a strip for a head band or pipe wrapping. It was allowable, however, for anyone to use the bear's claws for a necklace or other ornament. Some of the more adventurous wore a three or four-row necklace of their own killing, of which they were very proud.

One morning with Heavy Breast I went up on the

divide between Cutbank and Milk River.   He said that
we could easily ride through the pines there to the foot
of a bare mountain where there were always more or
less sheep.   We wanted some meat, and at that season
the mountain rams were even in better order than were
the buck antelope on the plains.   We found broad game
trails running through the timber, and soon came near
the inner edge of it.   Dismounting and securing our
horses, we went on carefully, and in a few moments
could see, through the interlacing branches of the pines,
a good-sized band of bighorn, all rams, trailing across
the shell rock at the foot of a cliff.   I let Heavy Breast
have the first shot, and he missed altogether.   Before
he could reload I managed to get two of the animals
with my Henry.   Both were very large ones with some
little fat on their ribs, and, having all the meat we cared
to pack, we loaded our horses and started homeward.
Passing out of the pines we saw, some four or five hundred yards distant, a large grizzly industriously tearing
up the sod on the bare hillside, in search of a gopher,
or ants' nest.

"Let us kill him," I exclaimed.

"Ok-yi (come on)," said Heavy Breast, but with an
inflection which meant, "All right, but it's your proposition, not mine."

We rode along in the edge of the timber down under
the hill, my companion praying, promising the Sun an
offering, and begging for success.   At the foot of the
hill we turned into a deep coulée and followed it up until
we thought we were quite near to the place where we
had seen the bear; then we rode up out of it, and, sure
enough, there was the old fellow not fifty yards away.
He saw us as quickly as we did him, sat up on his haunches
and wiggled his nose as he sniffed the air.   We both

fired and with a hair-lifting roar the bear rolled over, biting and clawing at his flank where a bullet had struck him, and then springing to his feet he charged us open-mouthed. We both urged our horses off to the north, for it was not a wise thing to turn back down the hill. I fired a couple of shots at the old fellow as fast as I could, but without effect. The bear meantime had covered the ground with surprisingly long bounds, and was already quite close to the heels of my companion's horse. I fired again and made another miss, and just then Heavy Breast, his saddle, and his sheep meat parted company with the fleeing pony; the cinch, an old, worn, rawhide band, had broken.

"Hai ya', my friend!" he cried, pleadingly, as he soared up in the air, still astride the saddle. Down they came with a loud thud not two steps in front of the onrushing bear, and that animal, with a dismayed and frightened "woof," turned sharply about and fled back toward the timber, I after him. I kept firing and firing, and finally by a lucky shot broke his back bone; it was easy then to finish him with a deliberately aimed bullet in the base of the brain. When it was all over I suddenly remembered how ridiculous Heavy Breast had appeared soaring on a horseless saddle, and how his eyes bulged as he called upon me for aid. I began to laugh and it seemed as if I never could stop. My companion had come up beside me and stood, very solemn, looking at me and the bear.

"Do not laugh, my friend," he said. "Do not laugh. Rather, pray to the good Sun, make sacrifice to him, that when you are sometime hard pressed by the enemy, or such another one as he lying here, you may as fortunately escape as did I. Surely the Sun listened to my prayer. I promised to sacrifice to him, intending to

hang up that fine white blanket I have just bought. I
will now do better. I will hang up the blanket and
my otter skin cap."

The bear had a fine coat of fur, and I determined to
take it and have it tanned. Heavy Breast took my
horse in order to catch his, which had run out of sight
into the valley, and I set to work. It was no small task,
for the bear was quite fat, and I wanted to get the hide
off as clean as possible. Long before I accomplished it
my friend returned with his animal, dismounted a little
way off, sat down, filled and lighted his pipe.

"Help me," I said, after he had smoked. "I'm
getting tired."

"I cannot do so," said he. "It is against my medicine; my dream forbade me to touch a bear."

We arrived in camp betimes, and hearing me ride
up beside the lodge, Nät-ah'-ki hurried out.

"Kyai-yo'!" she exclaimed, seeing the bear skin.
"Kyai-yo'!" she again exclaimed, and hurried back
inside.

I thought that rather strange, for when I came in
from a hunt she always insisted upon unpacking and
unsaddling my mount, and leading the animal over to
the lodge of a boy who took care of my little band. After
I had done this I went inside; a dish of boiled boss
ribs, a bowl of soup were ready for me. As I ate I told
about the day's hunt, but when I described how Heavy
Breast had sailed through the air and how he looked
when he cried out to me, Nät-ah'-ki did not laugh with
me. I thought that strange, also, for she was so quick
to see the comical side of things.

"It is a fine hide," I concluded; "long, thick, dark
hair. I wish you would tan it for me."

"Ah!" she exclaimed. "I knew you would ask that

as soon as I saw it. Have pity on me, for I cannot do it. I cannot touch it. Only here and there is a woman, or even a man, who through the power of their medicine can handle a bear skin. To others who attempt it some great misfortune befalls; sickness, even death. None of us here would dare to tan the skin. There is a woman of the Kut-ai'-im-iks (Do-not-laugh band) who would do it for you, another in the Buffalo-chip band; yes, there are several, but they are all far away."

I said no more about it, and after a while went out and stretched the skin, by pegging it to the ground. Nät-ah'-ki was uneasy, repeatedly coming out to watch me for a moment, and then hurrying inside again. I kept on at work; there was still a lot of fat on the skin; try as I would I could not get it all off. I was pretty greasy and tired of my job when night came.

I awoke soon after daylight. Nät-ah'-ki was already up and out. I could hear her praying near the lodge, telling the Sun that she was about to take the bearskin, flesh and tan it. She begged her God to have mercy on her; she did not want to; she feared to touch the unclean thing, but her man wished it to be worked into a soft robe.

"Oh, Sun!" she concluded, "help me, protect me from the evil power of the shadow (the spirit, or soul) of this bear. I will sacrifice to you. Let my good health continue, give us all, my man, my mother, my relatives, me, give us all long life, happiness; let us live to be old."

My first thought was to call out and say that she need not tan the skin, that I really did not care for a bear robe after all; but I concluded that it would be well for her to do the work. If she did not learn that there was nothing in the malevolent influence of the bear's spirit,

she would at least beget confidence in herself and her
medicine. So I lay still for a while, listening to the
quick chuck-chuck of her flesher as it stripped meat and
fat from the skin. After a little she came in, and seeing
that I was awake, built a fire for the morning meal. As
soon as it began to burn she washed herself in half a
dozen waters, and then, placing some dried sweetgrass
on a few live coals, she bent over its fragrant smoke,
rubbing her hands in it.

"What are you doing?" I asked. "Why burning
sweetgrass this early?"

"I purify myself," she replied. "I am fleshing the
bearskin. I am going to tan it for you."

"Now, that is kind," I told her. "When we go to
Fort Benton I will get you the prettiest shawl I can find,
and is there any sacrifice to be made? Tell me, that
I may furnish it."

The little woman was pleased. She smiled happily,
and then became very serious. Sitting down by my
side she bent over and whispered:

"I have prayed. I have promised a sacrifice for
you and for me. We must give something good. You
have two short guns (revolvers); can you not spare one?
and I, I will give my blue cloth dress."

The blue cloth dress! her most cherished possession,
seldom worn but often taken from its parfleche covering,
smoothed out, folded, refolded, admired, and then put
away again. Surely, if she could part with that I could
afford to lose one of my six-shooters. One of them—
they were the old Colt cap and ball affairs—had a trick
of discharging all the chambers at once. Yes, I would
give that. So, after breakfast we went out a little way
from camp and hung our offerings in a tree, Nät-ah'-ki
praying while I climbed up and securely fastened them

to a sturdy branch. All that day women of the camp came and stared at the tanner of the bearskin, some begging her to quit the work at once, all prophesying that she would in some way have bad luck. But she heeded them not, and in the course of four or five days I had a large, soft, bear rug with which I promptly covered our couch. But there it seemed it could not remain if I cared to have any visitors, for none of my friends would enter the lodge while it was inside. I was obliged to store it away under a couple of rawhides behind our home.

We remained on the Cutbank River until about the first of June. The flies were becoming troublesome and we moved out on the plains where they were not nearly so plentiful. Swinging over the ridge we went down the course of Milk River several days' journey, finally camping for a time just north of the east butte of the Sweetgrass Hills, where the rest of the Piegans were staying. There was much coming and going of visitors between the two camps. We learned that a great scandal had occurred in the Do-not-laugh band soon after leaving the Marias. Yellow Bird Woman, the young and pretty wife of old Looking Back, had run away with a youth named Two Stars. It was thought that they had gone north to the Bloods or Blackfeet, and the husband had started in pursuit of them. There was much talk about the affair, much conjecture as to what would be the end of it. We soon learned.

One evening Nät-ah'-ki informed me that the guilty couple had arrived from the north, and were in the lodge of a young friend of theirs. They had eluded the husband when he arrived in the Blood camp, and doubled back south. He would probably go on to the Blackfoot camp in search of them, and they, meanwhile,

were going on to visit the Gros Ventres. After a time
they hoped he would give up the chase, and then, by
paying him heavy damages, they would be allowed to
live together in peace. The very next morning, however, soon after sunrise, our camp was aroused by a
woman's piercing, terror-stricken shrieks. Everyone
sprang from bed and ran out, the men with their weapons
thinking that perhaps some enemy was attacking us.
But no, 'twas Yellow Bird Woman who shrieked; her
husband had found and seized her as she was going
to the stream for water, he had her by one wrist and
was dragging her to the lodge of our chief, the woman
hanging back, crying and struggling to get loose. Breakfast was prepared in the lodges, but that morning the
camp was very quiet. There was no singing, no laughter,
no talking, even the children were still. I remarked
upon it to the little woman.

"Hush," she said, "she is to be pitied; I think something dreadful is about to happen."

Presently we heard the camp-crier shouting out that
there was to be a council in Big Lake's—our chief's—
lodge, and he called over the names of those requested
to be present; medicine-pipe men, mature hunters and
warriors, wise old men. One by one they went over to
the place; a profound silence settled over the camp.

We had our breakfast and I had smoked a couple of
pipes when the camp-crier was again heard: "All
women! all women!" he shouted. "You are to assemble at once at the lodge of our chief, where a punishment is about to take place. A woman has been
guilty of infidelity; you are to witness what happens to
one who so disgraces her husband, her relatives, and
herself."

I imagine that few women wanted to go, but following

the camp-crier were the Crazy Dog band of the All
Friends Society, camp police as it were, who went from
lodge to lodge and ordered the women out. As one
raised the flap of our doorway Nät-ah'-ki sprang over
to me and grasped me convulsively.

"Come," said the policeman, looking in. "Come,
hurry! Didn't you hear the call?"

"She is no longer a Piegan," I said quietly, although
I felt angry enough. "She is a white woman now, and
she does not go."

I thought there might be some argument about the
matter, but there was none; the man dropped the door
flap and went away without a word.

We waited in suspense. "What are they going to do?"
I asked. "Kill her or—the other thing?"

Nät-ah'-ki shuddered and did not answer, clinging to
me more closely than ever. Suddenly we heard again
those piercing shrieks; then again all was silence until
a man, our chief, began to talk.

"Kyi!" he said. "You all here standing, have witnessed what befalls one who proves untrue to her husband. It is a great crime, unfaithfulness. In the long
ago our fathers counselled together as to what should
be the punishment of a woman who brought sorrow and
shame to the lodge of her man and her parents. And
as they decided should be done, so has it been done to
this woman to-day that all you witnessing it may take
warning. She is marked with a mark she will bear as
long as she lives. Wherever she goes people will look
and laugh and say: 'Ha, a cut-nosed woman! There
goes a woman of loose character; isn't she pretty?'"

Then, one after another, several men made little
speeches, each one to the same effect, and when they
had finished the chief told the people to disperse. The

woman in the case went to the river to wash her bleeding face; her nose had been cut off. From the bridge to the lip it had been entirely removed with one deep concaved slash. She was a horrible sight, an animated human skull.

The youth? He had hurried away to his own camp and lodge as soon as the woman was caught. Nothing was said nor done to him. In that we civilised and uncivilised people are alike. The woman always suffers but the man goes free.

"You see," Nät-ah'-ki told me, "the woman was not to blame; she had always loved Two Stars, but he is very poor and her bad father made her go to bad old Looking Back, who had already five women, and is very mean and cruel to them. Oh, I pity her!"

CHAPTER XI

THE KUTENAI'S STORY

IT WAS after breakfast. Nāt-ah'-ki recombed and rebraided her hair, binding it with a bright blue ribbon, donned her best dress, put on her prettiest pair of moccasins.

"What now?" I asked. "Why all this finery?"

"This morning Lone Elk takes out his sacred pipe, carrying it about through the camp. We follow him. Will you not come?"

Of course I would go, and I also put on my finery, a pair of fringed buckskin trousers, with bright, beaded vine-work running along the outer seams; a fringed and beaded buckskin shirt, a pair of gorgeous moccasins. I fancy that I must have been rather picturesque in that costume, with my hair so long that it rippled down over my shoulders. The Indians hated to see hair worn cropped short. Many a time, in speaking of the old days, the various factors and other prominent men of the American Fur Company, I have heard them say: "Yes, so and so was a chief; he wore long hair. There are no more white chiefs; all those we now meet are sheared."

We were late. There was such a crowd in and around the lodge of the medicine man that we could not get near it, but the lodge skin was raised all around and we could see what was going on. With hands purified by the smoke of burning sweetgrass, Lone Elk was remov-

ing the wrappings of the pipe, or, to be exact, the pipe-
stem; singing, he and those seated in the lodge, the
appropriate song for each wrap. There was the song of
the antelope, of the wolf, the bear, the buffalo, the last
very slow, deep, solemn. At last the long stem—eagle-
plumed, fur-wrapped, gorgeous with tufts of brilliant
feathers, lay exposed—and reverently lifting it he held it
up toward the sun, down toward the earth, pointed it
to the north, south, east, and west as he prayed for health,
happiness, long life for all of us. Then, rising, and holding the stem extended in front of him he danced slowly,
deliberately out of the lodge, the men, I too, falling in one
by one behind him. So did the women and the children,
until there were several hundred of us in the long, snake-
like procession, dancing along, weaving in and out round
the lodges of the camp, singing the various songs, of the
medicine pipe. A song finished, we rested a little before
another one was started, and in the interval the people
talked and laughed. They were happy; not one there
but believed in the efficacy of their prayers and devotion;
that the Sun was pleased to see them there, dressed in
their very best, dancing in his honour. Thus we went
on and on, and around and around, until the whole circuit
of the camp had been made and our leader came to the
doorway of his lodge; there he dismissed us and we
wended our several ways homeward to resume our everyday clothing and occupations.

"Kyi," said Nät-ah'-ki, "Wasn't it a happy dance?
And how fine the people looked dressed in their good
clothes."

"Ai," I replied, "it was a joy dance and the people
looked fine. There was one girl I noticed, prettiest and
best dressed of all."

"Who was it? Tell me quick!"

"Why, the white woman who lives in this lodge, of course."

Nät-ah'-ki said nothing, turning away from me in fact, but I caught the expression of her eyes; she was pleased, but too shy to let me know it.

The June days were long, but to me they seemed to fly. To hunt, to sit in the shade of the lodges and idly watch the people at their various work, to listen to the old men's stories was all very interesting. One day there came to our camp three Kutenai Indians, bringing to Big Lake some tobacco from their chief and the proposal of a visit of his tribe to the Piegans. They had come straight to us from their country across the Rockies, up through the dense forests of the western slope, over the glacier-capped heights of the great mountains, down the deep cañon of Cutbank Stream, and then straight to our camp, a hundred miles out in the vast plain. How knew they whence to shape their course with such certainty, to go straight to the only camp in all that immense stretch of mountain and butte-sentinelled, rolling plain? Perhaps it was partly instinct. They may have struck the trail of some homing war-party, some marauding party of their own people may have given them the location of those they sought. Anyhow, straight to us they came from the headwaters of the Columbia, and our chiefs took the tobacco they brought, smoked it in council, and pronounced it good. Some there were who having lost relatives in war against the mountain tribe, objected to making peace with them, and talked earnestly against it. But the majority were against them, and the messengers departed with word to their chief that the Piegans would be glad to have a long visit from him and his people.

In due time they came, not many of them, no more

" 'This morning Lone Elk takes out his sacred pipe. . . .
Will you not come?' "

than seven hundred all told, which, I understood, was
the larger part of the tribe.   They were very different
physically from the Piegans, no taller, perhaps, but
much heavier built, with larger hands and feet.   This
was naturally the result of their mountain life; they were
great bighorn and goat hunters, and constant climbing
had developed their leg muscles almost abnormally.
The Blackfeet disdained that sort of life; they would not
hunt that which they could not ride to or near, and the
hardest work they ever did was to butcher the animals
they killed and pack the meat on the horses.   No wonder,
then, that their hands and feet were small and delicately
fashioned, the former as soft and smooth as those of a
woman.

Old Sah'-aw-ko-kin-ap-i, Back-in-sight,   the Kutenai chief, came on with a few of his head men some little
time in advance of the main body, and ere our chief Big
Lake was aware that the expected visitors were anywhere near, the door-flap of his lodge was raised and the
Kutenais entered.   Taken thus by surprise it was custom-
ary for the host to make the visitor a present, and by the
end of the first smoke the Kutenai chief was five horses
richer than when he entered the camp.

The Kutenais pitched their lodges close by our camp
and ere the women fairly got them up and fires burning,
visiting and feasting and exchanging presents between
the two tribes was in full swing.   The Kutenais brought
with them large quantities of arrowroot and dried camas,
the latter a yellow, sweet, sticky, roasted bulb which
tasted good to one who had not seen a vegetable of any
kind for months.   The Piegans were exceedingly pleased
to get these, and in return gave the Kutenai wives much
of their stores of choice pemmican and dried meats, and
they bartered buffalo leather and parfleche for the

tanned skins of sheep and moose, and other mountain animals.

Of course the young men of both tribes went courting. In the Kutenai camp were the Piegan youths, and vice versa, standing around in silent stateliness, decked out in all their gorgeous finery, their faces strikingly painted, their long hair neatly braided. The more fortunate of them carried suspended by a thong from the left wrist a small mirror which kept turning and flashing in the bright sunlight; sometimes the mirror was set into a rude wooden frame carved by the owner and brightly painted. Of course these gallants of the plains never spoke to any of the maidens about, nor could one be sure, from observation, that they even looked at them. They stood here, there, by the hour, apparently gazing away off at some far distant object, but on the sly they were really watching the girls, and knew intimately every feature of each one's face, every little trait of action and repose; and the maids, oh, they were, apparently, wholly unaware that there were any young men in the camp. You never caught one looking at them, but they did all the same, and then they would get together and discuss the looks of this one and that one, and his valour, and temper, just as do white girls. I am sure of this, for Nät-ah'-ki told me all about it, and how, in secret, they ridiculed and laughed at some vainglorious swain who did not please them, but who himself thought that he was the only perfect and charming beau of the camp.

There was much racing, much gambling and dancing by the younger men of the two camps. Their elders looked on at it all in quiet approval, and talked of their hunts and battles, and the strange places and things they had seen. Most of this talk was in signs, but there were a few Kutenais, both men and women, who could speak Blackfoot, having learned it when captives, or upon the occasion of a long sojourn in the tribe. Indeed, there was no surrounding tribe which had not one or two Blackfoot-speaking members. None of the Blackfeet, however, spoke any language other than their own, and the sign language; they held all other people as inferiors and regarded it as beneath their dignity to learn any other tongue. One Blackfoot-speaking Kutenai, a very aged but still fairly active man, was a frequent visitor to my lodge. He must have felt that he was welcome there, for a bowl of food and plenty to smoke were always ready for him. In return for my hospitality and frequent gifts of a cut of tobacco, he told me stories of his travels and adventures. He had been a great wanderer in his time, an ethnologist in a way, for he had been among many tribes in various parts of the country, from the Blackfoot land to the coast, and south as far as the Great Salt Lake, and had made a study of their languages and customs. One evening he told us what he called his "Story of the Fish-eaters," which Nät-ah'-ki and I thought interesting.

"This happened long ago in my youthful days," he said, "We were four, all single, close friends to one another. We had been on several raids which were successful, and we were acquiring each a nice band of horses and things for the time when we should take women and have lodges of our own. There were many who wished to join us on our expeditions, but we did not care to have them, for we thought four the lucky number, one for each direction of the world. Indeed, among ourselves we did not call each other by our proper names, but by the different directions; thus, one was named North, another South, another East; I was West. Twice we had been out raiding on the plains; once we went

south; this time we started westward, having heard
that away down on a big river lived a people rich in
horses.   It was early in the summer when we started, and
we had made up our minds to travel on and on until we
found these fine herds of horses, even if they were two
or three moons' journey away.   We carried besides our
weapons and lariats and extra moccasins some awls and
sinew thread so that we could make for ourselves new
clothing, new footwear, if that we had should wear out.

"We went down by the lake of the Flatheads, camping and resting two days with them, and thence we
travelled on to the lake of the Pend d'Oreilles, through a
great forest where often there were no trails except those
made by the game.   At the lake, near the north end of
it, we saw the smoke of the Pend d'Oreilles' fires, and
several of their boats away out on the water.   But we
did not go near their camp.   They had good herds, from
which we might have taken our pick if we had wished
to, but we pressed on; we were bent on discovery; we
wanted to see the far land and its people.   The forest
grew denser, darker, as we went on; the trees were larger
than any we had seen before.   There was little game;
the animals and birds seemed never to have lived in it;
it was too dark and cheerless in there.   Animals and
birds, as well as men, love the sun.   The deer and the
moose may seek thick cover when they wish to rest, but
they never go far from some open place where they can
stand in the warm sunshine and see the blue above them.
And it is the same with men.   Those poor and horseless
tribes, whose stingy gods gave them only a forest for
their hunting ground, do not stay in its dark and silent
belly, but pitch their mean lodges on some opening by
the shore of a lake or river, or where a fire has cleared a
small space.   We did not like that great wood we

travelled through. Our food gave out, and were it not
for a few fish we shot with our arrows we must have
starved. We grew poor in flesh and in spirits, sitting
about our evening fires in silence, except to question if
there were any end to the timber, and if it were not better
to turn and take our back trail. Even East, who was
always talking and joking, now kept silent. We would
have turned back, I think, except that we hated to give
up what we had set out to do, for fear it would bring us
bad luck in the future. Little did we think that worse
than bad luck lay in wait for us ahead. Yet, I believe
we had the warning in a way, for I felt uneasy, afraid, but
of what I could not say. The others felt as I did, but
none of them would give in any more than I. Afterward
I took heed of that feeling! Three times I turned back
after starting on a raid, and on one of the times I know
I did what was wise, for my companions, who laughed at
me and kept on, never again saw their lodges.

"After many days we came at last to an open country.
There were bunches of timber here and there, but for
the most part the land was prairie, with many ledges
and buttes and boulders of dark-brown, bare rock. The
river had grown wider, deeper, and its current was strong.
Here there were elk, plenty of them, and deer, many
black bears, many grouse, and once more we heard the
little birds singing. We killed a young bull elk and
feasted upon it, and felt good. There was no sign of
people anywhere about; no horse trails, no smoke of
camp fires. We thought it safe to build a fire even then
in the middle of the day, and we lay about it until the
next morning, resting, eating, sleeping. With the sunrise we were off once more, travelling very cautiously,
climbing every butte and ridge to see what was ahead.
That day there was no sign of men, but on the next one

we saw smoke away down the river, and keeping within the fringe of timber which bordered the stream, we went on until we could see that it was rising on the opposite side. Away down there somewhere near the place of encampment, we could hear a roaring sound as of a big rapid, and even where we were the current was strong. Now here was something to talk over, and right there we considered it.   If we crossed over and took some horses, was there a trail on that side by which we could hurry them in a homeward direction; and if none, how were we to get them across the wide, swift river and on to the trail over which we had come.   At last he whom we had named South said:

"'We are wasting time talking about this now, when we have not yet seen the far side, nor the horses, nor even the people and their camp.   Let us cross over, see what is to be seen, and then decide what is best to do.'

"His words were wise, and we took them.   There was plenty of drift wood, and near sundown we rolled a piece of it, a short, dry log, down into the water, lashing another, a very small one, to it so that it would not turn over and over.   We decided not to wait until night to cross, for the river was wide and swift, and we wanted to see our course.   In one way it was not wise to start then, for some of the people of the camp might see us and give the alarm.   Still we had to take some chances; no one had yet appeared from the camp below, and we hoped to get across into the brush unobserved. Heaping our clothes and weapons on top of our raft, we pushed out into the stream, and all went well until we were part way across; there we struck very swift water, a low place into which the water from the sides of the river seemed to be running and sinking.   Try as we would we could not get out of it, for it was like going up hill to push for the far shore, or the one from which we had started, and all the time we were drifting faster and faster down toward the roar of the rapids, down toward the camp of strange people.

"'Let us leave the raft,' said North, 'and swim back to our shore.'

"We tried to do so, but we could no more leave that swift, sucking, down-pulling middle current than we had been so many helpless dead leaves adrift. One by one we turned back and hung on to our raft.

"'This is our only chance,' said South. 'We can hang on to this and perhaps pass the rapid and the camp without being seen.'

"We now turned a bend in the river, and before us saw a fearful thing that we were rushing into; the stream narrowed between two high walls of rock, and the green water leaped foaming along in great waves and whirls over and around huge black rocks.

"'Hold hard; hold on with all your strength,' cried South.

"I grabbed the smaller log harder than ever, but my strength was nothing in that place, nothing. Suddenly we went down, raft and all, down under the crazy, green, bubbling water; our logs struck a rock and I was pulled away from them and went whirling and rolling on. I was pushed up to the surface, went over the top of a big wave, and then was again drawn under, down, down, I knew not how far; my left foot caught in between two rocks, the water pushed me, and my leg broke just here above the ankle. For a little I hung there, then the water heaved back the other way, pulled me loose, pushed me up, and again I got a few breaths of air. Once more I went down, this time for so long that I was sure I would never rise. I had been praying, but now I stopped; 'it is no use,' I said to myself, 'I now die.' But I did roll up on top again; I was in smooth but swift water, a boat was above me, a short, stout, dark man was leaning over the side. I noticed that his hair looked as if it had never been cared for, that his face was very wide, his mouth very large. I felt him grasp my hair, and then I died (fainted).

"When I came to life I found that I was in a small, old and torn elk-skin lodge. I was lying on a couch, a robe of beaver skins thrown over me. An old gray-haired man was putting sticks on my broken leg and binding them, all the time singing a strange song. I knew he was a doctor. The man I had seen leaning over the side of the boat sat nearby. There were three women there also, one quite young and good looking. When I looked at her she turned her head away, but the others just sat and stared at me. Other men came in; they were all short and broad, with big muscles; they were also very dark coloured, very homely, and, worst of all, there was hair growing on their lip and chin. They looked much at me as they talked, and their talk was very strange; it seemed to come from down in their belly, and break out of their throat with the sound of bark being torn from a tree by jerks. I thought that I could never learn to speak such a language as that. The old doctor hurt me considerably as he bandaged my leg, but I kept very still. I was wondering if any of my friends had come through that terrible rapid alive and had escaped or been picked up as I was. I learned later that the water gods had claimed them, at least, none of them ever returned to the Kutenai country.

"I thought that these strangers were very kind to drag me from the river and care for me. I tried to make them understand how I felt, but it was impossible;

they did not understand the sign language, not a bit of it, which was very strange.

"After the doctor had fixed my leg they gave me food, some fish, a piece of a large, fat kind of trout. Fish, I found, was what they lived upon, spearing them in great numbers at the foot of the rapids, and drying them for winter use. It was a country of game, elk, deer, black bear, yet these queer men seldom hunted, being content to live upon fish and berries. Before I got well I suffered for want of meat. I was obliged to lie quite still in the lodge for a time, and then I hobbled out, a little farther each day, until I could go to the river and watch the fishing. Then I found work to do. I was given a pile of the fish, and a knife, and shown how to prepare them for drying. All at once I knew why I had been dragged from the river and cared for; I was a slave. I had heard that there was a people who made captives of their enemy instead of killing them, and made them work hard. I had found them; I, a Kutenai, broken-legged and unable to escape, was the slave of hairy-faced fish-eaters; I felt very sad. It was the women of these people, the women of the man who had captured me, that gave me work, showed me what to do. Not the young woman, his daughter, but the others. The girl never was anything but kind, sorry for me; when she could she did what had been given me to do, and when her mother objected, there was a quarrel, but the girl was never afraid.

"'When my leg is sound,' I kept saying to myself, 'I will escape. I will steal the weapons of this man and make my way once more to the Backbone-of-the-world.'

"But the break healed slowly, and before I could again walk well my plan was broken. One day everything was packed up, the bundles of dried fish, the lodges, everything placed in the boats, and we all set out down the river. Down we went, on and on, oh, very far, the river ever widening, passing great black forests, until at last we came almost to a great lake which had no other side, which was nearly all the time mad with great waves, and lost in thick fog. It was a dreadful place. There we made camp with many more of these same fish-eaters, and besides fish we now ate the flesh of water devils which could swim faster than an otter. It tasted very bad.

"Now, little by little I became able to speak some of this hard language, to make myself understood. After a time I was allowed to take a bow and arrows and hunt, and I killed many deer, a few black bears, some elk. But I was not happy; winter was coming on, there was no use in trying to start for my country until spring. When I did start, how was I, who could not manage a heavy, long boat, to get back up this great river, to cross others that we had passed? True, there was this shore we were camped upon. I could follow it back to the place of the terrible rapids and cross away above them, but the route was long, through deep forests, down-timber, thick brush. It was very bad, but I should have to try it.

"It was my dream that showed me the way. One night he said to me: 'Ask the girl; she likes you, will help you.'

"When I awoke in the morning I looked across the lodge at her; she was looking at me and her eyes were kind; she smiled. It was a good sign. I said that I would go hunting, and after eating I picked up the fish-eater's weapons and went out. But I did not hunt; I went back in the timber a little way and hid. She would be after wood some time in the day, and if alone

I could speak with her. When I went out I had given
her a strong look, which she seemed to understand, for
she came almost at once, and seeing me, began picking
up a piece of wood here, a piece there, but all the time
coming nearer, often looking back toward camp. I
slipped behind the roots of an overturned tree, and she
soon came around too and we stood side by side, watching through the little roots as we talked. I was afraid
to begin; I could talk but little of her language, so little,
I tried for the right words, but they would not come.
She looked up at me, put a hand on my shoulder, and
said: 'You wish to go to your people?'

"'Yes,' I told her. 'Yes, I want to go, but the big
river—don't understand boat.'

"She laughed a little, looked carefully to see if anyone was coming, and then said in little words I could
understand: 'I know boat—I take you—you be good
to me—I like you.'

"'Yes,' I said, 'I will be good to you. I make you
my woman. I give you everything, many horses, good
lodge, pretty things to wear.'

"She laughed low, a happy laugh, 'To-night, when
all sleep, we go.'

"I stopped her. 'It is far, much snow, we must wait
until leaves come.'

"She gave me a little shake, and went on: 'I said
to-night; I know where to go, what to do, you go with
me to-night; I take everything; when ready I call you,
so.' She pulled my arm a little.

"I sneaked away, but soon walked around to camp,
said I was sick and could not hunt. One of the old
women gave me some medicine. She was afraid her
slave would not be able to work, and hunt, and bring
in skins. I had to drink the medicine, and it tasted

very bad. I should have told some other lie. I thought
night would never come, but when it was time the sun
went down, we had our supper and lay down. The fire
went out, and it was very dark in the lodge. After a
while the fish-eater and his woman began to snore, and
at last I felt the little pull on my arm, for which I had
been waiting. I arose very slowly, picked up the bow
and arrows and the knife, which I had laid carelessly
by my couch when I came in from hunting, and stole
noiselessly out of the lodge. The girl took my hand and
led me down to the river, to a small boat which belonged
to another family. Already she had placed in it some
robes, some little food, a skin of good water, for the
water of that dreadful lake was salt, and every little
while it fought with the great river and beat back its
water from the snows and springs. We got into the
boat, I in front, the girl behind, pushed off without
making the least sound, and she paddled us out into the
darkness and stillness of the wide deep stream. After
awhile she gave me a paddle, and I pawed the water with
it, making much noise, but noise no longer mattered.
On we went, and on, speaking no word, until day began
to break; then we went ashore at a place where there
were many small rocks, with which we loaded the boat
until it sank out of sight. Then we went into the deep
timber and felt that we were safe; any pursuers could
neither see our boat nor us, nor even suspect that we
might be hiding there.

"Thus for three nights we went up that great river,
and then turned into a small one flowing from the north.
It was a beautiful stream, clear and quite swift, and
everywhere its shores were tracked with game. Half a
day we travelled up it, then cached our boat and walked
up a little narrow stream into high hills. There I killed

a deer, my woman made a little lodge of poles and brush. We built a small fire and feasted. We were in a safe place now. Here we were to stay until spring. I would hunt and get many skins, she would build a good lodge. That is what my woman said. And I, for the first time in many moons, I was happy. I had some one to care for, one who cared for me. When summer came we would travel together to my people and live happily. Oh, yes, I was happy; I would sing all day, except when I was hunting. At night we used to sit by our little fire and feast, and I would teach her my language, which she quickly learned, and I would tell her about my people and my country, the plains, the mountains, and the game.

"I was no longer impatient for summer to come; the days went fast and every one of them was a happy day. But soon the leaves began to show on the willows, the grass to grow, and one evening we got out our boat and floated down into the big river, travelling up it by night until we came to the terrible rapids. There we sunk our boat, that none might know we had passed that way, and started on the long trail over which I had come with my lost friends. The wide forest did not now seem so gloomy, nor the way so long. At last we came to the lake of the Pend d'Oreilles. 'From here on,' I said 'we will ride; I am going to take some horses from these people.'

"My little woman objected to this, but I would have my way. She was tired out from our long walk, more tired I could see every day. I felt that I must take at least one horse for her. I could see the camp and plenty of horses near it. After the people slept, although it was bright moonlight, I went right in among the lodges, stole a woman's saddle, and cut out two of the best horses

I could find and led them to where I had left my woman. She was terribly scared, for she had never ridden a horse. I saddled one, got on him, and rode around a little; he was gentle. So I fixed the saddle, put her up in it, shortened the stirrup straps, and showed her how to hang to the saddle. Then I mounted the other horse, and leading hers, we started over the trail I knew so well.

"We had not gone very far when it happened. The little woman cried out, her horse broke from me and began bucking around. By the time I had run back there she was dead. The saddle cinch had parted, she had fallen, her horse had kicked or trampled her.

"At first I could not believe it. I took her in my arms, called to her, felt her all over, and then at last I found the place; the top of her head was crushed. I must have gone crazy for a time. I jumped up and killed her horse; and then killed mine. I prayed to her gods and to mine, to bring her to life, but it was no use, no use. Morning came. I carried her to a place a little way off the trail and buried her as best I could. I looked back to the west, toward the country where I had suffered so, had lost my companions, been made a slave, had found a loving woman only to lose her, and I cried in anger and sorrow; then, alone, I tore myself away from where she lay and started once more on the trail to my people. I am an old man now, but many winters have not buried my sorrow. I still mourn for her, and I shall do so as long as I live."

Nät-ah'-ki often reverted to this story of the old man. "Kyai,-yo!" she would exclaim. "How poor, how sad."

"Who—what?" I would ask.

"Why, the Kutenai's young woman, of course. Only think, to die just as she had found happiness; never to see again the sunshine, and the mountains, and these beautiful plains."

"She never saw these plains," I said once, when we were talking about the story. "Hers was a country of forests and great rivers, of rains and fogs."

Nät-ah'-ki shivered. "I do not wish to see that country!" she exclaimed. "I hate the rain; always I want to live on these sunshine plains. How good Old Man* was to give us this rich country."

*The Blackfoot Creator, the Sun.

CHAPTER XII

THE GREAT RACE

THE visit of the Kutenais to our people wound up as several previous visits had done, in a fine row, which for a time threatened to be serious. It began also as another one had, over a horse race. The Kutenais owned a large, clean-limbed and very swift black mare which, with one horse after another, the Piegans had endeavoured to beat. Race after race had been run and each time the black had been victorious. The Piegans had lost heavily—guns, horses, blankets, finery of all descriptions—and were getting desperate. They claimed, for one thing, that the winners had managed secretly to rub something on their several horses which reduced the speed of the animals. In their extremity it was decided to send over to the Bloods for a certain horse which was known to be very fast, and to guard him night and day until the race was run. After a time the deputation sent to the Bloods returned with the horse, which was certainly a fine animal, a well-blooded American bay which had undoubtedly been taken from some unfortunate traveller on the Overland trail far away to the south. He was to have a rest of four days, and then the great race was to be run in which the Piegans expected to recoup their losses. During this time there is no question but that the horse was guarded. By day there were half a dozen young men with him out on the plain, where he grazed upon the richest grass that could be found, and at night he was fairly surrounded by interested watchers.

At last the great day came, and everyone in both camps, even the women and children, went out to the place where the race was to be run—a level stretch about 500 yards long. The betting was furious, and such a lot of stuff as was set out here and there on the plain I never saw before nor since. Specimens of everything the two tribes had for use or adornment were to be found in one or another of the heaps, and the many horses which had been staked upon the result were also there, their ropes held by some non-betting youth or boy. Even the women were betting; here you would see a brass kettle wagered against a beaded dress, there a parfleche of dried buffalo meat against a tanned elkskin, a yard of red cloth against a couple of copper bracelets. I stood with a crowd of others at the finishing point, where a furrow had been scraped across the dusty course. It was to be a standing start; we could see the two youthful riders, naked except for the inevitable breech-clout, guide their excited and prancing mounts up to the starting point, some 500 yards distant. They started; the spectators lining the course began to shout, encouraging the riders to do their utmost, an increasing confusion and clamour of Blackfoot and Kutenai exclamations, in which the shrill cries of the women played no unimportant part. We at the post could not tell which of the horses was ahead, as they came toward us with quick, long leaps; they seemed to be running side by side. Now, as they neared the goal, a sudden silence fell upon the crowd. Everyone held his breath; we could hear the broad thongs of the riders' rapidly plied quirts thwack against the straining sides of the racers. And now here they were; a few leaps more and they crossed the furrow almost neck and neck, the Kutenai horse, I thought, a few inches in the lead. Immediately a great clamour of tongues arose and there was a general rush for the stakes.

"We win!" the Piegans shouted, "We win!" and I presume that is what the Kutenais were saying in their unintelligible and angry words. What a scene ensued. Men seized upon the stakes and pulled and pushed each other for the possession of them. A Kutenai in the midst of a struggling group pulled an ancient flint-lock pistol and aimed it at his opponent, but someone knocked it upward in the nick of time, and the bullet went wide of its mark. At the sound of the shot the women fled in terror to their several lodges, dragging their crying children after them. The hot-headed Piegan youth and men began to call out to each other: "Get your weapons! Let's kill off these Kutenai cheats."

There was no more struggling over the things which had been staked upon the result of the race. Each bettor seemed to take that which was his without protest and hurry away to his lodge. In a moment or two the race ground was deserted save by the Kutenai and Piegan chiefs, a few of their leading men, Nät-ah'-ki and I. The latter was grasping my arm and there was real terror in her eyes as she begged me go with her at once.

"There is going to be a big fight; let us saddle our horses and ride away from it," she said. "Come."

"The fight will not concern me," I told her. "I am a white man."

"Yes," she cried, "you are a white man, and you are also a Piegan; the Kutenais will shoot at you as quickly as at anyone else."

I motioned her to keep silent, for I wanted to hear

what was being decided upon by the chiefs. Big Lake
sent his camp-crier home.

"Tell them," he said, "that these are my words: I
go now to the camp of my good friend Back-in-sight;
whoever would fight the Kutenais must fight me and
these here with me."

The camp-crier hurried away and then he turned to me.
"Come," he said, "you also are for peace; come with us."

I went with them over to the Kutenai camp. Nät-
ah'-ki, sorely troubled, closely following. We had
barely arrived there when we saw an ever-increasing
throng of shouting and excited riders bearing down upon
us from the other camp.

"Loan me a gun," said Big Lake, peremptorily.
"Some one loan me a gun."

When it was handed him he stepped out in front of
us and there was a look of grim determination on his
fine old face, an angry light in his eyes. Behind us, with
rustle of lodge-skin and rattle of poles, the lodges were
being hurriedly taken down, the baggage packed by
anxious and much-scared women, and near us the
Kutenai men were gathering, preparing to defend themselves and theirs. They were no match for the Piegans
they well knew; they were far outnumbered; but one had
only to look at their attitude of preparedness, their steady
eyes and compressed lips, to be satisfied that they would
do their best.

A young warrior named Little Deer was at the head of
the Piegans as they came riding fast toward us. I had
a strong dislike to him, for I felt that he hated me. I
had serious trouble with him later. He had a mean,
cruel face, pitiless and treacherous, with shifty eyes.
The most of this angry crowd of our people, we learned
later, had not heard the camp-crier in the excitement

and confusion or had left before he arrived among them, and here they were, determined to deal unmercifully with those whom they now considered their enemies. Big Lake hastened out to meet them, shouting to them, and making the sign for them to stop.   But as they paid no heed to him he ran on still farther, and levelling his gun at Little Deer, exclaimed: "If you don't stop I will shoot."

The latter unwillingly checked his horse and said: "Why do you stop me?   These Kutenai dogs have robbed us, cheated; we are going to have revenge."

He started to go on, calling out to his followers, and again Big Lake raised his gun: "Aim then at me," he cried, "I am now a Kutenai.   Aim, shoot; I give you a chance."

Little Deer did not raise his gun; he just sat there on his horse and glared at the chief, then turned in his saddle and looking at the crowd which had ridden up behind him, called upon them to follow him.   But the other Piegan leaders were now among them, by turns threatening, and coaxing them to return to their camp. None of them came forward; on the other hand, some started back toward their lodges.   Little Deer worked himself into a fine rage, alternately pointing at them and at the Kutenais, calling them all the evil names he could think of.   But in spite of his anger and defiance he made no attempt to advance; the chief's pointed gun, the steady cold, clear stare of his eyes wholly disconcerted him.   Muttering something or other in an unintelligible tone, he finally turned his horse and moodily rode back to camp in the wake of those whom but a few moments before he had so eagerly led.   The chiefs gave a long sigh of relief; so did I, so did Năt-ah'-ki, again close by my side.

"What hard heads these young men have," Big Lake remarked. "How difficult it is to manage them."

"You speak truth," said Back-in-sight. "Were it not for you, your strong words, many dead would now be lying on this plain. We go now back to the mountains, it may be long ere we meet again."

"Yes," agreed the Piegan, "it is best that we part. But the anger of our young men will soon die away. Next summer, somewhere hereabouts, let us meet again."

This was agreed upon, and with final handshakes all around, we left them. Arrived at our own camp, Big Lake gave orders that camp be struck at once, and the lodges began to come down in a hurry. He also instructed the Ai-in'-ai-kiks—seizers, holders—a band of the All Friends' Society which were, as one may say, police, to allow none of the young men to leave us under any pretext whatever. He feared that if they did go from us they would yet attack the Kutenais, who were already stringing out in a long column, westward over the rolling plain. A little later we too pulled out, heading south on the afternoon of the second day we went into camp on the Marias at the lower end of Medicine Rock bottom, right opposite the spot where, later, Fort Conrad was built, and where to-day the Great Falls & Canada Railroad crosses the stream.

At the extreme lower end of this bottom, about 100 yards from the river, and near the foot of the rising hill, unless the railroad vandals have taken them for construction work, lies a circle of large boulders partially embedded in the soil. The circle is about sixty-five feet in diameter; some of the boulders will weigh at least a ton. Who placed them there, and why, I could never learn. The Blackfeet have no tradition concerning them, saying merely that 'twas "done by the ancient ones," ahk'-kai-tup-pi. This, by the way, is an interesting word; as it stands, with the accent on the first syllable, its exact meaning is long-ago-people; but if the second instead of the first syllable is accented it means many people. However, in the first instance the word for time, sum-oh', is entirely omitted, most likely for the sake of euphony.

But if the Blackfeet know nothing of the boulder circle, they have much to say regarding the medicine rock. This lies by the side of the old travois trail about three miles above, near the top of the hill at the extreme upper end of the bottom. In the "Blackfoot Lodge Tales" is given the story of a rock, which, to avenge an insult, chased Old Man, and but for the timely interference of a bull bat would have crushed him flat. To a certain extent the Blackfeet are Pantheists, attributing life to, and worshipping many inanimate objects. This rock is one of several to which they sacrifice and pray, another one lying on a hill of the Two Medicine River, near the old Marias River—Belly River trail. It is a red mottled quartz—the red itself a "medicine" or sacred colour—a boulder of several tons' weight lying on a very steep sandy slope exposed to the southwest winds. The wind gradually moving the sand undermines the rock, and as the fine sand and soil is blown away it settles little by little, moving farther and farther down the hill. But although the Blackfeet are well aware of the cause of this movement, to them the rock is a sacred object. Passing it, they stop a moment and place on it a bracelet, a necklace, some beads or other offering, and beg it to take pity on them, to guard them from all evil things and grant them long life and happiness. The last time I passed this rock there was at

least a bushel of various small offerings lying upon, or
around it.   And there most likely they are to this day
unless the white settlers have picked them up.   Years
after I last rode by the rock, Nät-ah'-ki and I crossed
the bottom on a train of the new railway.   We sat out
on the platform of the rear sleeper, whence we could get
a good view of the country.   Oh, the dreariness and
desolation of it all.   Gone were the rich grasses, even
the sages, which once grew thick on flat and hillside.
Gone, too, were the grand old cottonwoods, the clusters
of willow, and cherry, and sarvis berry thickets which
bordered the river.   Nät-ah'-ki silently pressed my hand,
and I saw tears in her eyes.   I said nothing, asked no
question; well I knew of what she was thinking, and I
came near crying too.   What a—to us—terrible change
had taken place; gone were our friends, extinct the herds
of game; even the face of the country was changed.
Do you wonder that we felt sad?

CHAPTER XIII

THE SNAKE WOMAN

AT THE lower end of the bottom opposite that of the Medicine Rock, the Dry Fork of the Marias joins the greater stream. At times in spring it is a raging, muddy torrent, but for the larger part of the year is a shallow, sometimes dry, stream, the water standing in deep holes or where it has been backed up by the industrious beaver.—Why, why do I persist in writing in the present tense? As if there were any beaver there now! But I'll not change the line—The day after we went into camp on the river, there was to be a buffalo run out on the flat beyond the Medicine Rock, where an immense herd of buffalo had been located. Weasel Tail and I, however, chose to go up the Dry Fork on discovery. In our lodges were many a parfleche of dried meat; we wanted no summer skins of the buffalo, and, of course, we could kill what fresh meat was needed at almost any time and place. We crossed the river and rode through the bottom, then followed a broad, deep game trail running up the rather narrow valley of the Dry Fork, crossing and recrossing the stream. We passed a great many beaver dams and saw several of the animals swimming around in their ponds. Here and there were narrow strips of willow along the bank out of which an occasional white-tail deer would break for the hills, scared by our approach. There were solitary cottonwoods, stunted, many of them dead, their trunks worn quite smooth by the buffalo rubbing against them. Rattlesnakes were numerous; every little while we would be startled by one suddenly sounding his warning near the trail, and we killed all we saw save one or two which managed to escape into nearby holes. As we ascended the valley, antelope became more and more numerous. The plain lying between the Dry Fork and the next water to the south, Pend d'Oreille coulée, was one of their favourite feeding grounds in that part of the country. If possible, when we saw a herd of antelope or buffalo ahead, we would ride up a coulée on to the plain and go around them, for we liked not to have the game stampeding from us, betraying our presence and probable route to any chance enemy thereabouts.

It was at least eight or nine o'clock when we left camp, long after the departure of the buffalo runners, and by noontime we were well up the Dry Fork, twelve or fourteen miles from camp. Off to our right was a long ridge running east and west, the nearer point of it broken by sandstone cliffs. Thither we wended our way, riding up a coulée, which headed there. Arrived at the foot of the ridge we picketed our horses and climbing up, sat down on its crest to get a view of the country. I had brought some broiled antelope ribs, and, opening the little bag, laid them upon a convenient rock. "Take part of them," I said.

Weasel Tail shook his head. "What," I asked, "you will not eat? Take half; I brought them for you."

"It is not wise," he replied, "to eat when out on discovery, on the hunt, or when travelling anywhere away from camp. You should eat plenty after you arise in the morning, eat very much. Then you saddle up and strike out. You feel strong; you ride, and ride, and ride. You may be hunting, you are unlucky perhaps,

but you are not discouraged; you go on, and on, with
strong faith that the luck will change, that you will soon
find a band of antelope or buffalo, or game of some kind.
The sun mounts up, and up, arrives at the middle,
starts downward to his lodge beyond the edge (edge of
the world). You have food tied to your saddle, and
you say to yourself, 'I am hungry; I will stop and
eat.'

"On the crest of some ridge or butte you dismount,
and, half lying on the restful ground, you begin to eat,
meanwhile your clear, strong eyes search plain and valley or brush and mountainside for life of some kind.
You are very hungry, of course; the food tastes good
in your mouth, your stomach keeps crying for its fill,
and you keep on eating until the last morsel has disappeared. Then IIai-ya! what a change comes over
you! Your flesh suddenly becomes soft, your eyes no
longer seek to pierce the far distance, the lids close upon
them. The ground feels so good; it is a soft couch.
You become sleepy; it is only by great effort that you
keep awake. You lie there and the sun goes on, and on,
down toward his lodge. You know that you ought to
arise, that you ought to mount and ride until you can
see what is beyond that high, long ridge, but the food
has done its work and you lie to yourself, saying: 'Oh,
I don't believe that I would find any game over there;
I'll rest here for a time, and then start homeward. I
am sure to kill something on the back trail.' So you
recline there, as lazy and sleepy as a full-gorged bear,
and toward evening you arise and go homeward, finding
no game whatever by the way. You arrive at your
lodge, the people see that you bring neither meat nor
skins. Your women quietly unsaddle your horse; you
go inside and sit down upon your couch, much ashamed

and begin to lie, telling how very far you have ridden, how barren the country is, and how you wonder where all the game can be.

"No, friend, no ribs for me. You eat, if you will. Loan me your glass and I will have a look at the country."

What Weasel Tail said was all very true. Had I not time and again experienced the lassitude, the sleepiness caused by my midday lunch? I resolved never again to take food with me when going for a day's ride. But this time need not count. I ate most of the ribs, joined my friend in a smoke, and fell asleep.

Weasel Tail poked me in the ribs several times before he succeeded in awakening me. I sat up and rubbed my eyes. My throat felt dry; there was a fuzzy taste in my mouth all caused by my midday lunch and nap. I noticed that the sun was midway down toward the distant blue peaks of the Rockies. I had slept long. My friend was looking steadily through the glass at something to the westward of us and muttering to himself. "What do you see?" I asked, yawning lazily, reaching for his pipe and tobacco pouch.

"It does not seem possible," he replied, "that I see that which I see; yet, I am sure neither my eyes nor this glass deceive. I see a woman; a lone woman, a woman on foot walking along the crest of the ridge yonder and coming straight toward us.

"Let me look," I exclaimed, dropping the pipe and taking the glass. "Are you sure that you are awake?"

"See for yourself," he replied. "She is on the third rise from here."

I brought the glass to bear on the slope indicated, and, sure enough, there was a woman striding easily down the grassy incline. She stopped, turned, and, shading her eyes with her hand, looked away to the south,

then to the north, and lastly back whence she had come.
I noticed that she carried a small pack on her back, that
she stood erect, and was of slender figure. A young woman
undoubtedly. But why, why was she there, and afoot
on that great plain whose vastness and silence must be
appalling to one so alone and so defenceless.

"What do you think of this?" I asked.

"I don't think anything," Weasel Tail replied. "It
is useless to try to account for so strange a thing. She
comes this way; we will meet, and she will tell us the
reason of it all."

The woman passed out of sight into the hollow back
of the second rise of the ridge, but soon appeared on its
crest and kept on down into the next low place. When
she arrived at the top of the slope on which we sat, she
saw us at once, stopped and hesitated for an instant, and
then came on with her natural, easy, graceful stride. I
am afraid that we both rudely and coldly stared at her
but there was neither fear nor diffidence in her manner,
as she walked steadily up to us. My first impression was
that she had beautiful eyes; large, clear, kindly, honest
eyes, and my next was that her face was exceedingly
comely, her long hair glossy and neatly braided, her
figure all that one expects a woman's form to be. She
came on, quite up to us, and said: "How?"

"How, how?" we answered.

She unslung her pack, sat down, and began to talk in a
language unintelligible to us. By signs we interrupted
and said that we did not understand her talk.

"She is a Snake woman," said Weasel Tail. "By the
cut and pattern of her moccasins I know that she is one
of that tribe."

Who was he, I wonder, of what tribe and time, who
conceived the idea of the sign language, by means of

which all the tribes of the plains from the Saskatchewan to Mexico are able to converse with each other and tell all that their tongues may not utter. Here were we, unable to understand one word of this woman's language, yet by means of this wonderful invention of some ancient one, language mattered not.

"Who are you?" Weasel Tail asked, "and whence come you?"

"I am a Snake," the woman signed, "and I come from the camp of my people far to the south." She paused, and we signified that we understood. For a moment or two she sat thinking, brow wrinkled, lips pursed, and then continued:

"Three winters ago I became Two Bears' woman. He was very handsome, very brave, kind-hearted. I loved him, he loved me; we were happy." Again she paused, and tears rolled down her cheeks. She brushed them away repeatedly, and with much effort resumed her story: "We were very happy for he never got angry; no one ever heard cross words in our lodge. It was a lodge of feasts, and song, and laughter. Daily we prayed to the Sun, asking him to continue our happiness, to let us live long.

"It was three moons ago, two before this one which is almost ended. Winter had gone, the grass and leaves were coming out. I awoke one morning and found that I was alone in the lodge. My chief had arisen while I slept and gone out; he had taken his gun, his saddle and rope, so I knew that he had started on a hunt. I was glad. 'He will bring home meat,' I said, 'fat meat of some kind, and we will give a feast.' I gathered wood, I got water, and then I sat down to await his return. All day I sat in the lodge waiting for him, sewing moccasins, listening for the footfalls of his hunting horse. The sun went down, and I built a good fire. 'He will come soon now,' I said.

"But no, he did not come, and I began to feel uneasy. Far into the night I sat waiting, and fear pressed harder and harder on my heart. Soon the people of the village went to bed. I arose and went to my father's lodge, but I did not sleep.

"When morning came the men rode out to look for my chief; all day they hunted through the little prairies, through the forests, along the river, but they did not find him, nor any signs of him, nor of his horse. For three days they rode the country in all directions, and then gave up. 'He is dead,' they said; 'he has drowned, or a bear or some enemy has killed him. It must have been an enemy, else his horse would have returned to its mates.'

"My own thought was that he lived; I could not believe him dead. My mother told me to cut off my hair, but I would not do it. I said to her: 'He is alive. When he returns should he find my long hair gone he will be angry, for he loves it. Many a time he has himself combed and braided it.'

"The days passed and I waited, waited and watched for him to come. I began to think that he might be dead, and then one night my dream gave me hope. The next night and the next it was the same, and then on the fourth night, when my dream again came and told me I knew that it was true, that he lived. 'Far away to the north,' said my dream, 'on a river of the plains, your chief lies wounded and ill in a camp of the prairie people. Go find him, and help him to get well. He is sad and lonely, he cries for you.'

"So I got ready and, one evening after all were asleep, I started; it was the only way. Had they known what I was about to do, my father and mother would have stopped me. I carried some food, my awl and sinews, plenty of moccasin leather. When my food was gone I snared squirrels, rabbits, dug roots, so I was never hungry. But the way was long, very, very long, and I feared the bears prowling and snuffing around in the night. They did not harm me; my dream person must have kept them from doing me wrong. The camp, my dream said, was in sight of the mountains. After many days I came to the Big River, and for many more days I followed it down, until I came in sight of the white men's houses, but I found no camp of those I sought. I turned north, and coming to the next stream, followed it up to the mountains; still I found no people. Then I went north again until I came to this little creek and now I meet you. Tell me, is my chief in your camp?"

Crazy, say you? Well, that depends upon the point of view. Some there are who believe in "a prophet's paradise to come." Some, for instance, have faith in the revelations said to have been made to a certain Joseph Smith; some believe in Allah; others in Christian Science; still others in divers creeds and faiths. If they are crazy then indeed was this Indian woman also, for she had faith in a dream, doubted not for one instant that by following its instructions she would find her loved, lost man. Dreams, to most Indians, are a reality. They believe that they really do commune with spirits in their sleep, that their shadows—souls—temporarily released from the body, then travel far and meet with strange adventures. If a Blackfoot, for instance, dreams of seeing green grass he is absolutely certain that he will live to see another season of spring.

We were, of course, obliged to tell the wanderer that her lost one was not in our camp. Weasel Tail also informed her that some North Blackfeet and some Bloods were visiting us, and advised her to accompany us and question them. She readily consented to that, and we started homeward. My friend was riding a vicious little mare which would not carry double, so I was obliged to take the woman up behind me, and we created a big sensation when we rode into camp about sundown. Weasel Tail had agreed to give her a place in his lodge, and I had hoped to drop her near it unobserved by the mistress of a certain home a little farther along. But no such luck. I espied Nät-ah′-ki from afar standing and gazing at us, at the handsome young woman perched behind me, her arms tightly clasped about my waist. But when I rode up to my own lodge there was no one to greet me, and for the first time I was permitted to unsaddle my animal. I went inside and sat down. Nät-ah′-ki was roasting some meat and neither spoke nor looked up. Still in silence she brought me water, soap, a towel and comb. After I had washed she set before me a bowl of soup, some meat, and then what a sad, reproachful look she gave me. I grinned foolishly, vacuously and, although I had been guilty of no wrong, somehow I could not return her gaze and quickly busied myself with my food. The little woman fled to the other side of the lodge, covered her head with her shawl, and began to cry. Somehow, although I had thought I was hungry, my food did not taste good. I nervously ate a little of it and then went out and over to Weasel Tail's.

"Send your mother over to my lodge," I said, "and have her tell Nät-ah′-ki all about it."

"Ah ha!" he laughed, "the young ones have quarrelled, have they? The little one is jealous? Well, we'll soon fix it out," and he bade his mother go over.

An hour or two later, when I went home, Nät-ah′-ki

was all smiles and welcomed me joyously, insisted that I should have another supper, and gave me a pair of gorgeous moccasins which she had been surreptitiously making for my adornment.

"Oh, that poor Snake woman," she said just before we fell asleep, "how I pity her. To-morrow I shall make her a present of a horse."

CHAPTER XIV

NÄT-AH'-KI was the proud owner of a little band of horses, some of which had sprung from mares given her by relatives at various times. She loved to talk about them, to describe the colour, age, and peculiarities of each one. A Blackfoot who was horseless was an object of reproach and pity. Horses were the tribal wealth, and one who owned a large herd of them held a position only to be compared to that of our multi-millionaires. There were individuals who owned from one hundred to three and four hundred. Were the owners sonless, each employed some orphan boy to herd them, to drive them twice and thrice daily to water. And they liked to sit out on the plain or hills for hours at a time to be among them and gloat over them as they cropped the rich grass. When a man died, the bulk of his property was divided among the male relatives, and they were so numerous that it was rare for one to inherit any number of animals. He who could count his horses by the hundred, had gained them by a strenuous life, by many a long raid against bordering tribes, by stealing into their camps at night, by hand to hand conflict with them on many a field. No wonder then, that he was proud of them, and of himself, and that the people honoured him.

Nät-ah'-ki's band was herded by her uncle, Fish Robe, who himself had a large herd. When they were driven in the morning after our discovery of the Snake woman,

she selected a fat, pot-bellied roan, begged an old
woman's saddle from an aunt, placed it in position and
led the animal over to Weasel Tail's lodge. She handed
the end of the lariat to the Snake woman; at first the
stranger did not comprehend the meaning of the act;
but when Nat-ah'-ki signed that the horse was to be
hers, was a gift, her joy was pleasant to witness. The
two women became great friends, and she lived a part of
the time with us. "I am resting," she said, "and questioning arriving visitors from other tribes. If I do not soon
hear of my chief, I shall again set forth in quest of him."

But that was not to be. One day when she and Nät-
ah'-ki were gathering wood, a party of Bloods passed
by on their way to our camp, and she ran after them as
fast as she could, Nät-ah'-ki following and wondering
if the poor woman had lost her wits. The visitors dismounted and entered our chief's lodge. The Snake
woman, excited, trembling, pointed at one of the horses
they rode, a black and white pinto, and signed: "I
know it; my chief's horse. Ask the man where he got it."

Nät-ah'-ki went inside and made known the request
to one of the women of the lodge, and the latter, as soon
as there was a break in the conversation, repeated it to
Big Lake. All heard her, of course, and one of the visitors spoke up: "The pinto is mine," he said, "my
taking."

"Bring the woman in!" Big Lake ordered, and he
told his guests about our finding her alone on the plain,
about her dream and her quest.

She came inside all eagerness, the inbred diffidence of
a woman facing a number of chiefs and men of dis-
tinction forgotten. "Who, who," she quickly signed,
"is the rider of the pinto horse?"

"I am," the Blood signed. "What about it?"

"It is my horse—my man's horse, the one he rode away one morning three moons ago. And what of my man? Did you see him? How came you by his horse?"

The Blood hesitated for a moment, and then replied: "We went to war. Away south of the Ground-of-many-gifts,* at daylight one morning, a man riding the pinto horse surprised us, and I killed him. I took the animal for my own."

As he gestured his answer, the woman suddenly noticed a bear's claw necklace he wore, and pointing to it, she gave a fearful, heartbroken, gasping sob, and fled from the lodge. She went crying through the camp, and at the edge of the timber sat down, covered her head with her robe, and began to wail for the one who was dead.

Did you, reader, ever hear a woman of the plains mourn for a lost loved one, calling his or her name heart-brokenly, despairingly, over and over again for hours at a time? Nothing else in all this world is so mournful, so expressive of the feelings of one whom death has bereaved of a dear child, relative, companion. I can liken but one thing to it, and that is the cry of the mourning dove. It embodies all the feelings, the thoughts, of one utterly desolate, forsaken. Somewhere I have read, or heard, that an Indian's loss of to-day is forgotten on the morrow. That is certainly not true of the Blackfeet, nor of the Mandans. Often and often I have heard many of the Blackfeet mourn for one dead

---

*The country in the vicinity of Helena, Montana, which city, by the way, the Blackfeet have given the same name. It was a land rich in game and berries, hence the appellation:

Ah-kwo' to-kwü-si sak-ŏm.
Much   giving   ground

long years since. The Mandans used to care for the bones of their departed ones. Those of each family were placed in a little circle on the burying ground, and thither the survivors would repair frequently to deposit choice food, and to talk to the skulls of their dear ones, just as if they were alive and in the flesh. It is not for the Anglo-Saxon to boast of affection, of constancy, for he can take lessons from the despised red men. Never, with the Indians—I speak only of the two tribes before mentioned—was there a separation except for adultery, and that was rare indeed; nor did they ever abuse or desert their offspring. The affection of parents for their children, their pride in them, their sacrifices for them, were practically limitless. And such also was the regard in which the young held their elders. Family ties were something sacred.

I have often heard the Blackfeet speak of various white men as utterly heartless, because they had left their parents and their youthful home to wander and seek adventure in a strange land. They could not comprehend how one with right feeling might absent himself from father and mother, as we do, for months and years. "Hard hearts," "stone hearts," they call us, and with some reason.

The Snake woman continued to mourn, passing the greater part of the time up on the hill, or at the edge of the timber, wailing. She cut off her hair, scarified her ankles, ate little, grew thin and listless; and finally a day came when she remained on her couch instead of arising with the others in Weasel Tail's lodge. "I am to die," she signed, "and I am glad. I did not understand my dream. I thought that I was told to seek my chief in the flesh. Instead, it was meant that my shadow should look for his shadow. I see it plainly now, and in a few nights I start. I know that I shall find him."

And start she did. She died on the fourth day of her illness, and the women buried her decently, respectfully, in a not far distant tree.

CHAPTER XV

T HE long summer days went one by one, lingeringly, peacefully, happily. No war parties attacked us, and the young men who went out to war upon other tribes returned spoil-laden, without loss to their numbers. Perhaps in those times I was not much given to thinking about things; but I knew when I was content, was fully satisfied with the returns of each day and hour, and looked not to the future nor what it might have in store for me. But one thing troubled me, the insistent letters from home, commanding me to return. They were several months old when I got them, as were my New York *Tribunes* and other papers. I ceased reading any more than the headlines of the papers; they had no more interest to me, but I could not help worrying about the contents of the letters. There were grave reasons why I should heed them, should go home on or before the date that I became of age. Many an unpleasant half hour I passed after breaking their seals, and then, consigning them to the flames of the lodge fire, I would go out with Nät-ah'-ki for a ride, or to some feast or social gathering. It was interesting to note the extreme care with which my mail was handled. It was securely bunched up by my Fort Benton friends, and then those to whom it was intrusted re-wrapped and re-bound it in various coverings. The Blackfeet ever regarded the arts of writing and reading as the greatest of accomplishments. Some of them would sit for hours inspecting the pictures in my magazines and papers, and although they persisted in holding them sideways, or even upside down, they seemed, nevertheless, to grasp their significance. Nät-ah'-ki was wont to spread out my letters and endeavour to learn what they told, although, of course, she knew not even a letter of the alphabet. She early came to know my mother's handwriting, and when I received letters from others written in characteristically feminine style, she would watch me closely as I read them and then question me as to the writers. "Oh," I would carelessly answer, "they are from relatives, women of our house, just telling me the news and asking if I am well and happy."

And then she would shake her head doubtfully, and exclaim: "Relatives! Oh, yes, relatives! Tell me truly how many sweethearts you have in the land from whence you came?"

Then I would truthfully answer, swearing by the Sun, calling upon him to bear witness that I had but the one sweetheart, she there present, and she would be content —until I received another bundle of letters. As the summer wore on these letters became more frequent, and I realised with ever-increasing regret that my days of happy, irresponsible wandering were about over, that I must go home and begin the career which was expected of me.

We left the Marias not long after the death of the Snake woman, moved south by the way of the Pend d'Oreille Coulée and the Knees, and camped on the Teton River, the stream which Lewis and Clark named the Tansy, and which the Blackfeet rightly call Un'-i-kis-is-i-si-sak-ta, Milk River, for its waters in its lower course are ever of a milky colour. Late in August we moved to a point on this stream only three miles north of Fort Benton, and every day or so I used to ride in there, often accompanied by Nät-ah'-ki, whose desire for various bright-coloured prints, ribbons, shawls, and beads, was well nigh insatiable. There we found Berry and his good wife, his mother, and the Crow woman, the two latter recently returned from a sojourn with the Mandans. And thither, one day, came Sorrel Horse and his outfit. He and Berry were making preparations for the winter trade. I was beginning to feel pretty blue. I showed them my letters, told them what was expected of me, and declared that I must return east. They both laughed long, loudly, uproariously, and slapped each other on the back, and I gazed solemnly, reproachfully at them. I could not see that I had joked or said anything funny.

"He's goin' home," said Sorrel Horse, "and he's goin' to be a good, quiet little boy ever after."

"And go to church," said Berry.

"And walk the straight and narrer path, world without end, and so forth," Sorrel Horse concluded.

"Well, you see how it is," I said. "I've got to go— much as I would like to remain here with you; I simply must go."

"Yes," Berry acquiesced; "you have to go all right —but you'll come back. Oh, yes! you'll come back, and sooner than you think. These plains and mountains, the free life have you, and they'll never let go. I've known others to return to the States from here, but unless they died back there right quick, they soon came back. They couldn't help it. Mind you, I've been back there myself; went to school there, and all the time old Montana kept calling me, and I never felt right until I saw the sun shining on her bare plains once more and the Rockies looming up sharp and clear in the distance."

"And then," Sorrel Horse put in, speaking Blackfoot, which was as easy to him as English, "and then, what about Nät-ah'-ki? Can you forget her, do you think?"

He had, indeed, touched the sore spot. That was what was worrying me. I couldn't answer. We were sitting in a corner of Keno Bill's place. I jumped up from my chair, hurried out, and mounting my horse, rode swiftly over the hill to camp.

We ate our evening meal: dried meat and back fat (o-sak' i), stewed dried apples—how good they were— and yeast powder bread. In due time I went to bed, and for hours I rolled and tossed uneasily on my couch. "Nät-ah'-ki," I finally asked, "are you awake?"

"Ah."

"I want to tell you something: I must go away for a time; my people call me."

"That is not news to me. I have long known that you would go."

"How did you know?" I asked. "I told no one."

"Have I not seen you read the little writings? Have I not watched your face? I could see what the writing told you. I know that you are going to leave me. I have always known that you would. You are no different from other white men. They are all unfaithful, heartless. They marry for but a day."

She began to cry; not loud, just low, despairing, heart-broken sobs. Oh, how I hated myself. How I did hate myself. But I had opened the subject. I felt that I must carry it through, and I began to lie to her, hating myself more and more every moment. I told her that I was now twenty-one, at which time a

white youth becomes a man. That there were papers
about the property which my father had left, that I
must go home to sign. "But," I said, and I called on the
Sun to witness my words, "I will return; I will come
back in a few moons, and we will once more be happy
While I am away Berry will look out for you and your
good mother. You shall want for nothing."

And thus, explaining, lying, I drove away her fear and
sorrow, and she fell peacefully asleep. But there was
no sleep for me. In the morning I again rode in to the
Fort and talked long with Berry. He agreed to look
after the girl and her mother and keep them supplied
with all necessary food and clothing, until such a time,
I explained, "as Nät-ah'-ki will forget me and become
some other man's woman." I nearly choked when I
said it.

Berry laughed quietly. "She will never be another
man's woman," he said. "You will be only too glad to
return. I shall see you again inside of six months."

The last steamboat of the season was discharging
freight at the levee, and was to leave for St. Louis in
the morning. I went back to camp and prepared to leave
on it. There was not much to do, merely to pack up a
few native things I wished to take home. Nät-ah'-ki
rode back with me, and we passed the night with Berry
and his family. It was not a festive time to me. Berry's
mother and the faithful old Crow woman both lectured me
long and earnestly on the duty of man to woman, on
faithfulness—and what they said hurt, for I was about
to do that which they so strongly condemned.

And so, in the morning, Nät-ah'-ki and I parted, and
I shook hands with every one and went on board. The
boat swung out into the stream, turned around, and we
went flying down the swift current, over the Shonkin

Bar and around the bend. The old Fort, the happy
days of the past year were now but a memory.

There were a number of passengers aboard, mostly
miners from Helena and Virginia City, returning to the
States with more or less dust.

They gambled, and drank, and in a vain effort to get
rid of my thoughts, I joined in their madness. I remember that I lost three hundred dollars at one sitting,
and that the bad liquor made me very ill. Also, I nearly
fell overboard near Cow Island. We had run into a
large herd of buffalo swimming the river, and I tried to
rope a huge old bull from the bow of the boat. The
loop settled fairly over his head, but we had not counted
on such a shock as I and the three others helping me got
when the rope tightened. In an instant it was jerked
from our hands. I lost my balance, and would have
followed it into the water had not the next man behind
happened to catch me by the collar and draw me back.

We tied up to the shore each night; there were constant head winds after we entered Dakota, and when
early in October we arrived at Council Bluffs, I was glad
to leave the boat and board a train of the Union Pacific.
In due time I arrived in the little New England town,
where was my home.

I saw the place and the people with new eyes; I cared
for neither of them any more. It was a pretty place,
but it was all fenced up, and for a year I had lived in the
beyond, where fences were unknown. The people were
good people, but, oh! how narrow-minded. Their ways
were as prim and conventional as were the hideous fences
which marked the bounds of their farms. And this is
the way most of them greeted me: "Ah! my boy, so
you've come home, have you. Been a hull year in the
Indian country. It's a wonder you wasn't scalped.

Those Indians are terrible bad people, so I've heard. Wall, you've had your fling; I suppose you'll steady down now and go into business of some kind."

To only two men in the whole place could I tell anything of what I had seen or done, for they were the only ones who could understand. One was a humble painter, ostracised by all good people because he never went to church, and would occasionally enter a saloon in broad daylight. The other was a grocer. Both of them were fox and partridge hunters, and loved the ways of the wild. Night after night I would sit with them by the grocery stove, long after the staid villagers had retired, and talk of the great plains and the mountains, of the game and the red people. And in their excitement, as their minds pictured that wonderful land and its freedom, they would get up and pace the floor, and sigh, and rub their hands. They wanted to see it all, to experience it all as I had, but they were "bound to the wheel." It was impossible for them to leave home, and wife, and children. I felt sorry for them.

But even to them I said nothing about a certain other tie which bound me to that land of sunshine. There was not a moment of my waking hours in which I did not think of Nät-ah'-ki and the wrong I had done her. Across the several thousand miles which separated us, I could see her in my mind's eye, helping her mother in the various occupations of the lodge, and her manner was listless; no more her hearty infectious laughter rang out, and in her eyes there was an expression which was far from happy. Thus I pictured her by day, and in my dreams at night, awakening to find myself talking Blackfoot to her, and trying to explain away my faithlessness. The days passed for me in deadly monotony, and I was in constant strife with my relatives. Not

with my mother, I am thankful to say. I think that
she rather sympathised with me. But there were uncles
and aunts, and others, old friends of my long dead father,
all well meaning, of course, who thought that it was in-
cumbent on them to advise me, and shape my future.
And from the start we were antagonistic. They brought
me to task for refusing to attend church. To attend
church! To listen to a sermon, forsooth, upon predes-
tination, and the actual hell of fire and brimstone awaiting all who lapsed from the straight and narrow path.
I no longer believed that. My year with old Mother
Nature, and ample time to think, had taught me many
things. Not a day passed but what I got a lecture from
some of them, because, for instance, I drank a harmless
glass of beer with some trapper or guide from the North
Woods. There was more real human kindliness, more
broad-mindedness in one of those simple men of the
woods, than there was in the hearts of all my perse-
cutors.

Diagonally across the way from us lived a good old
Methodist. It was his habit to ascend to the attic of a
Sunday and pray. On a summer day, when windows
were open, one could hear him for hours at a time, entreating his God to forgive his many and grievous sins—
he had never committed one—and to grant him an humble place in the life hereafter. He also came and besought me to change my ways. To change my ways!
What had I done, I wondered, that made all these people
so anxious about me? Was this man's life a happy one?
No: he lived in constant fear of a jealous God. What
had I done? I had been friendly to certain black sheep
who longed for a pleasant word. I had entered the hotel
bar and in broad daylight clinked glasses with them.
These were not, in my estimation, sins. But, deep

down in my heart, there lay a heavy load. One wrong thing I had done, a grievous one. What of Nät-ah'-ki?

There came a certain night when all the well-meaning ones were gathered at our home. They had decided that I should buy out a retiring merchant, who, in the course of forty or fifty years, has acquired a modest competency. That was the last straw. I arose in my wrath, and tried to tell them what I thought of the narrow life they led; but words failed me, and, seizing my hat, I fled from the house. It was past midnight when I returned, but my mother was waiting for me. We sat down by the fire and talked the matter out. I reminded her that from earliest youth I had preferred the forests and streams, rifle and rod, to the so-called attractions of society, and that I felt I could not bear to live in a town or city, nor undertake a civilised occupation of any kind, especially one which would keep me confined in a store or office. And she, wise woman, agreed that as my heart was not in it, it would be useless to attempt anything of the kind. And she also admitted that, since I had come to love the plains and mountains so well, it was best that I should return to them. I said nothing about Nät-ah'-ki. Some time in the future, I determined, when I had done the right thing, she should learn all. For the first time in weeks I went to bed with a light heart. Two days later I boarded a train, and in due time arriving in St. Louis, put up with genial Ben Stickney of the Planters' Hotel. There I fell in touch with things once more. I met men from Texas and Arizona, from Wyoming and Montana, and we talked of the fenceless land, of the Indians and the buffalo trade, of cattle and miners, and various adventures we had experienced. We would congregate in the lobby of an evening and sit there talking and

smoking until long after midnight, or we would go out
in a body and see the town in true Western style. If we
were a trifle hilarious, the police were good, and kindly
looked the other way when our sombreroed crowd
tramped by, singing perchance, at the top of our voices.

Also, I did not forget Nät-ah'-ki. I bought another
trunk, and prowling around among the stores picked up
various washable things of quaint and pretty pattern,
strings of beads, a pair of serpent bracelets, a gold necklace, and various other articles dear to the feminine
heart. At last the trunk was so full that I could barely
lock it, and then, gathering up my things, I boarded a
train for Corinne, Wyoming. We were, I believe, four
days and nights en route. From there by stage to
Helena a week, and on to Fort Benton two days more.
My first inquiry was for Berry. He was down at the
mouth of the Marias, the trader told me, with the Piegans,
but his mother and the Crow woman were living in the
little cabin above, and, with a knowing wink, he added
that he believed a certain young woman named Nät-
ah'ki was with them.

It was very early in the morning. I hurried out and
up the dusty trail. A faint smoke was beginning to
arise from the chimney of the little cabin. I pushed open
the door and entered. Nät-ah'-ki was kneeling before
the fireplace blowing the reluctant flame. "Ah," she
cried, springing up and running to me, "he has come!
My man has come!" She threw her arms around my
neck and kissed me, and in another instant she was in
the next room crying out: "Awake, arise; my man has
returned!"

Berry's mother and the Crow woman hurried out and
also embraced and kissed me, and we all tried to talk at
once, Nät-ah'-ki hanging to my arm and gazing at me

with brimming eyes. "Ah," she said, over and over, "they kept telling me that you would not come back, but I knew that they were wrong. I knew that you would not forget me."

Truly, these were my people. I had returned to my own. Come what might, I vowed never to even think of leaving the little woman again, and I kept my word. Kept it, say I—I never had cause nor wish to do anything else.

That was a queer breakfast Nät-ah'-ki and I had; in fact, no breakfast at all. We gave up attempting to eat, and she recounted all that had happened during my absence. Then she questioned me: What had I been doing all this time? What had I seen? Was my good mother well? I had nothing to relate. I wanted to hear her talk, to watch her happiness, and in that I was happy too. In due time my trunks were brought over, and handing her the key of one, I said that it and its contents were all hers. What exclamations of surprise, of admiration there were as she unwrapped and unfolded the various things and spread them out here and there on table and couch and chairs. She threw the necklace on over her head, clasped on the bracelets, ran over and gave me a silent kiss, and then laid them away. "They are too nice, too good," she said. "I am not handsome enough to wear them."

Then she came back and whispered: "But all these are too many for me. May I give some of them to my grandmothers?"—meaning Mrs. Berry and the Crow woman.

In the lot there were several quiet dress patterns, a couple of shawls, which I had intended for them, and I said that they would be appropriate gifts for women of advanced age. How happy she was as she picked them up and presented them to the faithful friends. I look back upon that morning as the pleasantest one of my life.

After a while I strolled out and down to Keno Bill's place. It was December, but there was no snow on the ground. The sun shone warm, a gentle chinook was blowing. I thought of the far-away New England village shrouded in three feet of snow, and shivered.

I found the usual crowd in Keno's place. Judge D., a brilliant lawyer and an ex-commander in the Fenian war, was playing the marshal a game of seven-up for the drinks. Some bull-whackers and mule-skinners were bucking faro. A couple of buckskin-clad, kit-fox-capped, moccasined trappers were arguing on the best way to set a beaver trap in an ice-covered dam. They were all glad to see me, and I was promptly escorted to the bar. Several asked casually, what was new in the States? Not that they cared anything about them; they spoke of them as of some far-off and foreign country.

"Hm!" said Judge D., "you didn't remain there long, did you, my boy?"

"No," I replied, "I didn't; Montana is good enough for me."

"Montana!" cried the Judge, lifting his glass. "Here's to her and her sun-kissed plains. Here's to her noble mountains; her Indians and buffalo; and to those of us whom kind fortune has given a life within her bounds. Of all men, we are most favoured of the gods."

We all cheered the toast—and drank.

So it used to happen in the frontier towns. One man begins in the morning to assuage a suddenly acquired thirst, and one by one, and by twos, and threes, and fours, the rest join in, merchants, lawyers, doctors, and all, until not a sober man is left, until all are hilarious, and half seas over. Judge D.—peace to his ashes—started it;

by 4 o'clock in the afternoon things were pretty lively. I left the crowd and went home. The buffalo robe, couch and a pipe, the open fire and Nät-ah'-ki's cheerful presence, were more to my liking.

At sundown, who should roll in but Berry and Sorrel Horse, with their women. How glad I was to see them all again. "You didn't think that I would return?" I hazarded.

They laughed. "Didn't I tell you that you would," said Berry. "I only wonder that you didn't come sooner."

We sat by the fire until late, the women chattering in another room. We went to bed. "Little woman," I said taking her hand, "pity your man; he is not so good as he might be; there are bad places in his heart——"

"Stop!" she exclaimed. "Stop! You are good, all good. I would not have you different from what you are. You have come back to me. I cannot tell how happy I am—I have not power to do so."

CHAPTER XVI

THE STORY OF RISING WOLF

WHEN Berry and Sorrel Horse returned to the mouth of the Marias, Nät-ah′-ki and I, of course, went with them. Word of our coming had preceded us, and when we arrived in the great camp at dusk there we found our lodge set up between those of Talks-with-the-buffalo and Weasel Tail. Beside it was a pile of firewood; within a well-built fire was burning cheerfully; at the back our couch of soft robes and warm blankets was spread, guest seats with the comfortable backrests arranged, and in their proper place were our parfleches and cooking utensils, the former well filled with dried berries and choice dried meats and tongues and pemmican. All this had been done by Nät-ah′-ki's good mother, who greeted her daughter with a hearty hug and kiss and me with a shy but sincere welcome. She was a good woman; I may say a noble woman. Yes, a noble, high-minded, self-sacrificing woman, always doing something to alleviate the suffering of the sick and the sorrow of the bereaved.

I had no sooner got down from the wagon and gone inside, leaving Nät-ah′-ki and her mother to bring in our possessions, than my friends began to arrive, and right glad they seemed to be to see me again, as pleased as I was to meet them and hear them say, as they heartily grasped my hand: "Ah′-ko-two-ki-tuk′-ah-an-on"— our friend has returned.

They told me briefly of the happenings during my absence, and then asked for the story of my trip. While Năt-ah'-ki prepared a little feast, and they smoked, I gave it to them as well as I could, giving the number of days that I had travelled on the steamboat, and then on the train, in order to reach my home, a distance in all of 100 nights' sleep were one to travel it on horseback. I had to repeat the story several times that night, once in the chief's lodge. When I had finished the old man inquired particularly about the railroad and its trains, fire-wagons—is-tsi' an'-e-kas-im—as he called them. He wanted to know if any of them were heading for his country.

"No," I replied, "none are coming this way; there is but the one, that which runs east and west far south of here, through the land of the Wolf People and the Sheep Eaters."

"Ai!" he said, thoughtfully stroking his chin, "Ai! that one many of us have seen on our raids to the south. Yes, we have seen it, the wagons, crowded with people, roaring across the plain, killing and scaring the buffalo. Some day you write to our Grandfather (the President) and tell him that we will not allow one to enter our country. Yes, tell him that I, Big Lake, send him this word: 'The white men shall neither put a fire-wagon trail across the country of my people, nor settle here and tear up the sod of our valleys in order to plant the things they feed upon.'"

I attended many a feast that night, no sooner finishing a visit at one lodge than I was invited to another one. It was late when I finally returned home and lay down to rest, the song and laughter of the great camp, the howling of the wolves and coyotes lulling me to sleep. I thought of the far-away New England village buried

in deep snow, and of its dreary monotony. "Thrice
blest am I by propitious gods," I murmured.

Nät-ah'-ki nudged me. "You talk in your sleep,"
she said.

"I was not asleep; I was thinking aloud."

"And what thought you?"

"The gods pity me," I replied. "They have been
kind to me and given me much happiness."

"Ai!" she acquiesced; "they are good; we could ask
of them nothing that they have not given us. To-
morrow we will sacrifice to them." And while she
prayed I fell asleep, having determined that, save perhaps for an occasional visit, the East should know me
no more.

The following day the chiefs and leading men held a
council and decided that we should move out to the
foot of the Bear's Paw Mountains. Thither we went
across the wide, brown and buffalo-covered plain, en-
camping on a little stream running down from a pine-
clad coulée, remaining there for several days. There
were vast numbers of elk and deer and bighorn here,
and in our morning's hunt Wolverine and I killed four
fat ewes, choosing the females instead of the rams, as
the rutting season of the sheep was nearly over. So
numerous were the bands of these now scarce animals
that I doubt not we could have slaughtered twenty or
more of them had we been so minded; but we took no
more than our horses could carry.

When I returned to camp I found Nät-ah'-ki busily
chipping the hide of a cow buffalo I had killed. She
had laced it to a frame of four lodge poles and frozen
it, in which condition the surplus thickness of the hide
was most easily removed with the short elk-horn, steel-
tipped hoe used for the purpose. But even then it was

exceedingly hard, back-breaking labour, and I said that I would be pleased if she would cease doing that kind of work. I had said something about it on a previous occasion, and this time, perhaps, I spoke a trifle too peremptorily. She turned away from me, but not before I saw the tears begin to roll down her cheeks.

"What have I done?" I asked. "I did not mean to make you cry."

"Am I to do nothing," she in turn queried, "but sit in the lodge in idleness? You hunt and provide the meat; you buy from the traders the various foods we eat. You buy my clothes and everything else I wear and use. I also want to do something toward our support."

"But you do. You cook and wash the dishes, you even provide the firewood. You make my moccasins and warm mittens; you wash my clothes; when we travel it is you who take down and set up the lodge, who pack and unpack the horses."

"Yet am I idle most of the time," she said brokenly, "and the women jest and laugh at me, and call me proud and lazy, lazy! Too proud and too lazy to work!"

Thereupon I kissed her and dried her tears, and told her to tan as many robes as she wanted to, taking care not to work too hard nor too long at a time. And immediately she was all smiles and danced out of the lodge; presently I heard the monotonous chuck, chuck of the hoe tip against the stiff hide.

One night a dimly luminous ring was seen around the moon, and the next morning a brighter ring encircled the sun, while on either side of it was a large sun-dog. The rings portended the arrival of a furious storm at no distant date; the rainbow-hued sun-dogs gave certain warning that the enemy, perhaps a large war party, was approaching our camp. This was a bad combination, and a council was called to consider it. The tribe was not afraid to meet any enemy that might do battle with them, but it was certain that in the night of a severe storm a party could approach unseen and unheard, steal many horses, and that the driving, drifting snow would effectually blot out their trail, so that they could not be followed and overtaken. It was decided to break camp at once and move to the mouth of Creek-in-the-middle, on the Missouri. If much snow fell and severe, cold weather set in there would be better shelter in the deep valley of the river; the horses could be fed the rich bark of the cottonwood and kept in prime condition; by moving camp the certainly approaching enemy would probably never run across our trail, especially if the promised storm came soon. By 10 o'clock the last lodge was down and packed, and we strung out east by south for our destination. At noon snow began to fall. We camped that night on Creek-in-the-middle, so named because it has its source midway between the Bear's Paw and Little Rocky Mountains. The early voyageurs named it Cow Creek.

Snow was still lightly falling the next morning and it was much colder; nevertheless, we again broke camp and moved on, arriving at the river before dusk. Here we intended to remain for some time, and the hunters rode far and near on both sides of the valley and out on the plains setting deadfalls for wolves. Strychnine had not then come into general use. These deadfalls were merely a few six to eight foot poles set up at an angle of about forty-five degrees and supported by a two-stick trigger. They were covered with several hundred-weight of large stones; when the wolf seized the bait at the back end of the fall, down came the heavy roof and crushed him.   Berry and Sorrel Horse did all they could to encourage the trapping of the animals, as a large demand had sprung up for their skins in the States, where they were converted into sleigh robes.   Prime skins were selling in Fort Benton at from $4 to $5 each.

The storm did not amount to much, and in a few days a warm chinook again set in.   Nor did the expected war party appear.   My friends, the traders, were doing such a good business that they were obliged to go after more goods every two or three weeks, or whenever they could join a party bound on a visit to Fort Benton.

I had heard much of a certain white man named Hugh Monroe, or, in Blackfoot, Rising Wolf—Mah-kwo-i-pwo-ahts.   One afternoon I was told that he had arrived in camp with his numerous family, and a little later met him at a feast given by Big Lake.   In the evening I invited him over to my lodge and had a long talk with him while we ate bread and meat and beans, and smoked numerous pipefuls of tobacco.   We eventually became firm friends.   Even in his old age, Rising Wolf was about the quickest, most active man I ever saw.   He was about five feet six in height, fair-haired, blue-eyed, and his firm, square chin and rather prominent nose betokened what he was, a man of courage and determination.   His father, Hugh Monroe, was a colonel in the British army, his mother a member of the La Roches, a noble family of French emigrés, bankers of Montreal, and large land owners in that vicinity. Hugh, Jr., was born on the family estate at Three Rivers, and attended the parish school just long enough to learn to read and write.   All of his vacations, and many truant days from the class-room, were spent in the great forest surrounding his home.   The love of nature, of adventure and wild life was born in him.   He first saw the light in July, 1798. In 1813, when but fifteen years of age, he persuaded his parents to allow him to enter the service of the Hudson's Bay Company and started westward with a flotilla of their canoes that spring. His father gave him a fine English smooth-bore, his mother a pair of the famous La Roche duelling pistols and a prayer book. The family priest gave him a rosary and cross, and enjoined him to pray frequently. Travelling all summer they arrived at Lake Winnipeg in the autumn and wintered there. As soon as the ice went out in the spring the journey was continued, and one afternoon in July, Monroe beheld Mountain Fort, a new post of the company, built on the south bank of the Saskatchewan River, not far from the foot of the Rockies.

Around about it were encamped thousands of the Blackfeet waiting to trade for the goods the flotilla had brought up, and to obtain on credit ammunition, fukes, traps, and tobacco sufficient to last them through the coming season. As yet the company had no Blackfoot interpreter, their speech having first to be translated into Cree, and then into English. Many of the Blackfeet proper, the North Blackfeet, spoke good Cree, but the more southern tribes of the confederacy, the Bloods and Piegans, did not understand it. The factor, no doubt perceiving that Monroe was a youth of more than ordinary intelligence, at once detailed him to live and travel with the Piegans and learn the language, also to see that they returned to Mountain Fort with their furs the succeeding summer. Word had been received that, following the course of Lewis and Clark, American traders were yearly pushing farther and farther westward, and had even reached the mouth of the Yellowstone, about the eastern line of the vast territory claimed by the Blackfeet as their hunting ground. The company feared their competition; Monroe was to do his best to prevent it.

"At last the day came for our departure," Monroe told me, "and I set out with the chiefs and medicine men at the head of the long procession. There were 800 lodges of the Piegans there, about 8,000 souls. They owned thousands of horses. Oh, but it was a grand sight to see that long column of riders, and travois, and pack animals, and loose horses trooping over the plains. Yes, 'twas a grand, an inspiring sight. We travelled on and on southward all the long day, and about an hour or two before sundown came to the rim of a valley through which flowed a fine cottonwood-bordered stream. We dismounted at the top of the hill, and spread our robes intending to sit there until the procession passed by into the bottom and put up the lodges. A medicine man produced a large stone pipe, filled it and attempted to light it with flint and steel and a bit of punk, but somehow he could get no spark. I motioned him to hand it to me, and, drawing my sun-glass from my pocket I got the proper focus and set the tobacco afire, drawing several mouthfuls of smoke through the long stem. As one man, all those sitting round about sprang to their feet and rushed toward me, shouting and gesticulating as if they had gone crazy. I also jumped up, terribly frightened, for I thought they were going to do me harm, perhaps kill me; but for what I could not imagine. The pipe was wrenched out of my grasp by the chief himself, who eagerly began to smoke and pray. He had drawn but a whiff or two, however, when another seized it and from him it was taken by still another. Others turned and harangued the passing column; men and women sprang from their horses and joined the group, mothers pressing close and rubbing their babes against me, praying

earnestly meanwhile. I recognised a word that I had
already learned—natos'—Sun; and suddenly the meaning of the commotion became clear; they thought that
I was great medicine; that I had called upon the Sun
himself to light the pipe, and that he had done so. The
mere act of holding my hand up above the pipe was a
supplication to their God. They had perhaps not noticed
the glass, or if they did, had thought it some secret
charm or amulet. At all events, I had suddenly become
a great personage, and from then on the utmost consideration and kindness was accorded me.

"When I entered Lone Walker's lodge that evening—
he was the chief, and my host—I was greeted by deep
growls from either side of the doorway, and was horrified
to see two nearly grown grizzly bears acting as if about
to spring upon me. I stopped and stood quite still, but
I believe that my hair was rising: I know that my
flesh felt to be shrinking. I was not kept in suspense.
Lone Walker spoke to his pets and they immediately
lay down, noses between their paws, and I passed on to
the place pointed out to me, the first couch at the chief's
left hand. It was some time before I became accustomed
to the bears, but we finally came to a sort of understanding with one another. They ceased growling at me as
I passed in and out of the lodge, but would never allow
me to touch them, bristling up and preparing to fight if
I attempted to do so. In the following spring they
disappeared one night and were never seen again. Lone
Walker was disconsolate; he went about for days hunting
and calling them, but in vain. It has been said that a
grizzly cannot be tamed; those two at least appeared to
be tame enough, seemed to have a real liking for their
master, who alone fed them; they were never tied up
and followed the travois of his family along with the dogs

when we moved camp, always sleeping where I first saw them on either side of the doorway."

Is there one of us latter-day hunters, amateur explorers, who does not rejoice when he finds, far hidden in some deep forest a lakelet, or in the remote fastnesses of the mountains a glacier, which he is certain no white man has ever seen before, or who climbs some hitherto unclimbed and unnamed peak, and himself names it as his fancy wills, a name which is afterward accepted and printed on the maps of the Government survey? Think then how the youth, Rising Wolf, must have felt as he journeyed southward over the vast plains, and under the shadow of the giant mountains which lie between the Saskatchewan and the Missouri, for he knew that he was the first of his race to behold them. And to enhance his pleasure, he was travelling with an absolutely primitive people; a people many of whom still used flint arrow and spear points, and flint knives; a people whose language and customs no white man understood, but which he was to learn in due time. Would that we could have had that privilege, brother! We were born a little too late!

Monroe often referred to that first trip with the Piegans as the happiest time of his life. Journeying by easy stages, sometimes skirting the foot of the mountains, and again traversing the broad plains forty or fifty miles to the eastward of them, they came, at the season of falling leaves, to the Pile of Rocks River (Sun River, as the whites named it), and there they remained for three months, passing the remainder of the winter on the Yellow River (the Judith). They had crossed Lewis and Clark's trail, and here again was a vast region which no white man had ever traversed. When spring came, they went still further south to the Musselshell, down that to

its confluence with the Missouri, and, crossing the great
river, they wandered westward along the foot of the Little
Rockies, and thence by the Bear's Paw Mountains to the
Marias and its tributaries. It had been long since decided
that they would not return to Mountain Fort until the
following summer. Rifle and pistol were now useless,
as the last rounds of powder and ball had been fired. But
what mattered that? Had they not their bows and great
sheafs of arrows? After all, what had the white trader
in his stores absolutely necessary to their welfare and
happiness? Nothing; not even tobacco, for in the
spring they had planted on the banks of the Judith a
large patch of their own Nah-wak'-o-sis,* which they
would harvest in due time.

One by one young Rising Wolf's garments were worn
out and cast aside. The women of the lodge tanned
skins of deer and bighorn, and from them Lone Walker
himself cut and sewed shirts and leggings, which he wore
in their place. It was not permitted for women to make
men's clothing. So ere long he was dressed in full Indian
costume, even to the belt and breech-clout, and his
hair grew so that it fell in rippling waves down over his
shoulders. He began to think of braiding it. Ap'-ah-ki,
the shy young daughter of the chief, made his footwear—
thin, parfleche-soled moccasins for summer, beautifully
embroidered with coloured porcupine quills; thick, soft,
warm ones of buffalo robe for winter. Once, he told me
the story of this girl's and his little romance. He
was a temperate man in all things, but on this particular
New Year's night he had taken enough good hot-spiced
Scotch to make him bare his inmost thoughts, and I
doubt not that those thoughts were mostly of the loved
one who was dead and gone.

*See "Blackfoot Lodge Tales" for an account of this narcotic weed, and
the quaint ceremonies attending the planting of it.

"I could not help but notice her," he said, "on the first night I stayed in her father's lodge.   She was some three years younger than I, yet already a woman.   Of good height and slender but well-formed figure, comely face and beautiful eyes, long-haired, quick and graceful in all her movements, she was indeed good to see.   I fell into the habit of looking at her when I thought no one was observing me, and before long I found that it suited me better to stay in the lodge where I could at least be near her than it did to go hunting or on discovery with the men.   I was always increasingly glad when night came, and I could take my place in the lodge opposite her.   Thus the days and weeks and months went by. I learned the language easily, quickly; yet I never spoke to her, nor she to me, for, as you know, the Blackfeet think it unseemly for youths and maidens to do so.

"One evening a man came into the lodge and began to praise a certain youth with whom I had often hunted; spoke of his bravery, his kindness, his wealth, and ended by saying that the young fellow presented to Lone Walker thirty horses, and wished, with Ap′-ah-ki, to set up a lodge of his own.   I glanced at the girl and caught her looking at me;   such a look! expressing at once fear, despair and something else which I dared not believe I interpreted aright.   The chief spoke: 'Tell your   friend,' he said, 'that all you have spoken of him is true;   I know that he is a real man, a good, kind, brave, generous young man, yet for all that I cannot give him my daughter.'

"Again I looked at Ap′ah-ki, and she at me.   Now she was smiling, and there was happiness in her eyes, along with that same peculiar expression which I had before noticed.   But if she smiled, I could not, for Lone Walker's words had killed any hope I might have had of getting her some day for my own.   I had heard him refuse thirty head of horses. What hope had I then, who did not own even the horse I rode? I who received for my services only £20 a year, from which must be deducted the various articles I bought. Surely the girl was not for me. And to make it worse, there was that peculiar expression in her eyes when she looked into mine which, even young and inexperienced in the ways of women as I was, I decided meant that she cared for me, even as I did for her. I suffered.

"After that night Ap'-ah-ki no longer cast down her eyes when I caught her looking at me, but returned my gaze openly, fearlessly, lovingly. We now knew that we loved each other. Time passed. Going out one evening, she came in just as I reached the doorway, and as we passed our hands met—and clasped. For an instant we stood there, gently but firmly retaining our grasp. I trembled. I could feel her muscles also quivering. Then some one called out, 'Shut the doorway; the lodge fills with smoke.' I staggered out and sat down on the ground. For hours I sat there trying to think of some way to accomplish my desire, but I could find no feasible plan, and went miserably to bed. It was a little later, perhaps a couple of weeks, that I met her in the trail bringing home a bundle of firewood. We stopped and looked at each other in silence for a moment, and then I spoke her name. Crash went the fuel on the ground, and we embraced and kissed, regardless of those who might be looking.

" 'I can stand this no longer,' I said at last. 'Come with me now, *now*, to your father, and I will speak to him.'

" 'Yes,' she whispered. 'Yes; let us take courage, and go to him. He has always been good to me, and perhaps he will be generous now.'

"So, forgetting the bundle of wood, we went hand in hand and stood before Lone Walker, where he sat smoking his long pipe, out on the shady side of the lodge. 'I have not thirty horses,' I said, 'nor even one, but I love your daughter, and she loves me. I ask you to give her to me.'

"The chief smiled. 'Why, think you, did I refuse the thirty horses?' he asked, and before I could answer he continued, 'Because I wanted you for my son-in-law; wanted a white man because he is more cunning, much wiser than the Indian, and I need a counsellor. We have not been blind, neither I nor my women. We have long seen that this day was coming—have waited for you to speak the word. You have spoken; there is nothing more to say except this: Be good to her.'

"That very day they set up a small lodge for us and stored it with robes and parfleches of dried meat and berries, gave us one of their two brass kettles, tanned skins, pack saddles, ropes—all that a lodge should contain. And, not least, Lone Walker told me to choose thirty horses from his large herd. In the evening we took possession of our home and were happy."

The old man paused and sat silent, thinking of the old days.

"I know how you felt," I said, "for we are experiencing the same thing."

"I know it," he continued; "seeing the peace and contentment and happiness in this lodge, I could not help telling you about my own youthful days."

After he had gone I told Nät-ah'-ki all that he had said. It affected her deeply, for when I had ended I saw tears in her eyes, and she said over and over again, "Oh, how I pity him! Oh, how lonely he is!"

The next evening when he had come in and taken his

accustomed seat, Nät-ah'-ki went over and kissed him, kissed him twice. "That," she said, brokenly, "is because my man has told me all that you told him last night; because——" but she could say no more.

Rising Wolf bent his head and I could see his bosom heave, the tears dropping down his smooth-shaven cheeks. Perhaps there was a queer lump in my throat. Presently he straightened up, gently laid his hands on the little woman's head and said, "I pray God that you may live long and that you may always be as happy as you are now."

Monroe remained in the service of the Hudson's Bay Company a number of years, raising a large family of boys and girls, most of whom are alive to-day. The eldest, John, is about seventy-five years of age, but still young enough to go up in the Rockies near his home every autumn and kill a few bighorn and elk, and trap a few beavers. The old man never revisited his home; never saw his parents after the day they parted with him at the Montreal docks. He intended to return to them for a brief visit some time, but kept deferring it, and then came letters, two years old, saying that they were both dead. Came also a letter from an attorney, saying that they had bequeathed him a considerable property, that he must go to Montreal and sign certain papers in order to take possession of it. At the time the factor of Mountain Fort, was going to England on leave; to him, in his simple trustfulness, Monroe gave a power of attorney in the matter. The factor never returned, and by virtue of the papers he had signed, the frontiersman lost his inheritance. But that was a matter of little moment to him then. Had he not a lodge and family, good horses and a vast domain actually teeming with game —wherein to wander—what more could one possibly want?

Leaving the Hudson's Bay Company, Monroe sometimes worked for the American Fur Company, but mostly
as a "free trapper" wandered from the Saskatchewan
to the Yellowstone, and from the Rockies to Lake
Winnipeg. The headwaters of the South Saskatchewan
were one of his favourite hunting grounds. Thither in
the early '50's he guided the noted Jesuit Father,
De Smet, and at the foot of the beautiful lakes lying
just south of Chief Mountain they erected a huge
wooden cross, and named the two bodies of water St.
Mary's Lakes. One winter after his sons, John and
François, had married, they were camping there for the
season, the three lodges of the family, when one night
a large war party of Assiniboins attacked them. The
daughters, Lizzie, Amelia, and Mary, had been taught
to shoot, and together they made a brave resistance,
driving the Indians away just before daylight with the
loss of five of their number, Lizzie killing one of them
as he was about to let down the bars of the horse corral.

Besides other furs, beaver, fisher, martin, and wolverines, they killed more than three hundred wolves
that winter, by a device so unique yet simple, that it is
well worth recording. By the banks of the outlet of the
lakes they built a long pen twelve by sixteen feet at the
base, and sloping sharply inward and upward to a
height of seven feet; the top of the pyramid was an
opening about two and one-half feet wide by eight in
length. Whole deer, quarters of buffalo, any kind of
meat handy, was thrown into the pen, and the wolves,
scenting the flesh and blood, seeing it plainly through
the four to six inch spaces between the logs, would
eventually climb to the top and jump down through the
opening. But they could not jump out, and there
morning would find them uneasily pacing around and

around in utter bewilderment. Powder and ball were precious commodities in those days, so the trappers killed the wolves with bow and arrows, and opening a door at one end, they allowed the coyotes to escape. The carcasses of the slain wolves were always thrown into the river as soon as skinned, so that there should be nothing of a suspicious nature about.

Dear old Rising Wolf! He was always bemoaning the decadence of the Indians—the Piegans in particular. "You should have seen them in the long ago," he would say; "such a proud and brave people they were. But now, whisky is their curse. There·are no longer any great chiefs, the medicine men have lost their power."

You will remember that the old man was a Catholic. Yet I know that he had much faith in the Blackfoot religion, and believed in the efficacy of the medicine men's prayers and mysteries. He used often to speak of the terrible power possessed by a man named Old Sun. "There was one," he would say, "who surely talked with the gods, and was given some of their mysterious power. Sometimes of a dark night, he would invite a few of us to his lodge, when all was calm and still. After all were seated his wives would bank the fire with ashes so that it was as dark within as without, and he would begin to pray. First to the Sun, chief ruler, then to Ai-so-pwom-stan, the wind-maker, then to Sis-tse-kom, the thunder, and Puh-pom', the lightning. As he prayed, entreating them to come and do his will, first the lodge ears would begin to quiver with the first breath of a coming breeze, which gradually grew stronger and stronger until the lodge bent to the blasts, and the lodge poles strained and creaked. Then thunder began to boom, faint and far away, and lightning to dimly blaze, and they came nearer and nearer until they seemed to be just overhead; the crashes deafened us, the flashes blinded us, and all were terror-stricken. Then this wonderful man would pray them to go, and the wind would die down and the thunder and lightning go on rumbling and flashing into the far distance until we heard and saw them no more."

All this the old man firmly believed that he had heard and seen. I cannot account for it, nor can you, except —if there be such a thing—the wily old magician hypnotised his audiences.

CHAPTER XVII

A FRIENDLY VISIT FROM THE CROWS

IN THE days of which I write the Blackfeet were not, as they are now, cursed with the different forms of tuberculosis. Yet there were, of course occasional cases. The wife of Four Horns, a young man of the Small Robe band, had it, and was growing steadily worse. As the lodge of the young couple was quite near ours, we naturally saw much of them. Four Horns was an exceedingly tall, well-built, pleasant-featured man of twenty-eight or thirty, and his wife was also good looking, neat in person and habits, but the disease had sadly shrunken her once fine form. The man was a famous raider, a tireless hunter, and, with what he had taken from the enemy, and by careful breeding, had acquired a large band of horses. In his lodge were always bundles of fine robes and furs, ready to be bartered for anything that was needed or which took his wife's fancy. Nothing was too good for his woman; he thought the world of her, and she of him.

When the disease appeared a doctor was called in, and given a fee of three horses. His medicines and prayers did no good, however, and another one was tried, fee, five horses, but with like results. In succession the doctors of the whole tribe attended the patient, and now the end was near. The fine herd of horses had shrunk to less than a dozen head. Robes, furs, costly blankets, and finery had also been given to the doctors. Late one evening a messenger hurriedly

entered our lodge: "You are called," he said, "by
Four Horns; he bids you, both of you, make haste."

We found the poor woman gasping for breath. Four
Horns was sitting on the couch beside her, his face
buried in his hands. An old woman, robe thrown over
her head, was feeding the fire. I poured out a large
drink of whisky, added some sugar and hot water to it,
and Nät-ah'-ki gave it to the sufferer. It revived her;
she soon breathed more easily, and then said to me,
speaking very slowly and interruptedly: "Never in
all my life have I done a wrong thing. I have never
lied, nor stolen, nor done that which brings shame upon
a woman's parents and upon her. Yet our gods have
forsaken me and I am near to death. You have gods
as well as we. I have heard of them. The Maker, His
Son, the Mother of the Son. Pray to them, I beg you;
perhaps they will take pity and make me well."

I cannot explain, I fear, how I felt upon hearing that
simple request. I wished that I could grant it, and
knew that I could not. How was it possible for one to
pray who had no faith? I cast about in my mind for
some excuse; for something to say, for some way to
explain my inability to do it. I looked up and found
Nät-ah'-ki earnestly, expectantly gazing at me. We
had talked about religion, the white man's religion,
several times, and she knew that I had no faith in it.
Nevertheless, I could see that she expected me to do what
the dying woman had requested. I made the sign of
negation; no. She moved at once to the side of the
sufferer and said: "I will pray to those gods for you.
Long ago, when I was a little girl, a Blackrobe and my
uncle taught me the way," and she began: "Ap'-ai-stu-
to-ki, kin'-ah-an-on, etc." 'Twas the Lord's prayer!
Some zealous Jesuit, perhaps Father De Smet himself,

had translated it into Blackfoot, and good Blackfoot,
too.

But even as the prayer ended, a dark stream flowed
from the woman's mouth, the last and fatal hemorrhage.
"That which kills you," cried Four Horns, "shall kill
me. I follow you soon to the Sandhills." And bending over he drank of the blood flowing from his loved
one's lips. With one last effort she clasped her thin arms
around his neck, and died. It was a dreadful scene.

"Come," I said presently, gently lifting him. "Come
with me to my lodge; the women now have their work
to do."

With one last, long look, he arose and followed me.
I gave him the guest couch, and handed him a cupful of
whisky which he quickly swallowed. After a time I
gave him another cupful; worn out with long watching,
overcome by the strong liquor, he lay down and I
covered him with a robe. He slept soundly until after
noon the next day; by that time Nät-ah'-ki and others
had bound the body in robes and blankets and lashed
it in a tree somewhere down the river. I know not
whether Four Horns had long before contracted the disease, or if he was infected there at the woman's death
bed. He died of the same dread scourge some six weeks
later. If there is a Sandhills, let us hope that his shadow
found hers, and that together the dreariness of that
abode of shadows became lightened.

The uncle Nät-ah'-ki had mentioned was a French
creole, one of the earliest employees of the American
Fur Company. He had married the sister of her mother,
and had been very kind to his various relatives. Nät-
ah'-ki had passed two winters in his quarters at Fort
Benton, and much time in his lodge when he travelled
with the tribe. A devout Catholic himself, he had tried

to spread the doctrine among his adopted people. I would have said nothing about the prayer she had made, but she opened the subject an evening or two later by asking me why I had not done what her dying friend asked of me.

"How could I, not believing, as I have told you, that which the Blackrobes and others tell us?" I asked in turn.

"Surely," she said, "if I can believe, I who can neither speak your language nor read the Blackrobe's sacred writings, then you should be able to do so, you who can understand it all."

"In that very writing," I explained, "the Maker says that we shall have no other god than Him, and that if you pray to others than Him, He will punish you in some fearful manner. Therefore, if you do pray to Him, you must no longer pray to the Sun, or to anything else whatever."

"Nevertheless," said Nät-ah'-ki, decidedly, "I shall pray to Him, and to our gods also. That writing was not meant for us; only for the white people. We are poor; we are like a blind person feeling his way along high cliffs; we need the help of all the gods we can find."

"Right you are," I told her. "We do need help; pray to them all; and since I cannot, why, pray for me."

"Ah!" she sighed. "As if I did not always do so! There is the Sun; you can see him every day. How good he is, giving us light and heat. Can you not believe in him?"

"Yes," I replied, "I do believe in him, he is the life of this earth."

That pleased her, and she went about her work happily singing.

In February we were visited by a deputation from

the Crows, who were wintering on Tongue River, away to the south of us. They came with tobacco and other presents from their chief to ours, and the message that their people offered to make a lasting treaty of peace with the Piegans. Their leader was one Rock Eater, half Crow and half Blackfoot. His mother had been captured by the former tribe when a young girl, and in due time became the wife of her captor's son. Rock Eater, of course, spoke both languages perfectly. The envoys were well received, and became guests of the more prominent men. Their proposition was one which required mature deliberation, and while the chiefs and head warriors were discussing it, they were feasted and given the best of everything in the camp. Rock Eater himself became my guest, and many an interesting talk I had with him by the evening fire.

"Is your mother happy with the Crows?" I asked him one night. "And how do you yourself feel—that you are Piegan, or Crow, or both?"

"It is this way," he replied. "My mother loves my father, and I love him, for he has always been kind to us. Generally, we are quite happy; but there are times, when a party returns with Piegan scalps, or horses taken from them, boasting loudly of their victory, calling the Piegans cowardly dogs. Ah! then we feel very sad. And often the proud young Crows have made fun of me, and joked about me, calling me bad names. Oh! yes, we are very miserable at times. Long ago my mother began to urge my father to talk with the chiefs and urge them to make peace with her people. I have also long been saying what I could to help the plan. But always the most of the people would object. One chief would arise and say, 'The Piegans killed my son; I want revenge, not peace.' Others would speak, crying out that they had lost a brother, or father, or uncle, or nephew in war with the Piegans, and that they could not think of making peace. Not long ago my father again called a council to consider this question, and as ever, he was opposed by many of the leading men. The last speaker said this to him: 'We are tired of being asked to talk about making peace with the Piegans. If you are so anxious to be friendly with them, why go and live with them; become a Piegan yourself.'

"'So I will,' cried my father in anger. 'So I will. I will become a Piegan, and fight with them against all their enemies.' And so saying, he arose and went home, I following him.

"Now, my father is a chief himself; a fearless man in war, so kindly and generous that he is loved by all but a few who are jealous of his position. When it was learned what he had said in the council, the people came to him and begged him to take back his words; also they went to the other chiefs and insisted that peace should be declared, provided the Piegans would agree to it. 'We have had enough of this war,' they said. 'See the widows and orphans it has made. We have our own great country, covered with buffalo, the Piegans theirs; the two tribes can live without killing one another.' So, after all, my father had his way, and we were sent to you. I hope we will carry Piegan tobacco back with us."

Rock Eater was called to a feast, and soon after Rising Wolf came in to smoke a pipe with me. I asked him to tell me something about the wars between the two tribes. "Ha!" he said, grimly laughing; "I was in one of the fights, and a sad day it was to us. But to begin: The Blackfeet are a northern people. They once lived in the Slave Lake country. The Crees named those lakes after them, because they made slaves of the enemies they captured. Gradually they began to journey southward and came to these great plains abounding in game, where the winters are mild. There they found different tribes, Crows, Assiniboins, Shoshones, and various mountain tribes, the Kutenais, Pend d'Oreilles, and Stonies, and drove all before them, taking possession of their country. There were times of peace between them and these tribes, but mostly they waged war upon them. In 1832 the Blackfeet made a treaty of peace with the Crows, at Fort Union, which lasted only two years. Again, in 1855, at the mouth of the Judith River, at what is known as the Stevens treaty between the United States and various tribes, the Blackfeet, Crows, Gros Ventres, Pend d'Oreilles, the Kutenais, Nez Percés and others agreed to cease warring against one another, and intruding upon each other's hunting grounds. The Musselshell River was designated as the boundary separating Blackfeet from Crow territory. In the summer of 1857 the Crows broke this agreement by raiding a camp of the Bloods, killing two men and running off a large number of horses. That reopened the old feud, the three Blackfeet tribes, Bloods, Piegans and Blackfeet proper, making common cause against the enemy. In the fall of 1858 I joined the Piegans with my family at Fort Benton, and we went south of the Missouri to winter. We camped for a time on the Judith River, and then determined to move over on the Musselshell, follow it down by easy stages, and return to the Missouri by way of the east slope of the Snowy Mountains. About noon of the second day we came to the divide separating the two streams. Our column was loosely scattered along four or five miles of the trail that day, and most

of the hunters were behind, away to the east and west,
skinning buffalo and other game they had killed; ahead
of us a mile or so rode our scouts, some thirty or forty
men. It was a warm day; the horses felt lazy as well
as their riders, and the big camp moved slowly along
the trail, widely scattered as I have said. The scouts
far ahead, gave no sign that they had seen anything to
make them suspicious. The old people dozed in their
saddles; young men here and there were singing war,
or hunting songs; the mother crooned to the babe at her
breast; all were happy. The scouts passed out of view
down the south slope of the gap, and the head of our
column was nearing the summit, when out from a large
pine grove on our right dashed at least two hundred
mounted Crows, and fell upon us. Back turned the
people, the women and old men madly urging their
horses, scattering travois and lodge poles along the
way, shrieking for help, calling on the gods to preserve
them. Such fighting men as there were along this part of
the line did their utmost to check the rush of the Crows,
to cover the retreat of the weak and defenceless. Hearing shots and shouts, back came the scouts, and from
the rear came charging more men to the front. But
in spite of stubborn resistance the Crows swept all before
them for a distance of at least two miles, strewing the
trail with our dead and dying people—men, women,
children, even babies. They took not one captive, but
shot and struck, and lanced to kill, scalping many of
their victims. But at last the Piegans bunched up in
some sort of order, and the Crows drew off and rode
away to the south, singing their songs of victory, taunt-
ing us by waving in triumph the scalps they had taken.
So badly had our people been stampeded, so stunned
were they by the terrible calamity that had befallen

them, that they simply stood and stared at the retreating enemy, instead of following them and seeking revenge.

"Right there in the gap the lodges were pitched, and search for the dead and missing begun. By night all the bodies had been recovered and buried. On every hand, in nearly every lodge, there were mourners cutting their hair, gashing their lower limbs, crying and wailing, calling over and over again by the hour the names of the loved ones they had lost. Yes, it was a camp of mourning. For weeks and months, when evening came, the wailing of the mourners, sitting out in the darkness just beyond the circle of the lodges, was pitiful to hear. It was a very long time before singing and laughter, and the call of the feast-giver were again heard. I happened to be with the scouts that day, and when we charged back did my best with them to check the Crows. But they so far outnumbered us, had so demoralised the people by their unexpected and fierce assault, that we were well-nigh powerless until our men in the rear came up. More than half of the scouts were killed. I got an arrow in the left thigh. In all, one hundred and thirteen Piegans were killed, while we shot down but seven of the enemy.

"After this happened, you may be sure that most of the war parties leaving the Piegan camp headed for the Crow country, and from the north came parties of their brothers, the Blackfeet and Bloods to harass the common enemy. In the course of two or three years they killed enough members of the Crow tribe, and drove off sufficient numbers of their horse herds, to more than offset their own losses in the massacre and in later fights—for, of course, our war parties were not always victorious.

"In the spring of 1867 the Gros Ventres—then at war with the Blackfeet tribes—concluded a treaty with the Crows, and there was a great gathering of them all on lower Milk River, to celebrate the event. A party of young Gros Ventres returning from a raid against the Crees brought word that they had seen the Piegan camp in the Divided—or, as the whites called them, Cypress—Hills. This was great news. The Crows had a long score to settle with their old-time enemy. So also felt the Gros Ventres. Although they had for a very long time been under the protection of the Black-feet, who fought their battles for them, and protected them from their bitter foes, the Assiniboins and Yanktonais, they had no gratitude in their make-up, and had quarrelled with their benefactors over a trivial cause. And now for revenge! What could the Piegans do against their combined forces? Nothing. They would kill off the men, capture the women, seize the rich and varied property of the camp. So sure were they of success, that they had their women accompany them to sort out and care for the prospective plunder.

"From a distant butte the war party had seen the Piegan camp, but had not discovered that just over a hill to the west of it, not half a mile further, the Bloods were encamped in force, some five thousand of them, or in all about one thousand fighting men. No, they hadn't seen that, and so one morning the Crows and Gros Ventres came trailing leisurely over the plain toward the Piegan camp all decked out in their war costumes, the plumes of their war bonnets and the eagle feather fringe of their shields fluttering gaily in the wind. And with them came their women happily chattering, already rejoicing over the vast store of plunder they were going to possess that day. An early hunter from

the Piegan camp, going with his woman after some meat
he had killed the previous day, discovered the enemy
while they were still a mile and more away, and hurried
back to give the alarm, sending one of his women on
to call out the Bloods. There was a great rush for
horses, for weapons; some even managed to put on a
war shirt or war bonnet. Luckily it was early in the
morning and most of the horse herds, having been driven
in to water, were feeding nearby. If a man did not
at once see his own band, he roped and mounted the
first good animal he came to. And thus it happened
that when the attacking party came tearing over the
little rise of ground just east of the camp they were
met by such an overwhelming force of determined and
well-mounted men that they turned and fled, firing
but few shots. They were utterly panic-stricken; their
only thought was to escape. Better mounted than
their women, they left these defenceless ones to the
mercy of the enemy, seeking only to escape themselves.

"From the point of meeting a fearful slaughter began.
Big Lake, Little Dog, Three Suns, and other chiefs kept
shouting to their men to spare the women, but a few
were killed before they could make their commands
known. There was no mercy shown to the fleeing men,
however; they were overtaken and shot, or brained
with war clubs. So sudden had been the call that many
men had found no time to select a swift horse, mounting
anything they could rope, and these soon dropped out
of the race; but the others kept on and on, mile after
mile, killing all the men they overtook until their horses
could run no more and their club arms were well-nigh
paralysed from striking so long and frequently. Few
of the fleeing party made any resistance whatever, never
turned to look backward, but bent forward in the saddle

and plied the quirt until they were shot or clubbed from their seats. For miles the trail was strewn with the dead and dying, through which fled their women, shrieking with terror—the women they had brought to care for their plunder. 'Let them go!' cried Big Lake, laughing. 'Let them go! We will do as did Old Man with the rabbits, leave a few for to breed, so that their kind may not become wholly extinct.'

"A count was made of the dead. Only five of the Blackfeet had lost their lives, and a few been wounded. But along the trail over which they had so confidently marched that morning three hundred and sixty Crows and Gros Ventres lay dead. Many of them were never touched, for the victors had become tired of cutting and scalping. Their arms were taken, however, and in many cases their war costumes and ornaments, and then the two camps moved westward a way, leaving the battlefield to the wolf and coyote.

"As you know, the Gros Ventres asked for peace, and are again under the protection of our people. And now come these messengers from the Crows. Well, we will see what we will see." And bidding us sleep well, Rising Wolf—I never could call him Monroe—went home.

When Berry was in camp, or anywhere within a reasonable distance of it, the Piegans did no business without consulting him, and they always took his advice. He was really their leader; their chiefs deferred to him, relied upon him, and he never failed to advise that which was for their best interests. So now he was called to attend the council to consider the Crow proposal, and I went, too, under his wing as it were. I wanted to hear the speeches. The Crow delegation, of course, was not present. Big Lake's lodge was well filled with the chiefs and leading men of the tribe, including the younger heads of the different bands of the All Friends Society. Among them I noticed mine enemy, Little Deer, who scowled at me when I entered. He was beginning to get on my nerves. To tell the truth, I impatiently looked forward to the day when we would have it out, being possessed of a sort of unreasoning belief that I was fated some day to send his shadow to the Sandhills.

Big Lake filled his big stone pipe, a medicine man lighted it, made a short prayer, and then it was passed back and forth around the circle. Three Suns opened the subject for consideration by saying that he and his band, the Lone Eaters, favoured the making of a peace treaty with their old enemy. He had no sooner finished than Little Deer began an impassioned harangue. He should have been one of the last to speak, older and men of higher position having precedence over the younger; but he thrust himself forward. Nevertheless, he was listened to in silence. The Blackfeet are ever dignified, and pass over without remark any breach of tribal manners and etiquette. In the end, however, the transgressor is made in many ways to pay the penalty for his bad conduct. Little Deer said that he represented the Raven Carrier band of the great society, and that they wanted no peace with the Crows. Who were the Crows but murderers of their fathers and brothers; stealers of their herds? As soon as green grass came, he concluded, he and his friends would start on a raid against the people of the Elk River (Yellowstone), and that raid would be repeated again and again while summer lasted.

One after another each one had his say, many declaring for a peace treaty, a few—and generally the younger men—voicing Little Deer's sentiments. I remember especially the speech of an ancient, blind, white-haired medicine man. "Oh, my children!" he began, "Oh, my children! Hear me; listen understandingly. When I was young like some of you here, I was happiest when raiding the enemy, killing them, driving off their horses. I became rich. My women bore me four fine sons; my lodge was always filled with good food, fine furs. My boys grew up, and oh, how proud of them I was. They were so strong, so active, such good riders and good shots. Yes, and they were so kind to me and to their mothers. 'You shall hunt no more,' they commanded. 'You grow old; sit you here by the lodge fire and smoke and dream, and we will provide for you.' I was happy, grateful. I looked forward to many pleasant winters as I aged. Hai-ya! One after another my handsome sons went forth to war, and one after another they failed to return. Two of my women were also killed by the enemy; another died, and she who remains is old and feeble. I am blind and helpless; we are both dependent on our friends for what we eat and wear, and for a place by the lodge fire. This is truly a most unhappy condition. But if there had been no war—ai! If there had been no war, then this day I would be in my own lodge with my children and grandchildren, and my women, all of us happy and content. What has happened will happen again. You who have talked against peace, think hard and take back your words. What war has done to me, it surely will do to some of you."

When the old man finished, nearly every one in the lodge cried "Ah!" "Ah!" in approval of his speech. Big Lake then spoke a few words: "I was going to make a talk for peace," he said, "but our blind friend has spoken better than I could; his words are my words. Let us hear from our friend the trader chief."

"I say with you," Berry agreed, "that the old man's talk is my talk.   Better the camp of peace and plenty than the mourning of widows and orphans out in the darkness beyond the fires.   Let us make peace."

"It shall be peace!" said Big Lake.   "Only six of you here have talked against it, and you are far out-numbered.   I shall tell the Crow messengers that we will meet their people at Fort Benton in the sarvis berry moon, and there make friends.   I have said.   Go you forth."

We went our several ways; I to my lodge, where I found Rock Eater talking with Nät-ah'-ki.   I saw at once that she was excited about something, and as soon as I had told our friend the decision of the council, she began: "See what we have discovered.   His mother," pointing at Rock Eater, "is my mother's cousin, my relative; he is my relative.   How queer it is; he came into our lodge a stranger, and we discover that he is of our blood, our very own family!   And you say that we are to meet the Crows when the sarvis berries ripen. Oh, I am glad; glad!   How pleased my mother will be to see her whom we thought was dead.   Oh, we will be good to her.   We will make her forget all that she has suffered."

I reached over and shook hands with Rock Eater. "Friend and relative," I said, "I am glad to hear this news."

And indeed I was glad.   I had taken a strong liking to the young man, who in his plain and simple way had told us of his sufferings and humiliations among a partly alien—one may say wholly alien—people, for, after all, the mother's kin, and not the father's, are almost invariably the chosen kin of the offspring of a marriage between members of different tribes or nations.

The All Friends Society gave a dance in honour of the visitors, a Parted Hair, or Sioux dance, which was indeed a grand and spectacular performance. Not to be outdone, the Crows decided to give one of their own peculiar dances, one called, I believe, the Dog Feast dance. But at the very mention of it, the Piegans suddenly lost all interest. Not but that they wanted to see the dance; they were anxious to see it. The hitch was about the dog. To them it was a sacred animal, never to be killed, nor worse still, to be used as an article of food. Dreading the wrath of the gods, none of them even dared to give the visitors one, knowing that it would be killed and eaten. I solved the problem by buying one of an old woman, pretending that I wanted it for a watch dog, and then giving it to the Crows. 'Twas a large, fat, ancient dog, well-nigh toothless, purblind and furred like a wolf. The Crows led it down into the timber by the river, and when next I saw it, it was hanging in a tree, dressed and scraped, its skin as white and shiny as that of a newly butchered pig. The next day they wanted a kettle in which to stew the dog, and no one dared loan one for such a purpose. Again I went to the rescue, "borrowed" two empty five-gallon alcohol cans from Berry and donated them. In these the dog meat was cooked to perfection.

These Crows had about the handsomest war costumes I ever saw. Every eagle tail feather of their head-dresses was perfect, and the hanging part of them swept the ground at their heels. Their shirts and leggings were elegantly fringed with weasel skins, scalp locks and buckskin, and embroidered, as were their belts and moccasins, with complex designs in perfectly laid

porcupine quills of gorgeous colours. The steaming cans
of dog meat were carried to a level, open place between
the camp and the river, and placed by a freshly
built fire. Two of the Crows began to beat a drum, and
the dance began, an immense crowd having gathered
around in a great circle to see it. No one cared to go
near the cans of forbidden food. As I remember it
through all these years, the dance song was very different
from any the Blackfeet sing, but the dance step, a forward spring on one foot and then the other, body slightly
inclined forward, was like that of the Parted Hairs.
Forth and back they danced, now to the right, again to
the left, every little while circling completely around
the fire and the cans, arms and hands extended, as if
they were blessing the food. After dancing the circle
there was a rest, during which a pipe was smoked, and
then the dance was repeated. The performance lasted
about an hour, and then the party removed the cans
from the fire and prepared to feast on their contents.
In less than two minutes the last Piegan had left the
vicinity, some of the women badly nauseated at the
thought of eating such proscribed food.

After remaining with us a couple of days longer, the
Crows prepared to depart, and many a present was given
them for themselves and for their chief. They carried
about ten pounds of tobacco as a token that the Piegans
accepted their overtures of peace, also a handsome
black stone pipe, a present from Big Lake to their head
chief. Then they were given a number of horses, fine
blankets, parfleches of choice dried meat and skins of
pemmican. Nät-ah'-ki had her little herd run in. "My
horses are your horses," she said to me. "Give Rock
Eater that four-year-old black." I did so. Then she got
together some things for his mother—a new four-point

"And many a present was given them for themselves and for their chief"

blanket, a blue, trade-cloth dress, various paints and trinkets, and lastly a lot of food for the traveller. Rock Eater could hardly speak when he was leaving. Finally he managed to say. "These days here with you have been happy. I go from you, my good and generous relatives, only to meet you soon with my mother. She will cry with joy when she hears the words you send her and receives these fine presents." And so they rode away across the bottom and over the ice-bound river, and we turned to our everyday affairs.

CHAPTER XVIII

A RAID BY THE CROWS

A BIG chinook wind in the latter end of February cleared the river of ice, and the little snow in the coulées soon melted away. There was no more cold weather thereafter, grass showing green in the bottom lands in March.

Life in camp was generally tranquil. One night some Assiniboins stole forty head of horses, and were not overtaken, although a large party followed their trail eastward as far as Hairy Cap butte. Their coup stick, a long arrow, to which was tied a large scalp, was found sticking in the ground in the heart of our camp the morning after the theft, causing the people much chagrin. It was practically a message from the enemy, reading something like this: "We present you with a scalp, which we tore from the head of a member of your tribe. We have taken some of your horses. We are Assiniboins," for the tribe was known by the peculiar make of the arrow. "They will hear from us as soon as summer comes," said the young men. The Blackfeet did not often start on raids in cold weather. On the other hand, Assiniboin war parties seemed to prefer the most inclement months of winter for their expeditions. They were a very cowardly people, and realised that they ran less risk of being discovered and made to fight at a time when the enemy went abroad only to hunt in the vicinity of camp.

I shall never forget another morning, when, for a

few moments, it seemed as if we all must face a terrible
death. The evening before a vast herd of buffalo had
been discovered two or three miles back from the river—
a herd so large that it was said the valley of Cow Creek
and the hills on each side of it were black with them as
far as one could see. Soon after sunrise many hunters,
with their women following on travois horses, had gone
out to run this herd and get meat. An hour or so later
they charged in among them on their trained runners.
splitting the herd in such a way that about a thousand
or more broke straight down the valley toward the
camp. This was the part of the herd that they chased,
for the nearer to camp the killing was done the easier
it was to pack in the meat. Down the valley the frightened animals fled, followed by their tenacious pursuers.
We in camp heard the thunder of their hoofs and saw
the cloud of dust they raised, before the animals themselves came in sight. Our lodges were pitched on the
lower side of the bottom, between the creek and the
steep, bare, rocky ridge to the east. Every man, woman,
and child of us had hurried outside to witness the chase,
for it was not every day that we had such an opportunity. It was really far more exciting to see such a
run near at hand than to take part in it. When one
mounted his runner and flung into the thick of the herd,
he saw only the particular animals he chased and shot
or shot at; he had not time nor sense for anything else.
But the spectator of the run saw much. First of all,
he was impressed with the mighty power of the huge,
shaggy, oddly shaped beasts charging madly by him
with a thunderous pounding of hoof and rattle of horns,
causing the ground to tremble as if from an earthquake;
and then to see the hunters, their long hair streaming in
the wind, guiding their trained mounts here and there

in the thick of it all, singling out this fat cow or that choice young bull, firing their guns or leaning over and driving an arrow deep into the vital part of the great beast; to see the plain over which they passed become dotted with the dead, with great animals standing head down, swaying, staggering, as the life blood flowed from mouth and nostrils, finally crashing over on the ground, a limp and lifeless heap. Ah! that was a sight! That is what we, standing by our lodges, saw that morning. No one cheered the hunters, nor spoke, nor laughed. It was too solemn a moment. We saw death abroad; huge, powerful beasts, full of tireless energy, suddenly stricken into so many heaps of senseless meat and hide. Paradoxical as it may seem, the Blackfeet reverenced, spoke with awe of, regarded as "medicine" or sacred, these animals which they killed for food, whose hides furnished them with shelter and clothing.

A band of horses drinking at the river became frightened at the noise of the approaching herd. They bounded up the bank and raced out over the bottom, heads and tails up, running directly toward the herd, which swerved to the eastward, crossed the creek, and came tearing down our side of it. The rocky ridge hemming in the bottom was too steep for them to climb with anything like speed, so they kept on in the flat directly toward the lodges. Such a scampering as ensued! Some in their terror ran wildly around, stopping behind one lodge a moment, then running to the shelter of another. Women screamed, children bawled, men shouted words of advice and command. I seized hold of Nät-ah'-ki, ran with her over to one of Berry's wagons, and got her up in it. In a moment both his and Sorrel Horse's wagons were filled with people, others crouching under and standing in lines behind them. Persons in the vicinity of the ridge clambered up among the rocks. Those near the creek jumped down in it, but many stood helplessly behind their lodges in the centre of the camp. Now, the leaders of the herd reached the outer edge of the village. They could not draw back, for those behind forced them forward, and they loped on, threading their way between the lodges, nimbly jumping from side to side to avoid them, kicking out wickedly at them as they passed. For all his great size and uncouth shape, the buffalo was an animal quick and active on his feet.

I had taken shelter behind one of the wagons with many others and watched the brown, living stream surge by, winding in and out between the lodges as a river winds past the islands and bars in its channel. Not one of us but was frightened; we held our breath in anxious suspense, for we well knew that almost anything—the firing of a gun or sight of some suspicious object ahead—might throw the herd into confusion, and if it turned or bunched up in a compact mass, people would surely be trampled to death by them, lodges overturned, the greater part of camp reduced to irreparable ruin. To us it seemed a very long time, but in reality no more than a couple of minutes elapsed ere the last of the herd had passed out beyond the outer lodges into the river and across it to the opposite side. No one had been hurt, not a lodge had been overturned. But long scaffolds of drying meat, many hides and pelts of various animals pegged out on the ground to dry, had either disappeared or been cut into small fragments. That, indeed, was an experience to be remembered; we were thankful to have escaped with our lives. When we thought what would have happened had we got in the way of the rushing herd, we shuddered. When

Nät-ah'-ki said: "How good was the Sun to keep us
unharmed through this great danger," I am sure that she
voiced the sentiment of all. The next day I noticed
that the trees and high bushes bordering the river were
bright with the people's offerings or sacrifices to their
god. They gave always of their best, their choicest and
most prized ornaments and finery.

The winter was now gone. Berry and Sorrel Horse
started for Fort Benton with their families and the last
loads of their winter's trade. They had done exceedingly
well, and concluded to remain for a time at the fort.
Berry declared that he would do no more freighting to the mines with his bull train; he would either
sell it or employ some one as a train-master. The
Piegans still had a large number of prime robes, wolf
pelts, and other skins on hand, which they were to trade
at the fort, but instead of going there direct, they
decided to circle southward, up the Judith River,
thence around to the north by way of Arrow Creek and
the foot of the Highwood Mountain. I went with them,
agreeing to meet Berry at the fort and plan with him for
the ensuing season's trade.

So, one warm, sunny day in the end of March, camp
was broken, and crossing the wide, shallow ford of the
river at Cow Island, we climbed the south slope of the
valley and strung out over the plain. At such times
Nät-ah'-ki and I frequently dropped behind and rode
along a mile or more to the right or left of the trail on
little side hunts. We were free to do this, for the good
mother and her uncle's family took charge of our pack
and travois horses, and herded them along with their
own. And when we came to camp in the evening we
would find our lodge put up, the couches made, wood
and water at hand, the tireless mother sitting by the fire

awaiting our arrival. Sometimes Năt-ah'-ki would remonstrate with her for doing all this, but she would always say, "Young people should be happy. This my mother did for me when I was newly married. Some day you will likely be doing it for your daughter." Which latter remark would cause the little woman to turn away in confusion, and she would pretend to be very busy about something. Alas! they thought that this care-free life was going to last forever. Even we white men little dreamed how soon the buffalo were to disappear.

On this lovely morning we rode gradually, slowly and obliquely away to the west until we were a couple of miles from the trail. Still farther out we could see several hunters now and then, as they passed over a rise of ground, and occasionally the long column of the moving camp was in sight. Sometimes we loitered, letting our horses feed as they walked, and again we would start them into a lope and keep it up until we were well abreast of the others. Năt-ah'-ki kept up a ceaseless chatter of gossip and story and questions about the country from which I came. She was ever wanting to know about the ways of white women, good and bad, and when I told some of the things I had known, had seen the bad ones do, she would be horrified and say over and over again, "Terrible, shameless! No Blackfoot woman would ever act like that."

Along toward noon we came to the head of a pine-clad coulée running into the far-away Judith, and in a little grove there was a small spring of clear, cold water. We drank, and then leading our animals up to the top of the slope, where we could obtain a good view of the surrounding country, we ate our lunch of bread, depuyer, and dried meat. A kit fox came trotting over the bench opposite us, ran down the slope into the grove and to the spring, and presently came out on our side, sniffing the air, undoubtedly having scented our food. It walked up to within thirty feet of us, stopped and stared at us and the grazing horses, then circled around and finally stretched out on its belly, head up, watching us intently, and frequently sniffing the air, curiously working its slender, delicately contoured nose. It was evidently reasoning like this, "There is something to eat over by those strange-looking animals. I'll wait here a while, and nose around the place after they leave." At least, that is what Nät-ah'-ki said the little creature was thinking, and I had reason to believe that in such matters she generally knew whereof she spoke. "Did I ever tell you," she asked, "about my grandfather and his pet fox? No? Well then, listen:

"One night my grandfather's dream commanded him to catch a kit fox, tame it, and be kind to it. He thought long over this, and counselled with others as to its meaning; but none could understand it any more than he. The next night his dream told him the same things, and again on the third night, and lastly on the fourth night. Four times his dreams commanded him to do this. Four is the sacred number. When he arose the fourth morning he knew that he must obey his dream. He no longer asked why, nor what was meant, but after eating went out to catch a fox. There were many foxes; every little way as he walked he saw them running onward or sitting by their dens, into which they disappeared as he drew near. He had a long lariat, to an end of which he had tied a length of fine buckskin string. Making a running noose of the string, he would lay it in a circle around the entrance to the den, then go back as far as the lariat extended and lie down, to watch for the animals. If one poked its head out, he would jerk the lariat, and the noose would tighten around its neck or body. In this way children catch ground squirrels—he had done it himself in youthful days—and he believed that in like manner he could capture a fox.

"These animals have more than one entrance to their den, often as many as five or six. If my grandfather set the noose around a hole into which he saw a fox go, the animal was certain to look out from another opening, and seeing him lying there near by, would dodge back and appear no more, even though he waited a long time. Thus passed the first day, and also the second. On the evening of the third he noosed one, but with a snap of its sharp teeth it cut the string and escaped. Tired and thirsty, and hungry, he was returning home that evening, when on the side of a coulée he saw five young foxes playing near the entrance to their den, the mother and father sitting nearby watching them. They were very small; so young that they were not quick and active on their feet, but tumbled over each other slowly and awkwardly. He sat down on the opposite side of the coulée and watched them until the sun set and night came on. Over and over he asked himself how he could catch one of the young. He prayed, too, calling upon the gods, upon his dream, to show him the way.

"Returning to his lodge, he ate and drank and filled and lighted his pipe, again praying for help in that which he had to do. And suddenly, as he sat there silently smoking, the way was shown him. The gods had taken pity on him. He went to bed and slept well. 'Go out and find a large buffalo shoulder-blade,' he said to my grandmother, after the morning meal, 'then take a cow-skin and accompany me.'

"They went to the den of young foxes. Very close

to the place where the little ones played was a large bunch of rye grass, and in the centre of it my grandfather began to cut away the sod, to loosen the earth with his knife. My grandmother helped him, using the shoulder blade as a white man does his shovel, removing the earth and piling it on the cowskin, then carrying the load away and scattering it in the bottom of the coulée. They worked and worked, cutting and digging, and scraping, until the hole was deep enough for my grandfather to stand in. His eyes were even with the top of the ground, the fringe of rye grass still standing made a good screen; the foxes might scent him, but they could not see him. 'Go home,' he said to my grandmother, when they had finished their work. 'Go home and make a sacrifice to the Sun, and pray that I may succeed in that which I have to do.'

"Then he got into the hole and stood very still, waiting, watching for the little ones to come out. Long he waited; the sun seemed to travel very slowly down toward the mountains. It was very hot; he became very thirsty; his legs ached, but he stood as motionless as the ground itself, always watching. A little while before sunset an old one came out, and walked half way around the rye grass bunch. Then, suddenly, it scented him, and ran swiftly away up the coulée, not daring to return whence the wind had warned it of some danger, unseen, but more to be feared for that very reason. Soon afterward the little ones came forth, one by one, slowly and lazily, yawning and stretching themselves, blinking their eyes in the strong light. They began to play, as they had done on the previous evening, and before long they gathered in a scuffle at the edge of the rye grass. Then my grandfather quickly reached out, and seized one by the back of the neck. 'Hai-ya', little brother,' he cried,

'I have caught you.' Climbing out of the hole he wrapped it in a fold of his robe and hurried to his lodge.   He was happy.   Four times his dream had spoken to him; on the fourth day he had fulfilled its command.   He felt sure that in some way the taking of the fox was to be for his good.

"Puh'-po-kan (dream) my grandfather named the little animal.   For the very beginning it had no fear of him, and soon made friends with the dogs of the lodge. An old bitch loved it at once, and if any strange dog came nosing around where it was she would drive the stranger away.   The fox ate readily the bits of meat my grandfather gave it, and learned to drink water and soup. He forbade anyone to pet it, or feed it, or call it by name, so it was friendly only with him.   It wanted to follow him wherever he went, and at night would crawl under the robes and sleep beside him.   When camp was moved, it had a little nest in a travois load, where it would lie quite still to the journey's end.   It was such a funny little one; always wanting to play with my grandfather or with the lodge dogs; and when it got scared at anything it would run to him, making short, gasping, hoarse little barks, just as we hear them at night out beyond the lodges.   I did so want to play with it, take it up in my arms and pet it, but always my mother would say: 'Don't you dare do it; 'tis a sacred one, and if you touch it something dreadful will happen to you.   Perhaps you would go blind.'

"As it grew older it would wander around at times during the night until chased by some dog, and then it would rush in and crawl into bed beside my grandfather. Not a mouse wandered in under the lodge-skin but Puh'-po-kan had found and killed it, and often he would bring home a bird or ground squirrel.   About the time when

Puh'-po-kan had seen two winters, we were camping on the Little River, just north of the Bear's Paw Mountains. One night, after the lodge fires had all died out and everyone was asleep, Puh'-po-kan awoke my grandfather by backing up against his head and barking in a way it had when scared. 'Stop that,' said my grandfather, reaching up and giving the little one a light slap. 'Stop barking and go to sleep.'

"But Puh'-po-kan would not stop; instead he barked harder than ever, trembling because he was so excited. My grandfather raised up on his elbow and looked around. The moon was shining down through the smoke-hole, so that he could make out the different objects in the lodge; over by the doorway there was something that did not belong there; a dark, motionless object that looked like a person crouching. 'Who are you?' he asked. 'What do you want here?'

"No answer.

"Then my grandfather spoke again: 'Tell me quickly, who you are. Get up and talk, or I will shoot you.'

"Still there was no answer. Puh'-po-kan kept on barking. My grandfather quietly reached out for his gun, which lay at the head of his bed, cocked it without noise, aimed and fired it. With a fearful scream a man—for such the object proved to be—sprang up and fell dead right in the hot ashes and coals of the fire-place, from whence my grandfather quickly dragged him. Of course the shot aroused the camp, and the screams of the frightened women in my grandfather's lodge brought every one to it. A fire was quickly built and the light showed that the dead one was an enemy of a far-away tribe, a Sioux. He had no weapon except a big long knife, still firmly gripped in his right hand. Evidently he had entered the lodge intending to steal a gun, and would have stabbed anyone who interfered with him. When the fox gave warning of his presence, he most likely thought that by remaining crouched to the ground he would not be discovered, and that those aroused would soon again fall asleep. He seemed to have come to the camp alone, for no trace of others could be found, no horses were stolen.

"All the talk in camp was about the fox, and my grandfather's dream. It was all great medicine. And my grandfather, how pleased he was. He made many sacrifices, prayed much, and loved Puh'-po-kan more than ever. Two more winters the little one lived, and then one summer night it was bitten by a rattlesnake and soon died. The women wrapped the swollen little body in robes and buried it on a scaffold they made in a cottonwood tree, just as if it had been a person."

I recinched our saddles. Nät-ah'-ki spread the remains of our lunch on a smooth flat stone. "Eat heartily, little brother," she said. We mounted and rode away, and looking back we saw the fox busily chewing a piece of dried meat. Later in the afternoon we arrived in camp, which had been pitched near a small lake on the high plateau. The water was bad, but drinkable when made into tea. We used buffalo chips for fuel. In the evening I was invited to a feast given by Big Lake. Rising Wolf, was also a guest along with a number of other staid and sober men. Young men seldom feasted and smoked with their elders, and in the camp were many coteries, or social sets, just as we find them in any civilised community, with the exception that there was no jealousy nor rivalry between them; no one of them felt that its members were in anyway better than the members of another set.

We had smoked but one pipe, I remember, when a

young man bounced in through the doorway, and said: "A war party of many men is near us."

"Ah!" all exclaimed, and then Big Lake, "Quick! tell us about it."

"I was hunting," said the young man, "and tied my horse to a bunch of sage while I crept up to a band of antelope. Perhaps I did not tie him securely; he got loose and ran away on his back trail and I started back afoot. At sundown I came to the top of a ridge and could see our camp, and over on another ridge near the Judith I saw at least fifty men. Saw them climb up and stand on its summit. They must have discovered our camp, by the smoke from the lodge fires, if nothing more. I waited until it was so dark that they could not see me, and then hurried in. They will certainly raid our horses to-night.

"Scatter out through camp all of you," said Big Lake, quickly and decisively. "Tell the men to come here at once, warn the women not to scream or cry or run. Hurry!"

I went home and told Năt-ah'-ki the news, removed the cover of my rifle, and filled my coat pockets with cartridges. "Wait!" she said, grasping the gun barrel. "What are you going to do?"

"Why, Big Lake told us to meet at his lodge," I explained. "He has some good plan, I suppose."

"Yes, he is wise," she agreed, "but you are not going out there to be killed by a war party. Stay here with me."

"But our horses. I cannot remain here in the lodge and let the enemy run them off."

"They do not matter. Let them go."

"But," I said, "if I remained here think what people would say. They would call me a coward, they would say to you: 'Your white man has a woman's heart; why don't you make some dresses for him?' "

That ended the argument. She just sat down on the couch, covered her head with a shawl, and thus I left her. I will acknowledge that I did not go forth with a mad desire for battle. The cheerful lodge fire, the restful couch and the long-stemmed pipe were dear to all save the rash young man whose only thought was of war. Big Lake was a born tactician. In the few moments required to assemble the men around his lodge he had thought out his plan of defence, and issued his orders in a few words. The various bands of the All Friends Society were told off into four groups, and ordered to steal quietly out to the north, south, east, and west of camp and there await the arrival of the enemy. All others not of the society were to go with any one of the bands they chose. It was not feared that a war party of fifty or of even three times that number would make an attack on camp. They came, of course, to steal horses, and the plan was to go out where the herds were grazing and lie in wait. The really valuable animals were all tethered, as usual, near the lodges of their owners, and passing by the herds of common horses, the enemy would try to get in to them, cut their ropes and lead them away one by one, and by twos and threes.

With the Crazy Dogs and Raven Carriers I moved out with thirty or forty others who, like myself, belonged to no organisation. We spread out in a wide line, and after walking slowly and silently for about half a mile, word was passed to stop, whereupon we sat down in the cover of the sage and grease-wood brush. There was a moon, low down in the western sky, and due to set about midnight, so it was not very dark;

we could see quite plainly the brush forty or fifty yards
distant. We remained there quietly a long time. The
man nearest me on the right slowly crawled over and
sat beside me.

"The night light is about to go out of sight," he
whispered. "The war party will appear somewhere
soon, if they come at all to-night."

He spoke truly, for a little later we heard indistinctly
away out beyond, a murmur of voices. Then there was
silence, and then with soft tread and harsh swish of
brush against their leggings, the raiders came into view,
unsuspectingly advancing, some of them to their death.
Some one on my left fired first, and then the whole line
shot an irregular volley. How the sparks of the cheap
black powder glowed and sparkled as they spouted
from fuke and rifle into the darkness. The flashes
blinded us for a moment, and when we could see again
the enemy were running away. They had fired a number of shots in answer to ours, but as we afterward
found, not one of their bullets had hit any of us. Almost as one man our line sprang forward, with cries of
"Now, Crazy Dogs! Now, Raven Carriers! Take courage; we must wipe them out." Here were bodies, five
of them, and one with life still in it. Thud went a war
club and the recumbent figure sprawled out, face up,
in the waning moonlight. In a trice the dead were
scalped, their arms taken by those who first came to
them. On sped our party, an occasional shot was fired
at a dimly seen retreating figure. Behind us now came
the three other divisions of the camp, shouting words
of encouragement. But now no enemy could be seen,
nor heard, and our party stopped; it was useless to look
further for them in the darkness. Big Lake came up.
"Spread out," he said, "spread out again and encircle

the camp.   Perhaps some of them are concealed in the
brush closer in, and with daylight we will find them."

I shouldered my rifle and went home.   Nät-ah'-ki
was sitting up with her mother for company and I
related all that had occurred.

"Why did you come back?" she asked, after I had
finished.   "Why didn't you stay out there with the rest
as Big Lake ordered?"

"Hai-yah!" I exclaimed.   "How peculiar are women;
one may not understand them.   You begged me this
evening to remain here with you.   I came back because
I am tired and hungry, and sleepy, and now you are
displeased because I returned.   Well, to please you
I'll go back and sit with the others until morning."

"Sit down, crazy man," she said, pushing me back
on the couch from which I had started to rise.   "You
will stay right there.   Here is your pipe; fill it and smoke
while I broil some meat and make tea."

"You are the chief," I said to her, contentedly leaning
back against a willow mat.   "It shall be as you say."

Ah, me!   Roll them back, you ruthless harvester
of the years.   Give back to me Nät-ah'-ki and my
youth.   Return to us our lodge and the wide, brown,
buffalo plains.

CHAPTER XIX

NÄT-AH'-KI'S WEDDING

AT DAYLIGHT an unusual stir and confusion in camp awoke us, and Nät-ah'-ki went out to learn what it was all about. She soon returned with the news that our enemy of the night proved to be Crows, that the bodies of seven in all had been found, and that they had succeeded in running off seventy or more horses. A large party had already started in pursuit of them, and we were not to break camp until they returned. I arose and dressed betimes, had breakfast, and went visiting. Turning into Weasel Tail's lodge I found him nursing a gash in the thigh, where a Crow bullet had creased him. I sat with him a long time, while other visitors came and went. All were calling the Crows any bad name their language contained, but unfortunately or fortunately, some may say, in this line their speech was exceedingly limited. The very best they could do was to call their enemy dog faces and present them to the Sun, begging him to destroy them.

I went on to the lodge of the chief, where I found many of the principal men assembled. "I for one" Big Lake was saying when I entered, "will talk against making peace with the Crows so long as I live. Let us all agree never to smoke their tobacco. Let us teach our children that they are like the rattlesnake, always to be killed on sight."

The visitors heartily agreed to this, and I may say here that they kept their word, sending party after party against their Yellowstone enemies until the Government interfered and put a stop to inter-tribal war. The last raid occurred in the summer of 1885.

There was much scalp dancing during the day, participated in by those who had lost most recently husband of father or some other relative in battle with the Crows. This was not, as has been often luridly pictured, a spectacular dance of fierce exultation and triumph over the death of their enemy. As performed by the Blackfeet, it was a truly sad spectacle. Those participating in it blackened their faces, hands, and moccasins with charcoal, and wore their meanest, plainest clothes. An aged man held the scalp of the enemy tied to a willow wand in front of him, and the others ranged in line on each side. Then they sang a low and very plaintive song in a minor key, which to me, at least, seemed to express more sorrow over the loss of their kin than it did joy for the death of the enemy. On this occasion there were seven scalps, seven parties dancing in different parts of camp at once, and one band of mourners after another took their turn, so that the performance lasted until night. There was really no dancing about it, the singers merely stooping slightly and rising in time to the song.

The pursuing party returned at dusk, having failed to overtake the enemy. Some were for starting at once on a raid into the Crow country, but there was now little ammunition in camp and it was decided that we should push on to Fort Benton with as little delay as possible. After obtaining a good supply of powder and ball there, the war party could turn back southward. Four or five days later camp was pitched in the big bottom opposite the Fort, Nät-ah'-ki and I crossed the river, and wended our way to the little adobe house. There we found Berry, his wife and mother, and the good Crow Woman. What a happy lot they were, those women, as they bustled around and got in each other's way trying to get supper ready. And I am sure Berry and I were happy too. We did not say much as we stretched out on a buffalo-robe lounge and smoked, but words are often superfluous. It was all good enough for us, and each knew that the other so felt. Berry had got my mail out of the office and there it lay on the table, a few letters, a bushel or more of papers and magazines. I read the letters, but the rest mostly remained unopened. I had lost all interest in States' affairs.

In the evening Berry and I went down to the Fort for a while, and, of course, we called in at Keno Bill's place. As usual, at that time of year, the town, if it could be so called, was full of people, traders and trappers, bull-whackers and mule-skinners, miners and Indians, all awaiting the arrival of the steamboats which had long since left St. Louis, and were soon due to arrive. Every table in Keno's place was so crowded with players that one couldn't edge in to watch a game. Keno himself and two assistants were busy behind the bar, as the kegs still held out despite the heavy draught on them during the winter months. There were even a few bottles of beer left. I gladly paid a dollar and four bits for one of them, and Berry helped me drink it.

We went into the Overland Hotel for a moment on our way home, and there among other guests I saw a man whom I thought to be a preacher; at any rate, a white tie adorned his blue-flannel shirt front, and he wore a black coat which, if not cut in approved ministerial style, was at least of the right colour. I went up to him and said: "Excuse me, sir, but I'd like to know if you are a preacher?"

"I am," he replied with a pleasant smile. "I am a minister of the Methodist Episcopal Church. I have been in the mountains for the past year, both preaching and mining, and am now on my way to my home in the States."

"Well," I continued, "If you'll go along with me I guess I can find a job for you."

He arose at once and accompanied us home.

"May I ask," he said on the way, "what is to be the nature of my services? A baptism or marriage, or is there some sick one in need of a few words?"

"It's a marriage," I replied; "that is, providing the other party is willing."

With that Berry shamelessly snickered.

The women were gaily talking and laughing when we arrived, but became silent at once when they saw our companion. They were always thus in the presence of strangers. I called Nät-ah'-ki into the back room. "He out there," I said to her, "is a sacred (more correctly Sun) white man. I have asked him to sacredly marry us."

"Oh," she cried. "How did you know my wish? It is what I have always wanted you to do, but I—I was afraid, ashamed to ask it of you. But, is he a real sacred white man? He wears no black robe, no cross?"

"He is of another society," I replied. "There are a thousand of them, and each claims that theirs is the only true one. It matters not to us. Come on."

And so, Berry acting as interpreter, we were married and we sent the preacher forth with a gold piece as a souvenir of the occasion. "I'm hungry," said Berry, "broil us a couple of buffalo tongues, you women."

Broiled tongue and bread, tea and apple sauce comprised the wedding feast, as we may call it, and that also was good enough for us.

"It is this," Nät-ah'-ki confided to me later. "Many white men who have married women of our tribe according to our customs, have used them only as playthings and then have left them. But those who took women by the sacred words of a sacred white man, have never left them. I know that *you* would never leave me, no never. But how the others have laughed at me, joked about me, saying: 'Crazy girl, you love your man, and you are a fool; he has not married you in the white man's way, and will leave you as soon as he sees another woman with a prettier face.' They can never say that again. No, never."

We had planned, Berry and I, to remain in Fort Benton during the summer and make a camp trade the following winter. The steamboats began to arrive in May and then the levee was a busy place. The traders were also rushed, the Indians crowding in to dispose of the last of their robes and furs. But we had no part in this, and in a few weeks we became restless. Berry decided to make a couple of trips to Helena with his bull train, although it was not necessary for him to go, as he had hired a train-master, or, in the language of the bull-whacker, a "wagon boss." The women decided that they wanted to go berrying. The Piegans had long since crossed the river and were camped on the Teton, only a few miles away. We proposed to join them, Nät-ah'-ki sending word to her mother to have our saddle and pack horses driven in.

A couple of weeks before this, I was sitting on the levee one day when a stranger came along and sat down by my side, and we fell to talking about various things.

I saw at once that he was a man of education and refinement, and from the moment I first saw him I took
a liking to him. He was tall and well built, brown-
eyed and brown-haired, and had a pleasing, frank expression of countenance, although it was rather a sad
one. Also, he seemed to have no enthusiasms. He
seldom smiled, never laughed outright, and was often
so lost in thought over—to judge from his sad eyes—
something near his heart that he was entirely oblivious
to his surroundings. I invited him over to the
little abode for dinner, and Berry immediately took
to him as I had done. So did the women, who were
usually very distant and dignified in the presence of
strangers. He soon passed the most of his time with us,
and nothing, in the estimation of our household, was good
enough for him. Old Mrs. Berry rigged up a fine robe
couch with willow back-rests for his especial use. The
Crow Woman gave him a beautiful pair of moccasins.
Nät-ah'-ki and Berry's wife got out their choice stores
of pemmican, and depuyer, dried meats and berries
for our little evening feasts.

"See here," I said to Nät-ah'-ki one day. "I'm getting jealous of this man. You women think more of
him than you do of Berry and me."

"He is so sad feeling," she said, "that we pity him.
What is it that troubles him? Has he lost some loved one?"

I knew no more than she what troubled him; that
he was grieving about something was evident. We never
questioned him, never even asked his name, nor whence
he came. And that is where the Western people differed
from those of the East. They never gossiped, never
tried to pry into one's secrets, nor demanded his pedigree.
They simply gave him the hand of good-fellowship and
used him as they wished to be used.

The women named him Kut-ai'-imi, Never-Laughs;
and thus among themselves they ever spoke of him.
It was a long time before he knew it, and then it didn't
matter. He told Berry and me that his name was—well,
what it was is not necessary for this story; we will call
him Ashton. He also informed us that his home was
in Boston, and that he had come west merely to see
something of Western life. When he learned that the
women and I were to join the camp, he asked to be allowed to go with us, and of course we were glad to have
him go. He purchased a horse and saddle, blanket and
rifle, and various other things necessary for the trip.

So, one evening we returned to camp, to our very
own lodge, which Nät-ah'-ki's mother had again set up
and furnished for our home-coming. On every hand
there was song and laughter, and beating of drums, and
calls for feasts. The women broiled some meat, made
some bread and tea, and we ate the simple meal with
relish. Then Ashton and I lay back on our soft lounges
and smoked, talking little. I was perfectly content;
my friend, judging by his dreamy and far-away expression, had gone back eastward, in thought, a couple
of thousand miles. The women soon washed the dishes,
and got out their porcupine quill, or bead embroidery
work. "Grandmother," I said, "tell me a story; something about your people in the long ago."

"Hai!" the Crow Woman exclaimed. "Just hear
him. He is always wanting stories. Before long, if
we are to keep him contented, we will have to make up
some, for he has heard about all we know."

"But just think how selfish he is," said Nät-ah'-ki,
looking at me mischievously. "He gets all of our stories,
but tells us none of his."

I was obliged to acknowledge that the little woman

was right, and promised to tell some later. Old Mrs. Berry, after some thinking, began:

THE STORY OF NO-HEART

"It was before my grandfather's time, yes, far back of that, for he said that the old people whom he had heard relate it, told about having heard it from their grandfathers. So it is surely a story of great age.

"It was in the spring time. The people were scattered out on the plain one day, busily digging the white root,* when a terrible thunderstorm came up. It was far to the lodges, so the diggers, knowing that they would get wet whether they ran or stayed, just sat down where they were, covered themselves with their robes, and waited for the storm to pass by. One family happened to be all near each other when the rain began to fall, and all huddled up closely together.

" 'This is a very cold rain,' said the mother. 'I am shivering.'

" 'Yes,' said the father, 'it is cold. Crowd closer together all of you.'

"Thus they sat, when thunder crashed above them, and a ball of lightning, falling in their midst, broke with a big noise, and knocked them all flat and limp on the wet ground. There they lay, the father and mother, two sons and a daughter, and none dared go to aid them, for fear the angry god would strike them, too. But when the storm passed by, the people ran to do what they could for the stricken ones. At first they thought that all of them were dead, and four of them surely were; the fifth one, the girl, still breathed. In a little while she sat up and, seeing what had befallen the others, wept so piteously that the women there wept with her,

---

* The *pomme blanche* of the French Trappers, *Psoralea esculenta*.

although none of them were related to her. The father
had been an orphan since childhood; so had the mother;
and the poor girl was now alone. In the whole camp
she had not one relation.

"Kind friends buried the dead, and the many different ones asked the girl to come and live with them;
but she refused them all. 'You must go and live with
some one,' said the chief. 'No one ever heard of a
young woman living by herself. You cannot live alone.
Where would you procure your food? And think of
what people would say should you do so; you would
soon have a bad name.'

"'If people speak evil of me, I cannot help it,' said
the girl. 'They will live to take back their bad words.
I have decided to do this, and I will find a way to keep
from starving.'

"So this girl lived on alone in the lodge her parents
had built, with no company save her dogs. The women
of the camp frequently visited her and gave her meat and
other food; but no man, either young or old, ever went
in and sat by her fire. One or two had attempted it,
but only once, for she had told them plainly that she did
not wish the society of any man. So the youths gazed
at her from afar, and prayed the gods to soften her heart.
She was a handsome young woman, a hard and ceaseless
toiler; no wonder that the men fell in love with her,
and no wonder that they named her No Heart.

"One young man, Long Elk, son of the great chief,
loved the lone girl so much that he was nearly crazy
with the pain and longing for her. He had never spoken
to her, well knowing that her answer would be that which
she had given to others. But he could not help going
about, day after day, where she could always see him.
If she worked in her little bean and corn patch, he sat

on the edge of the river bank nearby. If she went to the timber for wood, he strolled out in that direction, often meeting her on the trail, but she always passed him with eyes cast down, as if she had not seen him. Often, in the night, when all the camp was fast asleep, Long Elk would steal out of his father's lodge, pick up a water-skin, and filling it again and again at the river, would water every row in No Heart's garden. At the risk of his life he would go out alone on the plains where the Sioux were always prowling, and hunt. In the morning when No Heart awoke and went out, she would find hanging in the dark entrance way, choice portions of meat, the skin of a buffalo or the deer kind. The people talked about this, wondering who did it all. If the girl knew, she gave no sign of it, always passing the young man as if she did not know there was such a person on earth. A few low and evil ones themselves, hinted wickedly that the unknown protector was well paid for his troubles. But they were always rebuked, for the girl had many friends who believed that she was all good.

"In the third summer of the girl's lone living, the Mandans and Arickarees quarrelled, and then trouble began, parties constantly starting out to steal each other's horses, and to kill and scalp all whom they could find hunting or travelling about beyond the protection of the villages. This was a very sad condition for the people. The two tribes had long been friends; Mandan men had married Arickaree women, and many Arickaree men had Mandan wives. It was dreadful to see the scalps of perhaps one's own relatives brought into camp. But what could the women do? They had no voice in the councils, and were afraid to say what they thought. Not so No Heart. Every day she went about in the camp, talking loudly, so that the men must hear, scolding them and their wickedness; pointing out the truth, that by killing each other, the two tribes would become so weak that they would soon be unable to withstand their common enemy, the Sioux. Yes, No Heart would even walk right up to a chief and scold him, and he would be obliged to turn silently away, for he could not argue with a woman, nor could he force this one to close her mouth; she was the ruler of her own person.

"One night a large number of Arickarees succeeded in making an opening in the village stockade and, passing through, they began to lead out the horses. Some-one soon discovered them, however, and gave the alarm, and a big fight took place, the Mandans driving the enemy out on the plain, and down into the timber below. Some men on both sides were killed; there was both mourning and rejoicing in the village.

"The Arickarees retreated to their village. Toward evening No Heart went down into the timber for fuel, and in a thick clump of willows she found one of the enemy, a young man, badly wounded. An arrow had pierced his groin, and the loss of blood had been great. He was so weak that he could scarcely speak or move. No Heart stuck many willow twigs in the ground about him, the more securely to conceal him. 'Do not fear,' she said to him, 'I will bring you food and drink.'

"She hurried back to her lodge and got some dried meat and a skin of water, put them under her robe and returned to the wounded one. He drank much, and ate of the food. No Heart washed and bound the wound. Then she again left him, telling him to lie quiet, that in the night she would return and take him to her home, where she would care for him until he got well. In her lodge she fixed a place for him, screening

one of the bed places with a large cowskin; she also
partly covered the smoke hole and hung a skin across
the entrance, so that the interior of the lodge had but
little light. The women who sometimes visited her
would never suspect that anyone was concealed, and
especially an enemy—in a lodge where for three summers
no man had entered.

"It was a very dark night. Down in the timber
there was no light at all. No Heart was obliged to ex-
tend her arms as she walked, to keep from running
against the trees, but she knew the place so well that
she had little trouble in finding the thicket, and the one
she had come to aid. 'Arise,' she said, in a low voice.
'Arise, and follow me.'

"The young man attempted to get up, but fell back
heavily upon the ground. 'I cannot stand,' he said;
'my legs have no strength.'

"Then No Heart cried out: 'You cannot walk! I
had not thought but that you could walk. What shall
I do? What shall I do?'

" 'You will let me carry him for you,' said someone
standing close behind her. 'I will carry him wherever
you lead.'

"No Heart turned with a little cry of surprise. She
could not see the speaker's face in the darkness, only his
dim form; but she knew the voice. She was not afraid.
'Lift him then,' she said, 'and follow me.'

"She herself raised the wounded one up and placed
him on the newcomer's back, and then led the way out
of the timber, across the plain, through the stockade, in
which she had loosened a post, and then on to her lodge.
No one was about, and they were not discovered. Within
a fire was burning, but there was no need of the light to
show the girl who had helped her. He was Long Elk.

'We will put him here,' she said, lifting the skin in front of the couch she had prepared, and they laid the sick man carefully down upon it. Then Long Elk stood for a little, looking at the girl, but she remained silent and would not look at him. 'I will go now,' he said, 'but each night I will come with meat for you and your lover.'

"Still the girl did not speak, and he went away. But as soon as he had gone, No Heart sat down and cried. The sick man raised up a little and asked, 'What troubles you? Why are you crying?'

" 'Did you not hear?' she replied. 'He said that you are my lover.'

" 'I know you,' said the man. 'They call you No Heart, but they lie. You have a heart; I wish it were for me.'

" 'Don't!' the girl cried. 'Don't say that again! I will take care of you, feed you. As your mother is to you, so will I be.'

"Now, when night came again, No Heart went often out in the passageway, staying there longer and longer each time, returning only to give the sick man water, or a little food. At last, as she was sitting out there in the dark, Long Elk came, and feeling for the right place, hung up a piece of meat beyond the reach of the dogs. 'Come in,' she said to him. 'Come in and talk with the wounded one.'

"After that Long Elk sat with the Arickaree every night for a time, and they talked of the things which interest men. While he was in the lodge No Heart never spoke, except to say, 'Eat it,' when she placed food before them. Day after day the wounded one grew stronger. One night, after Long Elk had gone, he said, 'I am able to travel; to-morrow night I will start home-

ward. I want to know why you have taken pity on me,
why you saved me from death?'

" 'Listen, then,' said the girl. 'It was because war
is bad; because I pitied you. Many women here, and
many more in your village, are crying because they have
lost the ones they loved in this quarrel. Of them all,
I alone have talked, begging the chiefs to make peace
with you. All the other women were glad of my words,
but they are afraid, and do not dare speak for themselves.
I talked and feared not; because no one could bid me
stop. I have helped you, now do you help me; help
your women; help us all. When you get home tell
what was done for you here, and talk hard for peace.'

" 'So I will,' the Arickaree told her. 'When they
learn all that you have done for me, the chiefs will listen.
I am sure they will be glad to stop this war.'

"The next night, when Long Elk entered the lodge,
he found the man sitting up. By his side lay his weapons
and a little sack of food. 'I was waiting for you,' he
said. 'I am now well, and wish to start for home to-
night. Will you take me out beyond the stockade?
If any speak you can answer them, and they will not
suspect that their enemy passes by.'

" 'I will go with you, of course,' Long Elk told him.
Whereupon he arose, slung on his bow and quiver, the
sack of food, and lifted his shield. No Heart sat quietly
on the opposite side of the lodge, looking straight at the
fire. Long Elk turned to her: 'And you?' he asked.
'Are you also ready?'

"She did not answer, but covered her face with her
robe.

" 'I go alone,' said the Arickaree. 'Let us start.'

"They went out, through the village, through the
stockade, and across the bottom to the timber, where

they stopped, 'You have come far enough,' the Arickaree said, 'I will go on alone from here. You have been
good to me. I shall not forget it. When I arrive home
I shall talk much for peace between our tribes. I hope
we may soon meet again in friendship.'

" 'Wait,' said Long Elk, as he turned to go, 'I want
to ask you something: Why do you not take No
Heart with you?'

" 'I would if she were willing,' he answered; 'but she
is not for me. I tell you truly, this: She has been a
mother to me; no more, no less. And you,' he continued, 'have you ever asked her to be your woman?
No? Then go now; right now, and do so.'

" 'It would be useless,' said Long Elk, sadly. 'Many
have asked her, and she has always turned them away.'

" 'I have seen much while I lay sick in her lodge,' the
Arickaree continued. 'I have seen her gaze at you as
you sat talking to me, and her eyes were beautiful then.
And I have seen her become restless and go out and in,
out and in, when you were late. When a woman does
that, it means that she loves you. Go and ask her.'

"They parted, Long Elk returned to the village. 'It
could not be,' he thought, 'that the young man was
right. No, it could not be.' Had he not kept near her
these many winters and summers? and never once had
she looked at him, or smiled. Thinking thus, he wandered on, and on, and found himself standing by the
entrance to her lodge. Within he heard, faintly, someone crying. He could not be sure that was it, the sound
of it was so low. He stepped noiselessly in and carefully
drew aside the door skin. No Heart was sitting where
he had last seen her, sitting before the dying fire, robe
over her head, and she was crying. He stole past the
doorway and sat down beside her, quite close, but he

dared not touch her. 'Good Heart,' he said, 'Big Heart, don't cry.'

"But she only cried harder when she heard his words, and he was much troubled, not knowing what to do. After a little he moved closer and put his arm around her; she did not draw away, so then he drew the robe away from her face. 'Tell me,' he said, 'why you are crying?'

" 'Because I am so lonely.'

" 'Ah! You do love him then. Perhaps it is not too late; I may be able to overtake him. Shall I go and call him back to you?'

" 'What do you mean?' cried No Heart, staring at him. 'Who are you talking about?'

" 'He who has just left; the Arickaree,' Long Elk answered. But now he had edged up still closer, and his arm was tighter around her, and she leaned heavily against him.

" 'Was there ever such a blind one?' she said. 'Yes, I will let you know my heart; I will not be ashamed, nor afraid to say it. I was crying because I thought you would not return. All these summers and winters I have been waiting, hoping that you would love me, and you never spoke.'

" 'How could I?' he asked. 'You never looked at me; you made no sign.'

" 'It was your place to speak,' she said. 'Even yet you have not done so.'

" 'I do, now, then. Will you take me for your man?'

"She put her arms around his neck and kissed him, and that was answer enough.

"In the morning, like any other married man, Long Elk went out and stood by the entrance to the lodge which was now his, and shouted feast invitations to his father and friends. They all came, and all were pleased that he had got such a good woman. Some made jokes about newly married ones, which made the young woman cover her face with her robe. Yet she was so happy that she would soon throw it back and laugh with the others.

"In a few days came a party from the Arickarees, and the wounded young man was one of them—asking for peace. The story was told then, how No Heart had taken in the young man and brought him to life again, and when they heard it many women prayed the gods to be good to her, and give her and her man long life. Peace between the two tribes was then declared, and there was much rejoicing.

"There my son, I have finished."

.   .   .   .

"Well, what was all that about?" asked Ashton, rousing up and reaching out for his pipe and tobacco.

"Oh!" I replied, " 'twas the story of a girl and a man." And I proceeded to give him a translation of it. After I had finished, he sat quietly thinking for some time, and then remarked:

"This gives me a new and unexpected view of these people. I had not thought that love, that self-sacrifice, such as the story depicts, was at all in their nature. Really, it's quite refreshing to learn that there are occasionally women who are true and steadfast in their love."

He said this bitterly. I could have told him things, but contented myself by saying, "Keep your eyes open, friend. You may find much in these people to be commended."

CHAPTER XX

AFTER a couple of days camp was moved out to the Marias, in the bottom opposite the mouth of Black Coulée. Sarvis berries were very plentiful all along the river, and the women gathered large quantities of them to dry for winter use. Ashton had not yet fired a shot from his new rifle, so one afternoon I prevailed upon him to go for a hunt. I had some difficulty, however, in getting him out. He seemed to have no interest in anything, passing most of the time on his couch, smoking, smoking, and abstractedly refilling his pipe and smoking again. The women were right. Never Laugh was sorely grieving about something. I wished that I could find a way to make him forget it, whatever the trouble was.

We climbed on our horses, crossed the river and rode northward, near enough to the Black Coulée to look down into it occasionally. Game was not very plentiful, for the hunters had driven the most of the herds back toward the Sweetgrass Hills. However, we saw some antelope here and there, and several small bands of buffalo, with occasionally a lone old bull. We rode out five or six miles, and then down into the coulée to water our horses at a pool we saw in the bottom. It was a shallow, narrow stretch of water, about fifty yards in length, and I was surprised to see that the willows bordering its eastern side had been cut in considerable quantity by beavers. On the western side, there was a clay slope of twenty or thirty feet, up to a high-cut bank, and in the base of this bank was a deep, dark, low cavern, in which the beavers lived. Judging by the various-sized footprints about, a whole family of them lived there. I never before, nor since, found these animals in such a place. There was no water between this pool and the river, some miles distant; the pool was not deep enough to wholly cover them. But most unusual of all was the fact that they lived in a cave, the entrance to which was some distance from and above the pool. There were three or four old lodge poles lying nearby, and I tried to ascertain the depth of the cave with one of them, but failed. I found, however, that the roof of it sloped down so near the floor, that nothing larger than a fox could get into the innermost recesses. A fox, even a red one, would go hungry a long time before trying to make a meal of a beaver.

Before descending into the coulée we had seen a few head of buffalo feeding on the opposite side of it, and while we loitered at the pool they came in sight at the top of the slope, breaking into a trot, and finally on a 'lope hurrying down for water. "Now, then," I said to Ashton, "try your rifle; shoot that young cow, the third from the leader."

The band turned, when about a hundred yards away, in order to come into the bottom of the coulée above the cut bank, and when this particular animal swung broadside to us, he threw his gun up and, without a noticeable pause to sight the arm, sent a bullet into the right place, just back of the shoulder. Blood streamed from its nostrils almost at the crack of the gun, and after 'loping on a short distance, it suddenly stopped and then sank to the ground. "That was a fine shot," I remarked. "You have evidently handled the rifle before."

"Yes," he said, "I used to shoot a good deal in the Adirondacks, and in Maine and Nova Scotia."

We led our horses over to the fallen buffalo, and I bled it, then set it up to cut out the boss ribs, Ashton standing by watching the way I did it. "I'll not kill another one," he said, more to himself than to me. "It doesn't seem right to take the life of such a magnificent animal."

"Well," I remarked, "there isn't a bit of fresh meat in the lodge. I don't know what the women would say were we to return without some."

"Oh! we must eat of course," he agreed; "but I don't care to kill any more of these noble animals. Somehow I've lost all pleasure in hunting. Hereafter I'll loan some Indian my rifle, and he can furnish my share of the meat. That can be done, I presume?"

I told him that he could probably make some such arrangement. I didn't tell him though, that I would see that he got out and rustled some himself. I wanted to wake him up; to get him out of the trance he was in. There is nothing so conducive to good mental health as plenty of fatiguing work or exercise.

When we returned home with the boss ribs and the tongue, and several other parts of the animal which I had surreptitiously cut out and hurriedly placed in the sack I especially carried for them, I took pains to relate what a fine shot my friend had made. The women praised him highly, all of which I translated, and the Crow Woman told him if she was not already his mother, so to speak, she would like to be his wife, for then she would be sure to have plenty of meat and skins. Ashton smiled, but made no answer.

We had a dish for supper that evening at which my friend looked askance, as I had done when I first saw it, and then, after tasting it, he ate it all, and looked around for more, as I also had done. I had brought in the little sack, among other things, a few feet of a certain entrail which is always streaked or covered with soft, snowy-white fat. This Nät-ah'-ki washed thoroughly and then stuffed with finely-chopped tenderloin, and stuffed it in such a manner that the inside of the entrail became the outside, and consequently the rich fat was encased with the meat. Both ends of the case were then securely tied, and the long sausage-like thing placed on the coals to roast, the cook constantly turning and moving it around to prevent it burning. After about twenty minutes on the coals, it was dropped into a pot of boiling water for five or ten minutes more, and was then ready to serve. In my estimation, and in that of all who have tried it, this method of cooking meat is the best of all, for the securely tied case confines all the juices of the meat. The Blackfeet call this Crow entrail, as they learned from that tribe how to prepare and cook the dish. It remains for some enterprising city cook to give it an English name, and open a place where it will be the main feature of the food. I'll guarantee that all the lovers of good things in the town will flock to him.

A day or two later, in pursuance of my plan to get Ashton out more frequently, I pretended to be ill, and then Nät-ah'-ki told him, I interpreting, that the meat was all gone, and unless he went out and killed something, we would go hungry to bed. He appealed to me to find a substitute for him, offering to furnish rifle and cartridges, and also pay the hunter, and Nät-ah'-ki was sent out to find some one. But I had posted her, and she presently returned with a very sad expression on her face, and reported that no one could be found to go; that all who could were already gone to hunt.

"Well, then," said our friend, "if that is the case, there's no need of my going out. I'll buy some meat of them when they return."

I thought that I had failed after all in my little plan, but Nät-ah'-ki came to the rescue, as soon as I told her what he had decided to do.

"Tell him," she said, "that I did not think he wished to bring shame upon this lodge. If he buys meat, the whole camp will laugh and jeer at me, and say, what a useless man she has got. He can't kill enough meat to supply his lodge. His friend has to buy it to keep all from starving."

Ashton jumped up at once when he heard that. "Where's my horse?" he asked. "If that is the way they look at it, why, I've got to hunt. Send for the horse."

I saw him off with Weasel Tail, whom I told to make a wide circle that would require the whole day. And a long day they certainly had, returning home after sunset. I had also instructed the Indian to lose his gun caps—where he could conveniently find them again. So Ashton had been obliged to do the shooting, and they brought in plenty of meat. He was very tired, and hungry and thirsty that evening, and instead of smoking innumerable times, he filled his pipe but once after eating, and then went to sleep. From that day on, for a time, he had to do all the hunting. I remained ill, or hurt my leg, or my horse was missing, so I couldn't go out. And it was truly wonderful the amount of meat we used. Nät-ah'-ki carried out quantities of it every day, and gave it to the needy ones of the camp, widows and others who had no one to hunt for them.

But I did not remain in camp, because of this. As soon as Ashton and his hunting party, either Weasel Tail or some other friend, had departed, I would go berrying with the women, or Nät-ah′-ki and I would saddle up and have a ride somewhere in a direction opposite to that in which they were travelling. But for all his hard work, I could not see that Ashton became any more cheerful. The improvement was that he had less time to think, for he was generally sound asleep by eight or nine o'clock.

Twice the camp was moved, each time a few miles farther down the river. The berry season was about over, and the women began to talk of returning to Fort Benton, having gathered and dried all the fruit they needed. We had been out about six weeks, and I also was ready to return, as I was sure that Berry would be there awaiting us. We had a talk, a little council of our own one evening, and decided to move in the following day but one. Was it preordained that I should send Ashton out for a last hunt the morning before our departure? If I had not done so—but I did. You shall learn in time what was the result of it. He needn't have gone, we had plenty of meat. I sent him, and thereby changed the course of his whole life. Why, he might be living to-day had he remained in camp that morning. Looking back at it all, I don't know whether to blame myself or not.

Ashton and Weasel Tail rode away. The women began to pack up, getting out their parfleches and filling them with their store of berries and dried meats. It was about noon, and I had just signed to Nät-ah′-ki that I was hungry, when there suddenly appeared a number of riders tearing down the north slope of the valley, and the camp began to hum with excitement. One or two

of the riders were waving their robes, making the sign
for the "enemy." Men and boys grabbed lariats and
started on the run for their horses. Down into the camp
came the little bunch of riders, and a moment later
Ashton rode up beside me. He had a young girl in front
of him, whom he dropped into Nät-ah'-ki's outstretched
arms. He was terribly excited, his dark eyes fairly
shone, and he said over and over again, "The cowards!
Oh, the cowards! But I killed two of them, yes, I got
two."

The girl was crying, wailing: "My mother, my
father," she kept repeating, "both dead, both killed."

There was a great commotion in camp; men were
saddling horses, calling wildly for their weapons, mounting and riding away out on to the plain in an ever-
increasing stream. Ashton dismounted and I saw that
his left trouser leg was soaked with blood. He limped
into the lodge, and I followed and undressed him; there
was a long, open bullet furrow just below the hip. "It
was this way," he told me, while I washed and bandaged the wound, "Weasel Tail and I overtook a party
of hunters three or four miles out, and travelled on with
them. Some had their women along, to help skin and
bring in what they killed, I suppose. In a little while
we sighted a fine herd of buffalo, approached them,
and had a good run, the party killing something like
twenty of them. We were butchering the animals when
something like fifty riders appeared from God knows
where, and commenced shooting at us. We were only
seven or eight men, not strong enough to stand them
off, but we partly held them in check, while the women
got their horses, and we all lit out for home—that is,
all but three, two men and a woman, who had been
killed at the first fire. I killed one of the enemy before

I got on my horse, and another one a little later. And I'm glad I did; I just wish I could have killed them all.

"Well, they followed us quite a long ways, perhaps two miles, but we managed to stop them finally, or perhaps they thought they had better not venture too near to our camp. One of them creased me, didn't he? Well, he will not do any more shooting. I got him. He just tumbled off his horse on his head, and flopped over flat on the ground. The girl? They shot her horse, but before it fell I reached over and lifted her on to mine. After that I couldn't handle my rifle, or I might have done better. I'll tell you what, old man, if 'twasn't for those poor scalped corpses lying out there on the plain, I would say that it was great sport."

CHAPTER XXI

NEVER-LAUGHS GOES EAST

OWING to the ensuing stiffness and soreness of Ashton's leg, we deferred for a few days our departure from the camp. A Piegan who had been wounded in the fight on the previous day died during the night. The attacking party proved to be Assiniboins, and in all they lost seven of their number, the pursuing party which left our camp overtaking and killing two who were riding slow horses.

Nät-ah'-ki constituted herself protector and guardian of the orphan. The girl had two aunts, sisters of her dead mother, but they were married to a Blackfoot and were far away in the North. In the Piegan camp she had not a remaining relative. She was a shy, quiet slip of a girl, about thirteen or fourteen years of age. Just now she was more than usually quiet, never speaking except to answer a question, silently crying most of the time. Nät-ah'-ki remodelled some of her own clothes for her. The Crow Woman gave her a shawl. When she appeared dressed in a neat calico dress, her hair nicely braided and bound with a deep red ribbon, even Ashton's æsthetic sense was pleased. "She is a very comely girl," he remarked. "Poor thing! Whatever will become of her?"

"Well," I reminded him, "this is not a civilised community; she will be welcomed and provided for by any and every family in the camp."

Such was, indeed, the case. Many a woman came to

our lodge and asked that the girl might live with her, each one saying that the mother had been her particular friend, or that her own daughter was the friend and play-mate of the orphan, and for that reason she wished to give the lone one a home. Nät-ah'-ki invariably told them that the girl was free to go, or remain, and then the latter would say that they were all very kind, but she preferred to stay where she was for a time.

When I told Ashton what these visitors were asking, he seemed to be surprised, and said that he had rather doubted my view of their kindliness and charity. He sat silently musing and smoking a long time and then, more in the way of a joke than seriously, told me to say to the girl that as he had saved her from the Assiniboins, he thought that she belonged to him; that he was now her father, as it were. But this was no joke to her; she took it very seriously indeed, and replied: "I know it; he is now my chief; I take his words."

This unexpected answer certainly surprised Ashton, and made him very thoughtful.

In about a week we packed up and moved in to the Fort, Nät-ah'-ki's uncle accompanying us to drive the horses back to the herd, as we had no way of caring for them. We ought to have remained longer in camp, for the ride reopened Ashton's wound, and retarded his complete recovery. After reaching the Fort, he kept pretty close to his lounge for a couple of weeks, and the young orphan waited on him, highly pleased when she could save him a few steps. To pass the time, he taught her simple English words, and short sentences. It was really laughable sometimes to hear her mix them up, as for instance, when she would say, "The cow he is water drink." But we didn't laugh, for if we had, there would have been an end to the lessons. Many a promising

Indian scholar has been lost by the thoughtless ridicule
of his teacher.

Berry returned to the Fort a day or two after we
arrived, and we began to plan for the winter's trade and
to make lists of the goods needed.   Whether we should
make a camp trade, or build a post, and at what point,
would depend entirely on the Indians' plans for the
winter.   Ashton intended to winter with us wherever
we went, but one day he received a letter that changed
his plans.   He did not tell us more than the fact that
it was necessary for him to return to the States soon.
In fact, he had never spoken of his affairs, nor his family.
All we knew was that he had proved to be a good companion, a man of kindly nature, a wholly dependable
man.

"I am not very inquisitive, I hope," said Berry to me;
"but I'd just like to know what our friend's trouble is,
what he is always grieving about, and what it is that
causes him to go back.   It's plain to be seen that he
doesn't want to go."

I felt as Berry did, but no more than he could I say
anything to Ashton about it.

Several steamboats were yet to arrive before the close
of the season, and he deferred his departure.   One evening, when we were all congregated in the front room, the
conversation turned to his impending departure, and he
said that he would return to us as soon as possible; if not
sometime during the winter, then by the first boat in the
spring.   "And now," he continued, "say this to my
little girl; tell her that I wish to take her with me, and
put her in school down there with a lot of other nice little
girls, where kind, black-robe women will care for her, and
teach her to read, and write, and sew, and many other
good and useful things."

This proposition certainly surprised Berry and me, and when it had been interpreted, the women were simply lost in astonishment. A long silence ensued; we all waited for the girl to speak; all certain that she would refuse to leave us. We were still more astonished, if that were possible, when she at last replied that she would go. And then she ran to Nät-ah'-ki, hid her face in her lap, and cried. We men got our hats and strolled out.

"I have been thinking of this for some time," Ashton said to us, after we had sat down on the river bank and lighted our pipes. "I am curious to know what effect a really first-class education will have upon the girl, and what use she will make of it. Do you think it a good plan?"

"God only knows," Berry replied. "It may make her very unhappy; it certainly will if, in spite of high education and all accomplishments, the whites shall still avoid and despise her because she is an Indian. Again, it might make of her a noble and useful woman. I advise you to try it, anyway."

"But, Berry, old man!" I exclaimed, "the white people do not despise Indians. On the other hand, I am sure that they highly respect those of them who are really men."

"I guess I know what they think, what they do," he rejoined. "I am only half Indian, but I have been abused by them in my time."

"Who were 'they'?" I asked. "Were they men fairly representative of the white people? Or were they the ignorant and low-down ones?"

He acknowledged that he had ever been kindly and respectfully treated by the former class.

"Well," Ashton concluded, "The girl goes with me.

I'll take her to St. Louis and place her in some good
institution, preferably one managed by the Sisters.   All
that money can pay for shall be done for her; moreover,
I'll make my will and provide for her in case of my death.
I'd rather she should have what I leave, than anyone
else."

Early one morning we went to the levee to see them
off.   On the previous evening the girl had cried bitterly
while the few things that we could provide for her were
being packed, and Nät-ah'-ki told her that if she did not
wish to leave us, she need not do so, that Never-Laughs
would not think of taking her away against her will.
The girl replied that she would do as he wished.   "He
saved me," she said: "and I belong to him.   I know
that he means well."

The boat had steam up, the whistle blew, and the
passengers went aboard.   The young one was very quiet,
and dry-eyed.   She followed Ashton up the gang-plank,
shawl thrown over her head and partly concealing her
face, and they went up on the upper deck.   The boat
drew out into the stream, slowly turned, and then swiftly
disappeared around the bend.   We went thoughtfully
home.

"I do not like it at all," said the Crow Woman.   "What
have we to do with white peoples' ways and learning?
The Sun gave us these plains, and these mountains and
rivers, the buffalo and the deer.   They are all we
need."

"You speak truth," old Mrs. Berry said to her.   "Yet
I am glad that my son went down to the far white men's
country, for what he learned there is of use.   He can
make their writing and read it.   He is a trader, knowing
how to buy and sell.   He is above the chiefs, for they
come to him for advice."

"I think," I said, "that I ought to have sent Nät-ah'-ki along with them."

"Just hear him!" she cried, seizing me by the shoulder and pushing me out of the trail. "As if he couldn't teach me himself. But he will not, although I have asked him to do so more than a hundred times."

That was one thing Nät-ah'-ki always rather regretted, her inability to speak English. I did not teach it to her, for I early realised that she would never be able to master some of our consonants, especially b, f, l, and r, the sounds of which are wholly foreign to the Blackfoot language. Rather than hear her speak our tongue incorrectly, I preferred that she should not speak it at all. And then, I spoke her language, more and more fluently as time went by, and I thought that we were sufficient unto ourselves. I did not think that we would ever be much in the company of white people, especially white women. The majority of the latter, those who lived upon the frontier, hated the Indian women, especially those married to white men, and equally they hated, despised, the whites who had married them, and they lost no opportunity to show their ill-will.

Berry keenly realised this, and at times was actually sick at heart over the slights, real and imagined, but mostly the latter, put upon him. Once, and once only— it was soon after Ashton's departure with his protégée— he told me of an experience he had gone through, which, I think, was in many ways the most peculiar and pathetic one I ever heard. It so burned itself into my memory that I can repeat it word for word as he related it.

"When I was only a child," he said, "I can remember my father frequently mentioning the property, a farm, he owned in Missouri. After he left the service of the American Fur Company, he became an independent trader, and made almost yearly trips to St. Louis to dispose of his furs. He gradually made longer and longer stays down there, and finally gave up trading altogether, remaining down on his farm, and visiting us only occasionally. Young as I was, I had a great desire to become a trader myself, and worked hard for the men with whom he successively placed me, beginning with Major Dawson, the company's factor here. Dawson himself, as well as the clerks, seemed to like me, and they all helped me when they saw that I was trying to read and write. If I do say it, I believe that I made pretty rapid progress, more rapid that my father thought I would. He intended, when the time came, to send me to school in the States.

"There came a time when he had been away from us for two years, and my friends thought that they would take the matter into their own hands and send me to a school they knew about in St. Joe, Missouri. They gave me a pocketful of money, and shipped me on a batteau which pulled out early in September. The fare down, by the way, was three hundred dollars, but I was dead-headed through. It was a long and tedious trip, especially in the lower part of the river, where the current was slow and head winds delayed us. We arrived in St. Joe late in the fall, and I went at once to the place selected for me, a boarding school which also took in day scholars. Right there my troubles began. While a few of my schoolmates liked me and were very kind, the most of them abused me and made fun of me calling me 'low-down Injun' and many other names which hurt. I stood it as long as I could, until, in fact, they began calling me coward. *Me* a coward, when I'd already been in two battles where men were killed, and done my share of the shooting! Well, when they called me a coward, I just waded in and gave three or four of them a good pounding, although I was in no way used to that style of fighting.   After that they left me alone, but all the same they hated me.

"I had not written my father where I was, as I had planned a little surprise for him.   When the Christmas vacation came, I started to pay him a visit.   I went for some distance on a train, and thought that a grand experience.   Then I got on a stage, and one evening was set down a couple of miles from his home.   I went on, inquiring my way, and about dusk I came in sight of his house, a very nice, trim, white-painted one, surrounded by fine fruit and other trees.   Someone was coming along the road, and I saw that it was my father.   When he recognised me, he ran and threw his arms around me, and kissed me, and said that he loved me best of all.   I didn't understand what he meant by best of all, but I soon learned.   After asking me all manner of questions, how I had come, how my mother and all his friends were, he stood silent for some little time, leaning on my shoulder, and then he said: 'My boy, I hoped you would never learn what I have to say, at least not until after my death.   But now I must tell you all: In that house yonder is a woman to whom I am married, and there are a boy and a girl, our children.   I can introduce you there only as a friend, as the son of an old-time Montana friend.   Oh, shame on me that I have to say such a thing!   Will you come?''

" 'Yes,' I said, 'I will go with you,' and we went in.

"She was a very kind woman that, and the children, younger than I, were, as well as she, very good to me.   I couldn't help but like them, and at the same time I felt very sad about it all.   I belieye that I cried about it nights after I had gone to my room and to bed.

"My father and I had many talks in private, and he told me over and over again that he loved me best; that I was first in his thoughts. Of course, I could not remain there long: the situation was too trying. In the last talk we had there, he asked me if I intended to tell my mother what I had learned, and I replied that I had no intention of doing so. And so we parted, and I returned to school. To this day my mother does not know anything about his other life. He comes and stays with us, sometimes for a whole summer, and she loves him so that I am sure it would kill her to learn what he has done, as it would also kill the other woman to know it. And he is my father. I love him, too. I cannot do anything but love him, no matter what he has done."

I may add that the old gentleman was true to his word. So long as he was able, he continued to visit his Montana son and wife, and when he died, we found that his will, executed several years previous to the time Berry visited him, bequeathed the greater part of his property to the first and favourite son. He was a man of good education, and interested in everything that pertained to the West. He entered the service of the American Fur Company when it was organised, in 1822 or 1823, and rose to be one of its prominent factors. For many years he kept a diary of the daily occurrences in his active life, which included much regarding the Indians he met, their customs and traditions. He was preparing them for publication when they were destroyed in a fire which burned down his house. That was a loss which many of us regret.

CHAPTER XXII

THE WAR TRIP OF QUEER PERSON

IT WAS about time for us to be doing something besides loafing at the Fort. Berry saddled a horse one morning and rode out to the camp on the Marias to interview the chiefs. When he returned, a day or two later, he was more than satisfied with the result of the council, for it was agreed that the winter should be passed on the Marias. We could use the post that had been built two years previously. It needed some repairs, but by the middle of September we were well established there, with a good stock of goods. The chief difficulty in moving out was our inability to keep the bull-whackers sober. One of them, Whisky Lyons, was the worst I ever saw. He never was on hand to help load the wagons, and when we were ready to pull out we had to hunt him up, tie a rope under his arms and souse him in the river until he came to his senses. There was another, "Captain" George, whose specialty was a singing spree. He had a large store of quaint songs, which he would sing unendingly when drunk.

I have often wondered whatever became of the old-time bull-whackers, they who spent their money so freely and joyously whenever they had the opportunity. I never heard of them dying. I never saw them after the advent of the railroads and the close of transportation on the upper Missouri. They simply vanished.

There was little for us to do until the prime winter

robes began to come in. The Piegans had moved out
on Milk River back of the Sweetgrass Hills, and would
not return to stay until cold weather drove them in.   A
few were coming and going all the time, bringing in
beaver skins, some to exchange for ammunition, tobacco,
and liquor; others to obtain the same from us on credit.
We missed Sorrel Horse, who had gone down on the
Missouri somewhere below the mouth of the Judith, to
run a woodyard, and to trade with the Gros Ventres.
He was always good company.   During the time of slack
trade, Berry was as uneasy as the proverbial fish out
of water. Always a very nervous, active man, he could
not be happy unless he was doing something.   I have
seen him throw and shoe a bull that did not need shocing,
or repair an old wagon wheel that could never be of any
service.   But his most dangerous hobby was medicine.
An army surgeon had given him a fine, large medicine
chest, which contained dozens of bottles of drugs, drawers
full of knives, saws, probes, and various other instruments
of torture, lint, plasters, splints—an exceedingly large
variety of things.   When any of us felt sick we concealed the fact from him if possible, lest he should dose
us into our graves.

One day our friend, Four Bears, the camp-crier, a
man of great dignity, came in complaining that he felt
very ill.   Berry was interested at once.

"I think," he said to me, after he had diagnosed the
case, "that I have exactly the remedy he needs.   A
Seidlitz powder will fix him all right.   Yes, that's what
he needs for sure.   I'll give him a double dose."   Whereupon he emptied two of the white paper powders into a
glass of water and had the patient gulp it down.   He then
discovered that he had forgotten to put in the powder
contained in the green papers.

"Oh, well," he said, "'tisn't too late, I'll just dissolve them in more water. I guess they'll mix all right in his stomach."

They did. Four Bears swallowed them and instantly an expression of surprise, of terror, spread over his face. He began to gasp; he bent nearly double and pressed the pit of his stomach; then he dropped to the floor and rolled and rolled, while the foaming mixture spouted from his mouth and nostrils, as does the contents of a seltzer siphon when the lever is pressed. Fortunately, the agony didn't last long, and as soon as he could the orator sprang to his feet, and fled across the bottom to his lodge. We didn't see him again for a month or more. After that the Indians seldom applied to Berry for relief. When they did, they required him to take a dose of his prescription before they would touch it, and they would stand around for a while and watch to see how it affected him.

But if Berry was at his wit's end for something to do, 'twas different with me; no day was too long. Nät-ah'-ki and I went hunting, either in the river bottoms for deer, or out on the plains for antelope. Buffalo, of course, were everywhere; and down below the post some ten or twelve miles there were quite a number of bighorn. And then the evenings were as full of interest as the days. What more pleasant than to be with the women where the flames and glowing coals in the rude fireplace, lighting up the grim log walls of the room, seemed a fit accompaniment to the quaint tales they so earnestly and reverently told. My dingy old note-books contain the outlines of those happy days, and as I look over them it all comes back to me as vividly as if it all had happened yesterday, or last week. Here, for instance, is a story the Crow Woman related one evening which may interest

"Queer Person"

you as much as it did me.   She called it the "Story of
Three Stabs":

"In all the village there were none poorer than White
Flying and her young grandson.   Her man was long since
dead; her son-in-law had been killed by the Sioux, and
her daughter, while working in their little plantation one
day, had suddenly dropped to the ground and ceased
breathing.   The boy was still too young to go on the
hunt, so they lived on what small store of corn they could
raise, and what portions of meat were given them by the
kind hearted.   There were days when they went to bed
hungry, for their best friends sometimes forgot to provide for them, and White Flying was too proud to go
out and beg.   When this happened, the boy would say,
'Never mind, grandmother, wait until I grow up and
I'll kill more meat than you can take care of.'

"The boy's name was Sees Black, a name an old
medicine man had given him when he was born.   No
one but his grandmother so called him; he was nick-
named Queer Person, for he had ways different from those
of any other boy ever heard of.   He never played with
other children, never laughed nor cried, and scarcely
spoke to anyone except his grandmother.   He seemed
to be dreaming of something all the time; and would sit
on the bank of the river, or on the hill near the village,
often for half a day, looking straight away into the far
distance as if he saw there things of great interest—so
great that he never noticed people who passed near him.
He brought strange and forbidden things to his lodge;
once, a human skull, which he placed under the end of
his couch.   When making up his bed one day, the old
woman found it, and it frightened her so that she fell
right down and was dead for a while.   When she came
to life, she begged him to take it back to the place where

he had found it, and he did so as once, for he was a good
boy and always obeyed her.   When she asked him why
he had taken it, he replied, 'I am seeking a great medicine.
I thought that if I slept by it I might have a powerful
dream.'

"Sometimes he would leave the village and stay away
all night; and when his grandmother asked him where
he had been, he would tell her that he had gone upon the
plain, or down in the timber, or out on a sandbar, to
sleep, hoping that some of the spirits or animals who
wander about in the darkness, would have pity and give
him the medicine he sought.

"While other boys of his age still played, he made bows
and arrows.   He watched the flint workers, and became
as skilful as they in chipping out sharp, thin arrow
points.   He hunted, too; at first, rabbits in the rosebush
thickets; and then, one day, he brought home a fine deer
—a part of the meat at a time—which he had shot on a
trail they used in going to and from their watering place.
After that he seldom hunted rabbits, but often brought
in deer, and once in a while the hide and meat of a buffalo
which he crept up on and killed in a coulée, or at the
river where they went to drink.   Still, they were very
poor; all the family horses had long since been given
the doctors who had tried to cure the grandfather.
Without horses Queer Person could not go out on the
big hunts and bring in loads of meat sufficient to last
during the bad weather, or through the long sieges of
the Sioux against them.   In the summer time this enemy
came often in great numbers and stayed around the
village for a whole moon and more, hoping to starve
the people and fall upon them when at last they were
obliged to go out to hunt.

"The summers and the winters passed.   The boy

grew and grew, tall and strong, and very fine-looking. He was now old enough to go to war; to fight the enemy and drive away their horses. But no war party would let him join them. 'One who slept with skulls,' they said, 'who went forth to sleep where the ghosts wandered—there was surely something wrong with such a person; he would cause bad luck to befall them.'

"Of course, the young man felt very badly about this, grieving much; and the grandmother grieved with him. And then he became angry. 'I will make them take back their words,' he said to the old woman. 'I will go against the enemy by myself, and the time shall come when they will beg to go with me. Make me a boat and I'll float down the river to the camps of the Sioux.'

"White Flying went out and cut the willows, crossed and recrossed them, bent them to the proper shape, then stretched and bound upon the frame the fresh hide of a big bull, and the boat was done. No, it was not like the boats of the white men. It was flat on the bottom and round, like the tubs white people have for washing clothes. Unless one was accustomed to them, he was helpless, for, if he did not upset when he tried to paddle, he would only make the boat whirl around and around like a child's top, and it would drift wherever the current and the wind chose to push it.

"There was a full moon now, and one night when it rose, soon after the sun had gone down, Queer Person got into his boat and pushed it out from the shore. No one was there to see him leave, except his grandmother; no one else in the village knew that he was going away. 'Oh, be careful!' she said. 'Be ever on the watch for the dangers, and try nothing that you are not certain you can do.'

"'Take courage,' he called back to her. 'I will return

to you; I will surely return. My dream has told me that I will.'

"The poor old woman sat down on the shore, covered her head with her robe, and cried; cried for those loved ones who were dead, and for the young man who was going, perhaps, to join them and leave her alone in her old age. She was very unhappy.

"On and on Queer Person drifted in the bright moonlight, down the wide, deep river, never paddling except to keep facing down stream and to avoid the snags and sandbars. The beavers played and splashed around him, and he prayed to them: 'Pity me,' he said; 'give me of your cunning, so that I may escape all danger.'

"Where the water boiled and swirled under the shadow of a high-cut bank, some dim thing rose above the surface, and slowly sank and disappeared. He could not see it plainly; it might have been one of the people who live in the dark, deep places; he prayed to them also, and dropped a sacrifice to them. 'Do not harm me,' he said; 'let me pass over your waters in safety.'

"All the animals of the valley seemed to be gathered along the shores, feeding, drinking, the young of elk and deer running and playing along the sandbars. There were big bears snuffling and pawing at the water's edge; wolves and coyotes looked down at him as he passed under the low bluffs. But none paid any attention to him, for there was no wind, and they could not know that an enemy was near. Thus the night passed, and with the daylight he went to the shore, dragging his boat into some thick willows and then smoothing off the trail he had made across the sands.

"Thus drifting by night and hiding in the daytime, Queer Person kept on toward the country of the Sioux. Every morning, after going ashore, he would walk out to the edge of the timber, sometimes climbing a nearby slope, and look carefully up and down the valley for signs of people. He saw none until the fifth morning, when he discovered a great camp directly across the river in a big bottom. There was a long strip of cottonwoods bordering the stream; the lodges were pitched on the open plain back of it. A large number of horses were tied in the camp, people were just coming out and turning them loose to graze. 'My medicine is good.' he said to himself. 'I have come safely down the river, and here I am in sight of that which I seek.'

"During the day he slept for some time, feeling quite safe where he was, for the enemy had no boats, the river was very high, and they could not cross. He made plans for the night. 'I will cross over,' he said, 'after the light in their lodges dies out; I will take some of their horses, and ride homeward as fast as I can.' All the afternoon this thought pleased him, and then came into his heart another thing which he considered. Any one could go into a camp and take horses and have a good chance to escape with them. That was easy to do. His people had refused to let him go with them on raids; he wanted to do some great thing, to show them that he was a braver man than any of them. What should he do to prove this? What could he do? He considered many things, many plans, and could not decide. Toward evening he slept again, and then his dream helped him and showed him the way to make a great name for himself.

"This is what he did; listen to the cunning his dream gave him: In the night he crossed the river, put some stones in his boat, then cut a hole in the bottom, so that it filled with water and sank. Then he went into the timber and buried his things beside a large cottonwood log, buried his clothes, moccasins, weapons; nothing remained on him, except his belt and breech-clout. Lastly, he unbound his braided hair, washed it to straighten out the kinks, then tangled it and scattered dust in it. He smeared mud and dust on his body; soiled his breech-clout; scratched his legs with a rose bush; when he had done, he looked very wild, very poor. He went out of the timber, down to the lower end of the bottom, and remained there the rest of the night.

"When the sun came up and people were moving about Queer Person arose and walked toward the camp, sometimes stopping and looking around, sometimes running, again walking slowly, looking at the ground. Thus he approached the lodges, and the great crowd of people who stood staring at him. He pretended not to see them, walking straight on; they parted to let him pass and then followed him. He stopped by a fire outside a lodge, upon which some meat was roasting, and sat down. The women tending it fled. The people gathered around him and stood and talked. Of course, they thought him crazy. A man came up, asked him many questions in signs; he did not reply, except occasionally to point down the river. This man had a wide scar on his left cheek. Queer Person knew that he was a chief. He had heard his people talk about him as a terrible man in battle. After a time an old woman came and set some broiled meat before him; he seized it and ate it as if he had been starving for many days. He ate a great deal, and a long time. The people mostly went away to their lodges. The scar-faced man made signs again, but when he got no answer he took Queer Person by the arm, made him get up, and led him to his lodge, showed him a couch, made signs that it was his, that he should live in the lodge. Still the young man pretended not to understand, but he remained there, going out sometimes but always returning. People made him presents—moccasins, leggings, a buckskin shirt, a cowskin robe. He put them on and wore them. After a few days he would walk about in camp, and the people would hardly notice him. They had got used to seeing him around.

"Queer Person soon found that the scar-faced chief was a very cruel man. He had five wives, the first one older than he, and very ugly. The others were all young women, and good-looking, one very pretty. The old wife abused the others, made them do all the work and labour hard all day long. Sometimes she struck them; often she would talk to the chief, and he would get up and beat them or seize a couple and knock their heads together. They were very unhappy. The young man could not help but look often at the youngest one, she was so pretty and so sad. He would always walk around where she was at work, and met her often in the grove when she gathered wood, and then they would smile at each other. After many days, he found her all alone in the woods one evening; his time had come, and he quickly told her in signs who he was, that he was not crazy; that he had started all alone to war. And then he said that he loved her; that it made him sad to see her abused. He asked if she would go away with him and be his woman. She did not answer, but she just stepped up and clung to him and kissed him. Then they heard some one coming, and they parted.

"The next day they met again in the timber and went and hid in the thicket willows, and made their plans to leave. They could hardly wait for night to come.

"When the fire had died out and the chief and his old

wife snored, Queer Person and the young woman crept out of the lodge and went to the river. There they tied together two small logs and placed their clothes upon them, on top of a little pile of brush they had laid. The young man got his clothes and weapons which he had buried, and piled them there also. Then, with nothing but his knife, he went back to the lodge, leaving the woman by the raft. He crept in, and over to the chief's couch, raised his knife and gave him one deep stab right in the heart, then another and another. The man did not cry out, but he kicked a little and the old woman beside him awoke. Queer Person at once seized her by the throat and strangled her until she lay still. Then he scalped the chief, took his weapons, and ran back to the raft. The woman was waiting for him, and together they waded out, pushing the logs, and when they got into deep water they swam, holding on to the logs with one hand. Thus they crossed the river and dressed and started on the long walk to the Arickaree village. Back across whence they had come, all was quiet; the trouble there had not yet been discovered.

"What a proud old woman White Flying was when her grandson returned home with his pretty wife, with the scalp and the weapons of the terrible chief. He had made a great name: in time he himself would be a chief. And he did become one, the head chief of his people. No one any longer called him Queer Person: he took the name Three Stabs, and all were proud to call him that. He and his good wife lived to great age. They had many children and were happy."

CHAPTER XXIII

THE PIEGANS MOVE IN

"GET UP!" Năt-ah'-ki commanded, grasping my arm and nearly pulling me out of bed. "Get up! It is very happy outside."

"Why did you awake me?" I asked. "I was having such a good dream."

"Of course you were, and you were talking, too. That is why I awoke you; I don't want you to dream about her. Tell me, quick, what the dream was, and what she said."

"Well, if you must know, she said—she said—she said——"

"Yes, hurry! What did she say?"

"She said, 'It's time for you to arise and wash. I have your morning food cooked, and we are going hunting to-day.'"

"Oh, what a lie he can tell!" she exclaimed, turning to the Crow Woman. "He was not dreaming about me at all, because he spoke in his own language."

I insisted that I was speaking the truth. "In the first place," I said, "there is no 'her' but you, and even if there were, her shadow could not come away out here to visit me in my sleep, because it would be unable to find the trail."

This reasoning was convincing, and closed the argument. It was indeed a lovely morning. There had been a heavy frost during the night, the grass in the shadow of the Fort was still white with it, but the sun was shining in a clear sky, a warm southwest wind had started up—everything was auspicious for a perfect autumn day.

We breakfasted, saddled our horses, and rode out a-cross the river, up the slope of the valley, and out on the plain. Năt-ah'-ki began to sing one of the women's songs of her people. "Be still!" I told her. "This is no way to hunt; you will scare away all the game."

"I do not care if I do," she said. "What matter? We have still some dried meat on hand. I can't help singing; this happy morning just makes me do it."

As she said, it did not matter. It was pleasant to see her so happy, to see her eyes sparkle, to hear her laugh and sing. A not distant band of antelope scampered away over a ridge; out of a nearby coulée rushed a small band of buffalo and loped off westward; a lone coyote also appeared, sat down on his haunches, and stared at us. "Hai-ya', little brother," said Năt-ah'-ki, addressing him, "are you also happy?"

"Of course he is," she continued. "His fur is so thick and warm that he does not fear the coming cold, and he has plenty, oh, always plenty of food. Some he kills for himself, and he can always feast on the re-mains of the animals his big relations kill. Old Man gave him and the wolf great intelligence."

We rode on and on aimlessly across the plain, talking and laughing, very, very happy, as two young people should be who love one another and who haven't a care in the world. Often, on reaching the top of some little eminence, we would dismount and let the horses graze while I smoked and swept the country with my tele-scope. Năt-ah'-ki also loved to use the glass, and watch the various animals it would bring so near to one, as they rested or grazed, or the young bounded and

skipped and chased each other in their exuberance of
spirits. It was a powerful glass, that old telescope, revealing even the dead old cones and dark abysses on the surface of the moon.   But that was an object at which
I never succeeded in coaxing her to level the instrument.
Night Light to her was no dead old globe, but a real and
sacred personage—wife to the Sun—and not to be
scrutinised and studied by mortal eyes.

It was mid-afternoon when we decided that it was
time we should get the meat we had started after and
return home.   We were about to mount and ride toward
a coulée to the west, where a few buffalo were feeding,
when, away to the north, we saw columns of dust rising,
and nearer, some bunches of buffalo, loping in various
directions, but mostly toward us.   A few moments later
a number of horsemen came in sight, and behind them,
on the top of a long ridge, appeared a long column of
riders and loose animals.

"Ah!" I said, "the Pe-kun-ny are moving in."

"My mother is there. Let us go to meet them,"
said Nät-ah'-ki.

Some of the startled buffalo were making almost a
bee-line for the place where we stood, so I told her to
lead the horses back out of sight, and I myself moved
down, so that I could just look over the top of the ridge.
In a short time some thirty or forty of the animals came
within easy range.   I aimed at a big cow, and broke the
left front leg the first shot; she dropped behind the
others at once, and a second shot laid her low.   She
proved to be very fat, and her coat was fine, not quite of
full length, perhaps, but very dark and glossy.

I was about to cut the animal open on the back, intending to take only the boss ribs and the tongue, when
Nät-ah'-ki came up and insisted that I should properly

skin it for a head-and-tail robe, and cut up all of the
meat for packing. "We will give the hide to my
mother," she said, "and get her to pack in the meat for
us."

So I did as I was told, of course; the butchering taking
some little time. Meanwhile Nät-ah'-ki went to the top
of the ridge, but soon returned to say that the people
were pitching camp near where we had discovered
them, and that it would be pleasant to remain with them
for a night.

"All right," I said, "we'll go over and stop with
Weasel Tail. We'll take a little of the meat and leave
the rest and the hide for your mother to pick up in the
morning."

But that, it seemed, would not do. "Either the
wolves will feast upon it in the night," she said, "or
someone will find and take it in the early morning; so,
to be sure, let us pack it into camp."

I spread the great hide over her horse, entirely covering the animal, saddle and all, from neck to tail, and
then hung the greater part of the meat across it over the
saddle, covering it all by folding and refolding the hide.
The rest I put in two large meat sacks and tied behind
my saddle. Then I helped Nät-ah'-ki to get up and
perch on top of her load, mounted my animal, and we
wended our way to camp and in among the lodges.
There were pleasant greetings and pleasant smiles for
us on every hand, and some jokes were made about the
young married hunters. We dismounted in front of
Weasel Tail's lodge. My good mother-in-law ran and
met her daughter, the two affectionately embracing and
kissing each other, the former repeatedly saying, "My
daughter! My daughter! She has arrived."

And the good woman looked at me and smiled, but

gave me no greeting.   Even in being in my vicinity, to
say nothing of smiling at me, she had broken a strict rule
of Blackfoot etiquette, of which I have already spoken,
which is that mother and son-in-law must never meet nor
speak to each other.   For my part, I transgressed this
form at the very first opportunity.   I came upon the
good woman when she could not escape, nor help listening, and told her that with us it was to be different;
that white people had no such custom.   "Wherever
we are," I continued, "you are to come and live with us
when you will, and I shall go where you are when occasion to do so arises."

I am sure that my words pleased her, as they also
pleased Nät-ah'-ki.   In time she became used to the
new order of things, in a way, but was always rather
backward about directly addressing me.   Very often,
when I asked her for information about something, she
would turn to her daughter and say, "Tell him that it
was in this way," etc.

CHAPTER XXIV

WE CAMPED with Weasel Tail, whose good woman spread out a number of new robes for our use. Visitors came and went, and we were called to several smokes at different places. In the latter part of the evening, after the feasting and visiting was over, Weasel Tail and Talks-with-the-buffalo, the two inseparables, and I were again together, as we had been on many a previous night. There were no three smokes and then the polite dismissal when we got together, no matter which of us was host. We would sit together for hours, smoking when we felt like it, talking or idly silent, as the mood struck us. The women passed around some berry pemmican, which was fine. "Friend," said Talks-with-the-buffalo, after we had eaten and the pipe was again filled and lighted, "I have a present for you."

"Ah!" I replied, "I am always glad to get presents."

"Yes," he continued, "and I will be glad to get rid of this. I want you to take it to-morrow morning, lest something happen that you never get the thing. It is a wolverine skin. Listen and I will tell you what trouble it has caused me. First, as to the way I got it: One morning my woman here told me to kill some bighorn; she wanted their skins for a dress. I said that those animals were too difficult to get; that she ought to make her dress of antelope skins, which also make fine soft leather when well tanned. But, no; they would not do; they were uneven, thick on the neck, too thin on the belly; nothing would do but bighorn skins, because they were all of the right kind—neither thick nor very thin in any place. I tried to get out of it by saying that if she must have them I would require her to go on the hunt with me, and help pack down what I killed. I thought that when I said this, she would make up her mind that antelope skins were good enough. I was mistaken. 'Of course, I'll go with you,' she said. 'Let us start in the morning.'

"I made up my mind that I would pretend to be sick; but when I awoke in the morning I had forgotten all about the hunt, and after I had got up and washed, I ate a big meal. When I did remember, it was too late. I couldn't get her to believe that I was sick, after making her broil meat twice. We started, and rode as far as our horses could carry us, up the north side of the west Sweetgrass Mountain; then we tied the animals and went on afoot. It was pretty steep climbing; in places the pines grew so closely together that we could hardly squeeze between them. My hunting partner was always behind. 'Come on; come on,' I kept saying; and 'Wait, wait for me,' she was always calling, and when she caught up she would be breathing like a horse that has run a race, and sweat would just drip off her chin. 'It is very pleasant, this bighorn hunting,' I told her; and she said, 'You speak the truth. Just look how high up we are, and how far we can see the plains away northward.'

"After that I did not tease her, because she had good courage, and did her best to climb. I travelled slower, and she kept close behind me. We approached the summit. The top of that mountain—you have seen it —is a mystery place. When Old Man made the world he painted the rocks he placed there with pretty colours, red, brown, yellow and white.* Some say that it is a lucky place to hunt; others, that if one kills anything there, he will have bad luck of some kind. I thought of this as I climbed, and at last I stopped and spoke to my woman. I told her that we had, perhaps, better go back on account of the bad luck we might have if I made a killing there. But she just laughed and laughed, and said that I was getting to be very foolish.

" 'Well,' I said to her, 'if you must laugh, do so with your hand over your mouth, else you will scare everything on this mountain.'

"We continued climbing, and in a little while came to the summit. Looking out at it from the cover of some pines, I saw a band of bighorn, maybe twenty or more, all she ones, and their young, except a two-year-old male. I took a careful aim at him—he was close by and standing side to me—and as it was handy, I rested my gun on a limb of a tree. I took a very good aim, right for his heart, and fired. I don't know where the bullet went, but I am sure that it never hit him, for we could find neither hair nor blood where he had stood nor along his trail. When I shot, the smoke hung like a little cloud before me, and when it blew away, I saw the animals, just as they disappeared into the timber down the slope. I was much surprised that I had not killed the animal, most surprised when I found that I had not even hit him, for I had aimed so long and so carefully.

" 'You must have hit him,' said my woman. 'Let us look again. We will likely find him lying dead somewhere far away.'

"We followed his trail for some distance down in the

---

* They are porous burnt quartz, that seems to have been thrown up through a seam in the porphyry.

timber; it was easy to follow, for his track was larger than that of the others; but there was no sign at all that he was hurt. We climbed up on top again, and sat down at the edge of the bare rocks, in the shelter of a low pine. I thought that if we stayed here a while some more bighorn might come along. But none appeared, although we sat and watched until long after the middle of the day. We were about to leave, when a big wolverine appeared, walking among the rocks, smelling and snuffing, sometimes climbing up on top of a big rock to look all around. He looked very pretty, his hair just shining in the sun. He soon came near, and the next time he climbed upon a rock I shot him. He fell off it and hardly kicked. I told my woman to skin it carefully. I knew you would want it to go with those you got last winter. She said that she would tan it very soft, and we would make you a present of it. The bad luck began right there. She cut her hand—the knife slipped—before she had half got the hide off, and I had to finish the work. Then we started homeward. When we got to the horses I tied the skin behind my saddle and got astride. The horse had been standing with his head to the wind, and when I turned him he got the scent of the wolverine for the first time, and it frightened him so that he went crazy. He snorted and made a big high jump down the mountain, and when he struck, the jar threw me off, right on my back into a lot of stones. I thought I was broken in two. The horse went on, jumping, and kicking, and snorting, right into a pile of big rocks, where he got caught by a foreleg, and broke it. As soon as I got my breath and could walk and my woman found my gun I had to go down and shoot him. We were late getting home, for we rode double on the other horse, and had to hang on it my saddle and other things. One thing we had learned: It was bad luck to kill anything on the painted rocks. Maybe, if I had killed the sheep also, my back would have been really broken when I was thrown by the horse.

"It was some days before I recovered from the soreness caused by my fall. My woman could not tan the wolverine skin on account of her sore hand, so she got a widow to do it. The next morning the old woman brought back the skin. 'Take it,' she said. 'I have been sick all night, and in my dream a wolverine came and tried to bite me. It is bad medicine. I will not tan it.'

"You know old Beaver Woman? Yes? We gave the skin to her. She said that she wasn't afraid of wolverines, that her medicine was stronger than theirs. Well, she took it to her lodge and went to work, fleshed it, put on the liver and brains, rolled it up and laid it away for two or three days. When it was well soaked with the mixture, she cleaned it and began to dry it, working it over the sinew cord, when she suddenly fell over dead for a short time. When she came to life her mouth was drawn around to one side and she could hardly speak. She was that way about four nights. Of course, the skin came back to us. The cut on my woman's hand had healed, so she went to work and finished the tanning, and without any mishap.

"Day before yesterday we started to move in; my woman packed the skin with other things on the lodge-skin horse. When we made camp in the evening, the skin was missing. Everything else that had been placed in the pack was there, the skin only was gone. While we were wondering how it could have happened, a young man rode up and tossed it to us. 'I found it on the trail,' he said.

" 'We rode double on the other horse' "

"So, you see, this skin is powerful bad medicine. I
said that I was going to give it to you, and I now do so.
Also I have told you all the evil it has done. I shall not
blame you if you throw it in the fire, or otherwise dispose of it. All I ask is that you take it off our hands."

Of course, I accepted the skin. In time it became
part of a handsome robe; a small bear skin in the centre,
the border of six wolverines.

Nät-ah'-ki and I were in the saddle next morning long
before the lodges began to come down, and started homeward. It had been a very warm night. Soon after we
left camp a light wind sprang up from the north, cold,
damp, and with a strong odour of burning grass. We knew
the sign well enough; the smoky smell was always the
precursor of a storm from the north. "The Cold-maker
is near," said Nät-ah'-ki. "Let us hurry on."

Looking back, we saw that the Sweetgrass hills had
become enveloped in a dense white fog, which was sweeping southward with incredible swiftness. It soon overtook us, and was so thick that we could not see a hundred
yards ahead. The sweat on our horses instantly froze;
fine particles of frost filled the air; our ears began to
tingle, and we covered them with handkerchiefs. It was
useless to attempt to look out a course to the river, so we
gave our horses the reins and kept them going, and
arrived home before noon. The wind had steadily increased, the fog had gone, but snow had taken its place.
Winter had come.

Prime robes soon began to come in, and we were kept
pretty busy exchanging goods and spirits for them. For
convenience, we used brass checks in trading, each check
representing one dollar. Having some robes to sell, an
Indian would stalk in, followed by one or more of his
women carrying them, and, as a rule, he would stand at

a little distance, very silent and straight, his robe or blanket partly concealing his face, while we examined them and counted down the checks.   Unless he needed a gun or some such expensive article, he generally gave his women a part of the proceeds, and invested the rest himself in whatever took his fancy; tobacco always, generally some liquor.   They always wanted to taste of the liquor before buying, and we kept for that purpose a pailful of it and a cup behind the counter, which was four and a half feet in height.   There was seldom any objection to the strength of the article we sold, which was alcohol of high proof, mixed with five parts of water. A few moments after one of these extremely haughty customers had taken a drink, his manner changed.   He became quite affable and loquacious, and before leaving would sometimes wish to embrace and kiss all present, including the traders.   It was not often that any of them became cross with us, their quarrels generally taking place in camp.   Nor were they, on the whole, much more quarrelsome than so many white men.   We did little trading after dark, most of the people preferring to come in the morning to barter their fur and robes.   I never knew a trader who had not some especial and privileged friends, and we were no exception to the rule. Several of these would sometimes come and sit with us of an evening to smoke and tell stories, and every little while either Berry or I would pass around the cup, but not too frequently.   It was very interesting to listen to their tales, and queer conceptions of various things.

CHAPTER XXV

THEN there were days when the warm chinook was blowing, that simply drew one out of the Fort and away on the plain. Nät-ah'-ki and I would saddle a couple of horses and ride a great circle, returning home tired and hungry and ready to retire right after the evening meal, to sleep soundly through the long winter night. One fine day we were out, and along about 2 or 3 o'clock struck the river some five or six miles above the Fort and turned homeward down the valley. Riding along the trail through a grove of cottonwoods we met mine enemy, Little Deer, in quest of beaver, as he had some traps tied to his saddle. He leered at Nät-ah'-ki, who happened to be in the lead, and scowled savagely at me as we passed. I must confess that I bent in the saddle once or twice, pretending to adjust my stirrup leather, but really furtively looking back under my arm. I was certainly afraid of him and felt relieved when I saw him disappear around a bend of the trail without once, so far as I could determine, turning to look back at us.

Passing through the grove we crossed an open flat, went into another piece of timber, and then out on a wide, bare bottom. When about 150 or 200 yards from the last grove a gun boomed behind us and a bullet whizzed past my left side and kicked up the dust when it struck the ground farther on. Nät-ah'-ki shrieked, whipped up her horse and called to me to hurry, and we made pretty good time the rest of the way home. When the shot was fired I looked back and saw a thin cloud of smoke in front of some willows, but no man. It was Little Deer who had shot, of course, and he had come near hitting me. He had done just what I had always predicted he would do—attack me from behind; and from such a position as he was in it would have been folly to attempt to dislodge him.

Nät-ah'-ki was well-nigh speechless from terror and anger. I was angry, too, and swore that I would kill Little Deer at sight. Berry listened quietly, but made no comment until after supper, when we had quieted down.

"You see," he began, "that fish has some powerful relations in camp, and although they know well enough that he needs killing, they are nevertheless bound to avenge his death."

"Well?" I asked, "and am I to do nothing, and some day be potted from an ambush?"

"No," he replied. "We've got to kill him, but it must be done in such a manner that we will never be suspected. Just lay low and we will find some way to do it."

After that day Little Deer came no more to the Fort. If he needed anything he sent someone to purchase it for him. When Nät-ah'-ki and I rode we went out on the open plain, avoiding the coulées and the timber in the valley. Sometimes, of a night, Berry and I would try to devise some way to effectively get rid of my enemy, but we never succeeded. Could I have waylaid him, or shot him from behind, as he had attempted to do to me, I would gladly have done so—one should always fight the devil with his own weapons.

It was a day in the fore part of March when Little Deer was missed from the camp. The previous morning he had gone out with some other hunters on the plains north of the river to kill some meat. They had separated finally, but late in the afternoon several of them had seen the missing man on a butte skinning a buffalo. During the night his horse had returned and joined the band to which it belonged, still saddled and trailing its lariat. Relatives of Little Deer went out and continued to search for him for several days, and at last they found him a long distance from the carcass of the buffalo he had skinned and cut up. He was lying in a coulée and the top of his head was crushed in. His wives and female relatives buried him, but the wives did not mourn; he had been very cruel to them and they were glad to be free. The meat of the buffalo he had killed had all been neatly cut up and prepared for loading on the horse. It was thought that he had left the place to kill something else and had been thrown, or that, perhaps, his horse had fallen with him and had kicked him in its struggles to rise.

Nät-ah'-ki and I rejoiced when we learned this. She herself was the first to hear of it and came running in, all excitement, her eyes sparkling, and gave me a hearty squeeze.

"Be happy," she cried. "Our enemy is dead; they have found his body; we can ride where we please and without fear."

One night my old friend whom I have variously called Bear Head and Wolverine—he took the former name after a successful battle he was in—paid us a visit. He stayed long after all the others had gone, silently smoking, much preoccupied about something. Both Berry and I noticed it and spoke about it.

"He probably wants a new gun," I said, "or maybe a blanket or a new dress for his woman. Whatever it is I'll give it to him myself."

We were getting sleepy. Berry brought out a drink and handed it to him. "Well," he said, "tell us about it; what is on your mind?"

"I killed him," he replied. "I killed him and carried his body to the coulée and dropped it."

This was news indeed. We knew at once to whom he referred, none other than Little Deer. "Ah!" we both exclaimed, and waited for him to continue.

"I rode up to where he was tying his meat and got off my horse to tighten the saddle. We got to talking and he told about shooting at you. 'I don't see how I missed,' he said, 'for I took careful aim. But I'm not done. I'll kill that white man yet, and his woman shall be my woman, even if she does hate me.'

"His words made me mad. 'Kill him!' something said to me. 'Kill him, lest he kill your friend who has been so good to you.' He was bending over tying the last pieces of meat; I raised my rifle and struck him right on top of his head, and he fell forward, his shadow departed. I was glad that I did it."

He arose and prepared to leave. "Friend," I said, grasping his hand and heartily shaking it, "what is mine is yours. What can I give you?"

"Nothing," he replied. "Nothing. I am not poor. But if I ever am in need then I will come and ask for help."

He went out and we closed and barred the door. "Well, I'll be damned if that isn't the best turn I ever knew an Indian to do for a white man," Berry exclaimed. "He's sure a friend worth having."

For obvious reasons we kept what we had learned to ourselves, although I had a struggle to do so. It was years afterward when I finally told Nät-ah'-ki about it, and when the time came that our friend certainly did need help he got it.

We had with us that winter one Long-haired Jim,
bull-whacker, a man about forty years of age.   He wore
hair that was at least two feet long and which fell in
dark, rippling waves very gracefully over his back and
shoulders.   When on the road or out at work in the
wind he kept it braided, but in camp it was simply confined by a silk bandage bound around his head.   He
was very proud of it and kept it nicely washed and
combed.

Jim had made various trips, he claimed, on the Santa
Fé and the Overland Trails, and had drifted up into
Montana from Corinne.   According to his own story,
he was a great fighter, a successful gambler, but these
advantages, he said, were offset by the fact that he was
terribly unlucky in love.   "I have set my affections on
four different females in my time," he told us, "an' I'll
be dog-goned ef I got ary one of 'em."

"I come mighty close to it once," he continued.
"She was a red-haired widow what kept a boardin'
house in Council Bluffs.   We rolled in there one evenin',
an' as soon as we had corralled, all hands went over to
her place fer supper.   As soon as I set eyes on her I
says to myself, 'That's a mighty fine figger of a woman.'
She was small, an' slim, an' freckled, with the purtiest
little turn-up, peart nose as ever happened.   'Who is
she?' I asked a feller settin' next me.

" 'A widder,' he says, 'she runs this here place.'

"That settled it.   I went to the wagon-boss, told him
I quit, drew my pay, an' packed my beddin' and war-sack
over to her place.   The next evenin' I caught her settin'
out on the steps all by herself and walked right up to
her.   'Mrs. Westbridge,' I says, 'I've sure fell in love
with you.   Will you marry me?'

" 'Why, the idear!' she cried out.   'Jest listen to

the man; an' him a stranger. Scat! git out o' here!'
An' she up an run into the house, an' into the kitchen,
an' slammed an' locked the door.

"That didn't make no difference to me. I wa'n't
ordered to leave the house, so I staid right on, an' put
the question to her every chanct I got, sometimes twict
a day. She got sost she didn't run, took it kinder good-
natured like, but she always gave me a straight 'No'
for an answer. I wa'n't no way discouraged.

"Well, it run along a matter of two weeks, an, one
evenin' I asked her again; 'twas the twenty-first time,
which number bein' my lucky one, I considered it sure to
win. An' it did.

" 'Yes, sir, Mr. Jim What's-yer-name,' she says,
straight out, 'I'll marry yer on certain conditions:

" 'You must cut your hair.'

" 'Yep.'

" 'An' throw away them six-shooters an' that long
knife.'

" 'Yep.'

" 'An' quit gamblin.'

" 'Yep.'

" 'An' help me run this yere boardin' house.'

"Yes, I agreed to it all, an' she said we'd be married
the comin' Sunday. I asked her fer a kiss, but she
slapped my face an' run off into the kitchen. 'Never
mind,' I says, settin' down on the steps, 'I'll wait till
she comes out an' ketch her.'

"Wal, sir, I was a settin' there all peaceful an' happy
like, when along comes an ornery-lookin' one-leg cripple
an' asks, 'Is this whar Miss Westbridge lives?'

" 'It are,' I said. 'An' what might you want of her?'

" 'Oh, nothing', he says, ''cept she's my wife.'

"I allow I might have swatted him, even if he was a

cripple, if the woman hadn't come out just then. When she see him she just throwed up her hands and cried out: 'My Gawd! Wherever did you come from? I thought you was dead. They told me you was. Are you sure it's you?'

" 'Yes, Sairy,' he said. 'It's me all right; that is, what's left of me. It was reported that I died, or was missin', but I pulled through. I been trailin' you a long time. It's a long story——'

"I didn't wait to hear it. Went up to my room and sat down. After a while she come up. 'You see how 'tis,' she said. 'I've got to take care of him. Yer a good man, Jim; I admire yer spunk, a askin' and a askin', an never takin' "no" fer an answer. As it is, *ef* you care fer me I wisht you'd go.'

"I packed right up an' pulled out. No, I never did have no luck with women. Sence that happened I ain't had a chance to tackle another one."

Jim took great interest in Nät-ah'-ki and me. "My Gawd!" he would say, "just hear her laugh. She's sure happy. I wisht I had such a nice woman."

He spent much time in the trade room, and went often through the camp seeking to make a conquest of some fair damsel. He was really ridiculous, smiling at them, bowing and saying something in English which none could understand. The maidens turned away from him abashed. The men looking on either scowled or laughed and joked and named him the One-unable-to-marry, a very bad name in Blackfoot.

The main trouble was that he wore an immense moustache and chin whiskers. The Blackfeet abhorred hair, except that of the head. An old acquaintance never buttoned his shirt winter nor summer; his breast was as hairy as a dog's back. I have seen the Blackfeet actually shudder when they looked at it. But a happy day was coming for Jim. On a trip out from Fort Benton, Berry brought him a letter containing great news. A woman back in Missouri whom he had known from childhood had consented to marry him. He left for the States at once by the way of Corinne. We heard from him several months later: "Dear friends," he wrote, "she died the day before I got here. I'm sure grevin'. They's a nuther one here, but she's got seven children, an' she's after me. I take the Santy Fé trail to-morrer. Hain't I sure out of luck?"

By the same mail we heard from Ashton. He was in Genoa, Italy, and expected to be with us in the spring. He also wrote that he was getting good reports of his protégée's progress. A little later there came a letter for Nät-ah'-ki from the girl herself, which was very touching. It was in print, and read, including some additions by the Sisters: "I can read. I can write. The Sisters are good to me. I have pretty dresses. When I sleep I see the lodges and the people, and I smell the kak-sim-i' (sage). I love you. Diana Ashton."

Dear me! but Nät-ah'-ki was proud of that letter. She carried it around and showed it to her friends and had me translate it many times. She made several beautiful pairs of moccasins for the child, and after we returned to Fort Benton in the spring had me ship them on a steamboat with a lot of pemmican, dried meat and tongues, and a big bunch of sagebrush. I objected to sending the pemmican and meat, saying that the girl had all the food she wanted and the very best.

"Yes," she said, contemptuously, "white people's food; nothing food. I know she is hungry for real food."

We had a good trade that winter, but troublous times succeeded. A part of the Piegans, the Bloods and Blackfeet became a real terror to the whites in the country, and it was really unsafe to try to trade outside of Fort Benton. We passed the following two winters there. In January of the second one the Baker massacre occurred, and the Indians at once quieted down. In the spring of 1870 we began to plan for another season at some more or less distant point.

CHAPTER XXVI

A LAW prohibiting the sale of liquor to Indians, or even its transportation across the Indian country, had been practically a dead letter ever since Congress passed it. Along in the fall of 1869, however, a new United States marshal appeared in the country and arrested several traders who had liquor in their possession, confiscated their outfits, and made them all sorts of trouble. So long as this man remained in office it seemed as if the trade was doomed, and Berry wisely hit upon the plan of crossing the line into Canada and establishing a post there. True, there would be some trouble in transporting the forbidden goods from Fort Benton northward to the line, but chances had to be taken.

Miss Agnes E. Laut, author of "Lords of the North," "Heralds of the Empire," etc., in her "Tales of the Northwest Mounted Police" has this to say about the exodus: "It was in the early seventies that the monopoly of the Hudson's Bay Company ceased and the Dominion Government took over judicial rights in all that vast territory which lies like an American Russia between the boundary and the North Pole. The ending of the monopoly was the signal for an inrush of adventurers. Gamblers, smugglers, criminals of every stripe, struck across from the Missouri into the Canadian territory at the foothills of the Rockies. Without a white population, these riff-raff adventurers could not ply their usual 'wide-open' traffic. The only way to wealth was by the fur trade; and the easiest way to obtain the furs was by smuggling whisky into the country in small quantities, diluting this and trading it to the natives for pelts. Chances of interference were nil, for the Canadian Government was thousands of miles distant without either telegraph or railway connection. But the game was not without its dangers. The country at the foothills was inhabited by the Confederacy of the Blackfeet—Bloods, Piegans and Blackfeet—tigers of the prairie when sober, and worse than tigers when drunk. The Missouri whisky smugglers found they must either organise for defence or pay for their fun by being exterminated. How many whites were massacred in these drinking frays will never be known; but all around Old Man's River and Fort Macleod are gruesome landmarks known as the places where such and such parties were destroyed in the early seventies.

"The upshot was that the Missouri smugglers emulated the old fur traders and built themselves permanent forts; Robbers' Roost, Stand Off, Freeze Out, and, most famous of all, Whoop-Her-Up, whose name for respectability's sake has been changed to 'Whoop-Pup,' with an innocent suggestiveness of some poetic Indian title. Whoop-Up, as it was known to plainsmen, was palisaded and loop-holed for musketry, with bastions and cannon and an alarm bell. The fortifications of this place alone, it is said, cost $12,000, and it at once became the metropolis of the whisky smugglers. Henceforth only a few Indians were allowed inside the fort at a time, the rest being served through the loop-holes.

"But the Blackfeet, who loved a man hunt better than a buffalo hunt, were not to be balked. The trail by which the whisky smugglers came from Fort Benton zigzagged over the rolling prairie, mainly following

the bottoms of the precipitous coulées and ravines for
a distance of 200 miles to Whoop-Up. Heavy wagons
with canvas tops and yokes of fifteen and twenty oxen
drew the freight of liquor through the devious passes
that connected ravine with ravine. The Blackfeet are
probably the best horsemen in the world. There were
places where the defiles were exceptionally narrow,
where the wagons got mired, where oxen and freight
had to be rafted across rain-swollen sloughs. With a
yelling of incarnate fiends that would have stampeded
more sober brutes than oxen drawing kegs of whisky,
down swooped the Blackfeet at just these hard spots.
Sometimes the raids took place at night, when tethers
would be cut and the oxen stampeded with the bellowing of a frightened buffalo herd. If the smugglers
made a stand there was a fight. If they drew off, the
savages captured the booty."

Miss Laut's informants have most grievously imposed
upon her. The men who participated in the trade across
the line were not "criminals of every stripe," but honest,
fearless, straightforward fellows. Very many of them
are living to-day and they feel that they have been
wronged by Miss Laut's statements. Neither were
they smugglers into the country, for that part of Canada
was then to the Canadians an unknown land, without
any laws or white residents. Away up on the Saskatchewan was the Hudson's Bay Company selling rum
to the Indians, as they had been doing for many years.
In the opposition of the Americans they saw the end of
their lucrative trade, and complained to the Dominion
Government about it, finally getting relief with the appearance of the Northwest Mounted Police. Neither
were there any drinking frays in which whites were
massacred. One man named Joe Neufrain was killed

for cause by the Blackfeet at Elbow, about 100 miles north of Belly River. Two men, a Frenchman named Polite, and Joseph Wey, were killed at Rocky Springs, on the trail from Fort Benton north. The Assiniboins, not the Blackfeet, shot them. The fact is that the trail did not follow precipitous coulées and ravines but ran straight over the open rolling plain, the freighters thereon were not attacked by the Blackfeet, and their cattle stampeded. Nor did they freight whisky in heavy loaded bull trains. In crossing the Indian country south of the line they had the United States marshal to elude; the whisky was transported by four-horse teams which travelled swiftly across by a route which the marshal was unlikely to know.

In the fall of 1870 Berry established Stand-Off; after that Whoop-Up and Fort Kipp were built. There were one or two other minor posts at Elbow, on High River, and Sheep Creek. In all, from 1870 until the arrival of the Mounted Police in 1874, there were fifty-six white men at these various places or camped out on the plains wolfing. They were not massacred by the Blackfeet. When the Mounted Police came they also got along peaceably with the Confederacy, because the Baker massacre had taken all the fight out of them. So much by way of explanation.

.   .   .   .

Starting north from Fort Benton with a good outfit of stores, Berry, I, and several others arrived at Belly River, at a point some twenty-five or thirty miles above its mouth, and built Stand-Off, a place of a few rude cabins. This is why we gave it the peculiar name: The marshal got on our trail and overtook us soon after we had crossed the North Fork of Milk River and were descending the slope to the St. Mary's.

"Well, boys," he said, smiling grimly, "I've caught you at last. Turn around and hit the back trail with me."

"I don't think we will," said Berry. "We're across the line. Better turn around and go back yourself."

A warm argument ensued. The line had never been surveyed, but we knew that according to the treaty it was the 49th parallel. We were on the Arctic Slope watershed, and therefore we assumed that we were in Canada; the marshal said that we were not. Finally Berry told him that he would not turn back, that he would fight first, as he knew that he was right. The marshal was powerless to take us, as he was alone. We "stood him off," and he sorrowfully turned back.

Another time Berry went into Fort Benton for liquor and the marshal trailed him around day and night. Nothing was to be done there, so he hitched up his four-horse team and with another man travelled up to Helena. Still the marshal followed, but Berry was a man of resource. He went to a certain firm there and got them to deliver thirty cases of alcohol to him on the banks of the Missouri a few miles below town, where he made a raft for them, got aboard, and pushed out into the current. Meanwhile the marshal was watching the four horses and wagon at the livery stable. That night Berry's helper got them out and started on the back trail. In a little while the officer caught up with the outfit, but lo! the wagon was empty and Berry was missing. He turned back and stayed all that night in Helena, then started again and arrived in Fort Benton about the same time as did the team. There the man loaded up with straight provisions and pulled out for the north. The marshal was completely nonplussed.

Meanwhile Berry was having a hard time. A raft of alcohol, which has but little higher specific gravity than water, proved a difficult thing to handle, and in rapid water was sometimes completely submerged. Sometimes it stuck on a bar or was in danger of hitting a rocky shore and he had to jump off and push it into deeper water. For three days he played beaver, and practically fasted, for his provisions got wet, but on the third evening he reached the mouth of Sun River with the loss of but one case of alcohol, which the rocks had punctured. There a four-horse team awaited him, sent from Fort Benton by the driver of his own outfit. The two men at once loaded up the wagon and struck out over the trackless prairie, crossing the line and arriving at Stand-Off without trouble.

The Bloods and Blackfeet gave us a fair trade that winter. We realised, however, that with the building of Whoop-Up we were too far west to be in the centre of the trade; so the succeeding summer we moved down some miles and built another post. The main event of the succeeding winter was the killing of Calf Shirt, the Blood chief, and a terrible man. He was absolutely ferocious and his people feared him, he having killed six or eight of them—several his own relatives. He came into the trade room one day and pointing a pistol at the man on duty there, demanded some whisky. The trader raised his pistol and fired, the bullet taking effect in the Indian's breast. He did not drop, however, or even stagger; nor did he shoot, but turned and walked calmly out of the door toward his camp. Upon hearing the shot a number of men elsewhere in the post rushed out, saw the pistol in his hand, and thinking that he had killed someone, began firing. Shot after shot struck Calf Shirt, but he kept calmly on for many yards, and

then fell over dead.   He possessed extraordinary vitality.
The body was thrown into the river through a hole in
the ice, but it came up in an airhole below, and was found
there.   The chief had always told his wives that if he was
killed they were to sing certain songs over his body, and
he would come to life, if they kept it up for four days.
The women took the corpse home and did as they had
been told, and felt very badly when they found that
their efforts were fruitless.   All the rest of the tribe,
however, rejoiced that the terror was gone.

The next winter a row broke out among the traders
and the wolfers of the country, the latter demanding that
no more rifles and ammunition be sold to the Indians.
They formed what the traders named in derision the
"Is-pit-si Cavalry" and went around trying to get signatures to an agreement, both by threats and entreaty,
that the traders would comply with their request, but
they met with little or no success.   Miss Laut also refers
to this "cavalry," and says that they were organised
by the smugglers to escort the freighters and defend the
fort.   The freighters needed no escort, and I would like
to know how men could be called smugglers who broke
no known law; who, it may be said, practically settled
the country and made it possible for a little band of
Mounted Police to march into it.   Miss Laut says that
the latter were the result of protests to the Dominion
Government "from the fur company deprived of lawful
trade."   They sold tobacco, tea, sugar, blankets, guns
and various notions.   So did we.   They sold watered
Jamaica rum and Scotch whisky.   We sold watered
American alcohol and whisky.   I claim that we were
just as respectable as the honourable lords and members
of the Hudson's Bay Company, Limited.   The latter,
at this very day, are selling liquor in nearly every town

of Alberta, Assiniboia and other territory of Northwest Canada, but we long since went out of the business.

I don't blame Miss Laut; she couldn't have known the facts. The men who told her the story—well, they slandered some pretty good men. None of them were what might be called saints, but the kindly, generous, honourable acts I have known them to do!

Many of the traders had thousands of dollars worth of merchandise in stock when the Mounted Police drew near, and most of them were warned in time of their approach to bury, or otherwise conceal the liquor. A band of hunters brought the news. "Some men are coming," they said, "who wear red coats, and they are drawing a cannon."

That was sufficient for Berry and me, and we promptly cached the ten or twelve gallons of whisky we had. Only one trader, I believe, failed to get the warning; he had his whole stock confiscated because among it were found a few gallons of liquor. Of course, we were not glad to see the strangers, but we met them with courtesy and treated them well. Although they had come through a country teeming with game they were in an almost starving condition, and were very glad to buy our provisions. Their commander, Colonel Macleod, was a gentleman, and became a life-long friend with some of the "smugglers." Many of the traders remained in that country to continue trade with the Indians and the newcomers, while others returned to Montana. We went with the latter outfits. None "slid out," but went from time to time decorously and peaceably, and with such of their possessions as they had not sold or given away. Thus passed the trade in the north. I cannot say that we regretted it. Prices of furs had fluctuated and dropped in value 100 per cent., few had cleared anything worth mentioning. Four years later the last of the Alberta buffalo herds drifted south and never returned to that section of the country.

We again took up our quarters in Fort Benton at the little adobe house and wintered there. It was a relief to be out of the trade for a time and rest up. A few of those who had been in the North with us crossed the river and located ranches on the Shonkin and along the Highwood Mountains. Berry and I thought that we did not want any ranching in ours.

We had frequently heard from Ashton. He seemed to be a man of unrest, now somewhere in Europe, again travelling in the States, once in a while visiting his protégée in St. Louis. Diana also wrote quite frequently, and her letters were now models of chirography, correct in grammar and phrasing. In some she spoke only of her school work and the petty incidents of her daily life. These, I fancied, were the ones the good Sisters glanced over before mailing them. But the others told of her dislike of the city. "I could bear it," she said, "if I could only see the great mountains once in a while, and the plains." She also spoke of Ashton and told how good he was to her, how happy she was when he came to visit there. He desired her in another year to enter a seminary: she would go, of course, for what her chief wished she would do, although she so longed to see the dear land in which she was born, and to visit us, if only for a day; but she could not tell him that.

And in one letter she told Nät-ah'-ki that Diana meant Sahm'i-ah-ki (Hunter Woman), and she was one who lived in the long ago, was a Sun woman, and never married. "And I must do likewise," she concluded pathetically, "for no one I could care for would love me, a plain, dark little Indian girl."

"Kyai'-yo!" the Crow Woman exclaimed when I had read this out. "I guess any young man in camp would be glad to have her."

"I think that I understand," said Nät-ah'-ki, meditatively. "I think that I understand. The ways of her people are no longer her ways; she has become a white woman in all but colour."

Every winter since his departure Ashton had written that he would visit us in the spring, but he never fulfilled his promise. We had concluded that he never would come again, when he surprised us by coming ashore from a steamboat one day in June. We were certainly glad to greet him, and in his quiet way he seemed to be equally pleased. We all went over to the house and when the women saw him they clapped hand to mouth in surprise and came forward to shake hands with him. "Ok'-i kut'-ai-im-i," they said. You will remember that they had named him Never Laughs, but he did not know that.

He was the same Ashton we had known, not given to much speech, and with the sad look in his eyes, although upon his arrival he talked more than usual and joked with the women, Berry or I, of course, interpreting.

"You ought to be ashamed," Nät-ah'-ki told him, "to come alone. Why didn't you bring Diana?"

"Oh," he said, "she is busy; she has her studies; she could hardly leave them. You should see into what a fine lady she has grown. She sends you all her love and some presents, which I will hand you as soon as my trunk arrives."

Nät-ah'-ki wished me to tell him that the girl was grieving for the sight of her country, but I would not do so. "We are not to mix up in his affairs," I said to her.

Nät-ah'-ki and I gave Ashton our room, and moved

out to a tent set up beside the house. But that was not for long.

"In summer in this country one should not live in a house," he said, one morning. "Ever since I left here I have been longing to stay in that lodge of yours once more. Many a time I've thought of that robe couch, the cheerful little fire, the quaint things scattered around. It was a place to rest and to dream. I'd like to try it again."

I told him that he should. Our lodge was about worn out. So Nät-ah'-ki sent word to the Piegan camp to her mother—they were out on the Teton somewhere—to get us a good one and bring it in; and when it arrived we set it up, and there Ashton camped with us. He would sit or recline on his couch as he used to for hours at a time, smoking, smoking, and silent. And his thoughts were not happy ones, for the shadow was in his eyes. And, as before, Nät-ah'-ki and I wondered what his trouble might be. She grieved herself for him and said many times: "He is very, very poor. I pity him."

A steamboat came in one evening, but none of us went over to see her land; they had become a common sight. We had finished supper, Nät-ah'-ki had cleared the table and lighted the lamp. Ashton had not yet returned to the lodge, but was standing by the light repairing his pipe stem. There was a sound of swishing of silk and then a tall and graceful woman crossed the threshold, raising her veil with an impatient gesture, and almost ran up to him, holding out her hands appealingly. We recognised her instantly. It was Diana.

"My chief," she cried, "forgive me! I could not help it. I so longed to see my country before I went back to school, that I left Alice and came. Oh, don't be angry; forgive me!"

Ashton had grasped her hands when she held them
out to him, and almost drew her to him, and I had never
thought to see his face brighten so.   It fairly beamed
with love and pride and joy, I thought.

"My dear! my dear!" he said, almost falteringly.
"Angry? Forgive? Your desires are always mine. God
knows I always wish you to be happy. Why didn't
you tell me? We could have come out together?"

But the girl was crying now, and Nät-ah'-ki, almost
afraid of this tall and stately girl, dressed in a manner
unknown to her, walked up and said: "My daughter—
you are my daughter, aren't you?"

"Oh, yes!" she faltered, and the two embraced.

We men filed out and left them together. Ashton
went to the lodge, Berry and I strolled up the trail a way.

"Good God!" Berry exclaimed, "I never thought that
one of our blood could be like that. Why, she plumb
knocks the spots off of any white woman I ever saw, in
some way. I can't explain the difference between her
and them, but it's there sure. What is it?"

"Well," I said to him, "it's a matter of education, and
of association with refined people mainly, I guess; and
well, some women are that way. I can't exactly explain
it myself."

"And did you notice how she's dressed?" Berry
added. "Plain like, yet somehow you know that those
clothes cost a heap of money, and were made by some-
body who sure knew how. And that locket hanging
down on her breast; all pearls and a big diamond in the
centre. My, my!"

She was beautiful, as we imagine Diana, her name-
sake, must have been. But where the goddess was cold
and calm and all disdainful, our Diana was gracious,
and, as we had seen, she had a heart.

We went back. The tears were gone; the women, Berry's wife, Năt-ah'-ki, old Mrs. Berry and the Crow Woman were sitting around her breathlessly listening to some of her experiences. She had not forgotten her mother's language. She arose and shook hands with us, and said how pleased she was to meet us again; that she had never forgotten our kindness.

After a little she went over to the lodge with Năt-ah'-ki and me, daintily holding up her skirts, carefully circling the little fire and sitting down opposite Ashton, who looked well pleased that we had come in.

"Oh," she cried, clapping her hands, "how well I remember it all, even to the coals of different fuel. You are burning cottonwood." And so she talked on, sometimes to Ashton and me, sometimes to Năt-ah'-ki, and we passed a pleasant evening. Berry and his wife gave up their room to her, and came also to live in the lodge. Somehow we could not ask her if she would like to live in it, she seemed to be above the old life entirely, out of place in it.

I must say that the girl created a sensation in the Fort or town, as it was beginning to be called. The bull-whackers and mule-skinners and the wolfers stared at her open-mouthed when she passed. The gamblers did their best to get an introduction. The real men, to whom she was introduced, treated her with profound consideration. We daily had visitors from the Piegan camp, the women regarded her with awe, and timidly shook hands with her. The chiefs even shook her hand and talked to her; the young gallants came and stood at a little distance, posing, and watching her out of the corner of their eyes.

One morning Ashton proposed that we should pack up and go somewhere for a month or two with the

Piegan camp, or, if it was safe, by ourselves out to the Belt, or the foot of the Rockies. Diana objected. "I would rather not go," she said. "You know I must soon return to school."

Ashton seemed to be surprised at her objection and so were we.

"My dear," he said, "I hoped you would enjoy such a trip. There is ample time for you to make it and return east for the school opening."

But still she made excuses, and the subject was dropped. She told Nät-ah'-ki, however, that she longed to go out on the plains and roam about once more, but that she was in duty bound to go back soon. "You can't understand how good my chief is to me," she said. "Always I have money, more than any of the other girls, more than I can use. And I have the finest clothes, lovely jewellery. Oh, he is so good and kind to me, and seems so pleased that I learn things. I have seen you all and my country once more, and he was not angry that I came. Now, I am going back to study hard."

"Isn't she good!" Nät-ah'-ki exclaimed, after she told me this. "And isn't she beautiful! I wish she was my real daughter."

"You simple thing!" I said. "She might be your sister; you are but little older, you know."

"I don't care," she concluded, "she is my daughter in a way. Didn't I take care of her and wipe away her tears, and do all I could when Never Laughs brought her home that bad day?"

CHAPTER XXVII

THE STORY OF ANCIENT SLEEPER

AS DIANA would not agree to the camping trip, Ashton did all he could to make her visit pleasant in other ways. He bought a horse and saddle for her—a wholly unnecessary proceeding, as we had plenty of both—and went riding with her up over the plains, and across into the Teton Valley, or wherever she chose to go. Every evening she came into the lodge and sat with us, sometimes happily talking, again silent for long intervals, dreamily watching the flames of the little fire. The girl was a puzzle to me. I wondered if she were in love with Ashton, or merely regarded him as any girl would a kind and indulgent father. I asked Nät-ah'-ki if she had ever speculated about it, and she replied that she had, but could not make up her mind how the girl felt.

It may have been ten days after Diana arrived that one afternoon she requested Nät-ah'-ki to pass the night with her, and of course the latter complied. I thought it a girlish whim. Diana was unusually silent all that evening, and many times, when Ashton was unaware of her gaze, I saw her looking at him with an expression in her eyes which I could not interpret as anything but intense affection. We retired early and, as usual, slept soundly. We were none of us early risers, and Nät-ah'-ki's warning call aroused us for breakfast. We arose and went into the house and took our places at the table. Diana was not at hand, and I asked Nät-ah'-ki why she

did not call her.   For reply she handed Ashton a note
and fled from the room.   He glanced at it and turned
white. "She's gone back!" he said. "She's gone back!"
He sprang from his chair, seized his hat, and rushed out
toward the levee.

"What's all this?"   I asked Nät-ah'-ki, whom I
found in the old women's room, sitting scared and still.
"Where is the girl?"

"Gone back to her reading and writing work," she
replied.   "I helped take her things over to the fire-
boat, and it went away."   And then she began to cry.
"She's gone!" she wailed. "My beautiful daughter
is gone, and I know that I shall never see her again!"

"But why?"   I broke in. "Why did she leave without saying anything to Never Laughs?   It was wrong;
you should not have helped her; you should have come
and told us about her plan."

"I did as she asked me to, and would do so again,"
she said.   "And you must not blame me.   The girl
was worrying, worrying, worrying.   She believed that
her chief was not pleased because she had come up here
away from where he had placed her, and she goes back
alone, because she feared that he would feel he must
accompany her.   She does not wish him to lose a pleasant summer, a big hunt somewhere, on her account."

Ashton came back from the levee. "She has certainly
gone," he said, dejectedly. "What madness possesses
her?   See this!" handing me the note.

"Dear Chief," it read, "I go back in the morning at
daylight.   I hope you will have a good time and kill
lots of game."

"What possesses the child?" he continued. "And
to think that I could have a 'good time' while she is
travelling down this cursed river unprotected!"

I told him what I had learned from Nät-ah'-ki, and he brightened perceptibly. "She does care then," he said. "I didn't understand; I have never felt that I knew her; but if this is the reason she went—well, I'll go back too, and I'll be at the levee in Saint Louis to meet her."

And he was as good as his word, leaving on the stage the next day for the Union Pacific Railway, by the way of Helena and Corinne. My parting words to him were these: "Old man," I said, "never doubt but what your protégée loves you. I know that she does."

The days passed monotonously. Berry fidgeted around, and was cross, and I became nervous and cross, too. We didn't know what to do with ourselves. "My father always told me," he said one day, "that a man who stayed in the fur trade was a fool. One might make a stake one winter, but he would be sure to lose it another season. He was right. Let's give it up, buy some cattle with what we have left, and settle down to stock raising."

"All right," I agreed. "It's a go. Anything suits me."

"We'll do some ploughing," he went on, "and raise potatoes and oats and all kinds of garden stuff. I tell you, it'll just be fine."

Berry's bull train had just pulled in from a trip to Helena. We loaded it with some lumber, doors and windows, what furniture we had, plenty of provisions and some tools, hired a couple of good axe-men, and started it out, we going on ahead with the women with a four-horse team. We chose a location on Back Fat Creek, not far from the foot of the Rockies, and less than one hundred miles from Fort Benton. We selected a site for the buildings, and then, leaving me to superintend their erection, Berry went away with a couple of men to purchase some cattle. It did not take long to haul enough pine logs from the mountains for a six-room shack, a stable and corral, and by the time Berry returned with the cattle, about four hundred head, I had everything fixed for winter, even enough hay for a team and a couple of saddle horses.

The Piegans were scattered that winter. Some were on the Marias, some on the Teton, and a number of lodges of them occasionally trailed in and stopped near our place for several weeks at a time. Buffalo were fairly plentiful, and up in the foothills there were all kinds of game. We had some trouble with the cattle at first, but in a few weeks they located, and thereafter it required little riding to keep them close herded. I can't say that I did much of the riding, but Berry enjoyed it. We had a couple of men, so I went out on little hunts with Nät-ah'-ki, poisoned wolves, caught trout in the deep holes of the creek, and just stayed with the women, listening to Crow Woman's and old Mrs. Berry's tales of the long ago.

The room Nät-ah'-ki and I occupied had a rude stove and mud fireplace, as did all the others except the kitchen, where was a good big stove. Previous to this, except when in Fort Benton, the women had always used a fireplace for cooking, and they still used one for roasting meat, and baking beans in a Dutch oven. Besides a bed and a chair or two, our room had a bureau—one of those cheap, varnished affairs—of which Nät-ah'-ki was very proud. She was always washing and dusting it, although it was never in need of such care, and arranging and re-arranging the contents of the drawers. Also, we had curtains to the window, tied back with blue ribbons, and there was a table which I made of a dry goods box,

covered with a bright blanket. At one side of the fireplace was a buffalo robe couch, willow back-rests at each
end. We had some argument over that. When I explained what I wanted, Nät-ah'-ki objected to its construction. "You disappoint me," she complained.
"Here we have built a home, and furnished it with
beautiful things," pointing to the bureau, bed, and curtains, "and we are living like white people, trying to be
white, and now you want to spoil it all by fixing up an
Indian couch!" But of course I had my way.

One evening we visited a camp of some thirty lodges,
of which one, Ancient Sleeper, was the head man. He
owned a medicine pipe and various other sacred things,
and did some doctoring, in which, besides various con-
coctions of herbs that were given the patient internally
or externally, a mountain lion skin, and prayers to that
animal, played an important part. When we entered
his lodge, I was welcomed and motioned to a
place on his left, Nät-ah'-ki of course taking her seat
near the doorway with the women. Above the old man,
securely tied to the lodge poles, hung his medicine pipe,
bound in many wrappings of various skins, Spread
over the back-rest at the right end of his couch was the
sacred lion skin. In front of him his everyday pipe of
black stone rested upon a large buffalo chip. Long
before, I had heard, his dream had commanded this,
and ever since the pipe he smoked had never been laid
on the ground. As in the lodges of other medicine men,
no one was permitted to walk entirely around the fire,
thus passing between it and the medicines, nor could any
one remove fire from the lodge, for by so doing the power
of his medicine might be broken.

Ancient Sleeper mixed tobacco and l'herbe, chopping
it fine, filled his pipe, passed it to me to light, and we

smoked together by turns. When I received the pipe, I took it from him with one hand; when I passed it to him, he grasped the stem with both hands, palms down, spreading and crooking his fingers, seizing, pouncing upon it, in imitation of the way of a bear. Thus did all medicine-pipe men; it was a sign of their order. We talked a little—about the weather; the game; the whereabouts of the people. The women set before us some food, and I ate of it as in duty bound. I had gone to the lodge with a purpose, and I began to edge around to it. I told him I had at various times in various places killed mountain lions. "I see you have the skin of one there," I concluded. "Did you kill it, or was it a present?"

"The Sun was good to me," he replied. "I killed it. It was all ik-ut'-o-wap-i (very sun power; very—let us translate it—supernatural) that which occurred.

"I was a man. I had a lodge of my own, my three women whom you see here. My body was strong. I was successful in everything. I was happy. And then all this changed. If I went to war, I got wounded. If I took horses, I lost them again; they died, or were stolen, or crippled themselves. Although I hunted hard, somehow I often failed to bring home meat. And then came the worst of all, sickness. Some bad ghost or evil thing got inside of me, and at times would grip my heart, so that the pain was terrible. When it did that, no matter where I was, what I was doing, the pain was so great that I became dizzy and staggered, and sometimes I just fell over and died for a short time (fainted). I doctored; I had the medicine men pray for me, giving a horse here, a horse there. I did not get any better, and I became very poor. At last we had only enough horses with which to move camp. Parties would no longer allow me to go to war with them; they feared that I would die on their hands, or in some way bring misfortune. I heard of a man, a Gros Ventre, who had suffered with the same trouble. He had bought a medicine pipe of great power, and by its use he had got well. He would sell the pipe, I was told, but I could not buy it. I had no fifteen or twenty horses to give for it nor even one. I preferred to die rather than have my women go afoot. Neither had I relatives to help me nor had my women any who could do so. Oh! I was very poor. Still somehow, I kept up courage, trying in every way to get well, and to provide for myself and mine. At last my dying times became so frequent that I no longer went hunting nor anywhere, except when one of my women accompanied me. They would not let me go off by myself.

"She there, my last woman, went with me one day on a hunt. We were camping at the time on the Pi-is-tum-is-i-sak-ta (Deep Creek) away up toward the headwaters, and we went on foot up into the pines of the Belt Mountains in search of anything that was meat. The camp had been in that locality for more than a moon and the game had moved away to farther foothills, and high up on the mountain. We travelled far before we found much fresh sign. At last, away up high on the mountain side I saw a band of elk move across an opening and disappear in the timber which surrounded it. The wind was right and I followed them, my woman keeping close behind me. Down into a deep coulée they went, across the stream at the bottom of it, and up the other side. But when we came to the stream we stopped, for there in the trail, fresh on top of the hoof marks of the elk, were the footprints of a real bear, a very large one. He, too, was hunting, and he was before me on the trail of the

"'I preferred to die rather than have my woman go afoot'"

elk. I gave it to him and turned back. I did not wish to meet him there among the thick pines. We came again to the opening and went into the timber in another direction, up toward the summit of the mountain. We found more fresh elk sign and followed it very cautiously step by step, looking, looking everywhere for sight of the animals. At last we came to the foot of a high cliff. Under it were broken rocks, bushes, low pines. Right out where the sun shone on it full, lay an elk, a two-year-old bull, head bent around to its side, fast asleep. I had but my bow and arrows. To make a sure shot, I must get close either above or below it, for the animal lay lengthwise with the cliff, and I had approached it from behind. It were useless to shoot it in the haunches; I must send an arrow down through its back, or from below up into its side. I chose to go along the foot of the cliff, and shoot downward. Never did I step more carefully, more slowly. I had to get that elk, for we were without meat, had lived for some days on that given us by more successful hunters. My woman had stopped and sat down to give me more chance in the approach. I glanced back and saw her looking at me, at the elk, signing me to be cautious. I went even more carefully, if that were possible, and was at last in a good position to shoot. I drew back the bow and let go the string. I saw the arrow sink down into the elk, saw it struggle to rise, saw blood stream from its nostrils, and then the pain gripped my heart. I staggered and died.

"I was a very long time dead, for when I came to life the sun had set and the last of his colours were fading behind him. I was lying in a sort of cave where my woman had carried me. I felt too weak to get up. She brought plenty of wood and made a little fire at the mouth of the cave. Then she brought water in a piece

of the elk skin, and some meat. I drank, and she fed
me, some roast liver, a marrow bone, a kidney, but I
was not hungry; I could eat only a few mouthfuls.
Neither could she eat; we felt very sad; both knew
that this time I had almost really died. She came and
lay down beside me and smoothed my forehead, speaking
words of courage, and after a little time I fell asleep.
Then my shadow went forth from my worn body. I
was free, as light as the bubble of the stream. I felt able
to travel wherever I wished to, and to understand all
things. Thus, as if I had been led, or shown the way,
I came to a fine, new, big lodge standing all by itself
at the edge of a grove, in a deep, wide valley in which
was a beautiful stream. Without hesitating, without
bashfulness, I raised the door skin and entered the lodge.
An old, old man was its owner, and he welcomed me,
gave me a seat beside him, told his woman to prepare
food. We smoked, and he asked many questions. I
told him all, all the story of my life, how I now suffered.
'Yes,' he kept saying, and 'Yes,' and 'Yes.' 'I know—
I understand.'

"We ate that which the women set before us, and he
again filled the pipe. 'Listen,' he said, as we smoked.
'Listen. Once I suffered as you do, and, like you, I
sought everywhere, in many ways for help, and at last
it was given to me. I regained my health. My hair
has turned white, my skin wrinkles, I am very, very old;
yet still my body is strong and sound, and I provide
myself the meat for this lodge. All this because I found
a powerful helper. I pity you. As I was told to do,
I will now tell you; heed my words and follow the advice,
and you, too, will live to great age.

" 'First, as to your sickness: Some ghost, perhaps
that of an enemy you have killed, has in some way

entered your body and set up an evil growth in your stomach. It must be removed, for it grows larger and larger, pressing against the heart, and unless it is checked, will soon press so hard that the heart cannot work; then death. You must kill a mountain lion, have the skin tanned, leaving the claws on the feet. You must take good care of this skin, and at night hang it or place it near the head of your couch. So, when you lie down to sleep you will pray, saying, 'Hai'-yu! maker of claws; Hai'-yu! maker of sharp, cutting claws, I pray you to aid me; claw away this thing which is threatening my life, and will surely kill me without your aid!' Thus you must pray to the maker of claws, to the shadow of the ancient lion himself. Also, you must learn these songs— and he taught me three [here Ancient Person sang them, needless to say, with all the deep, sincere feeling that the devout express in their sacred songs]. Also, he said, that I must always lay my pipe on a buffalo chip, for the buffalo was a sacred animal, and that when I prayed, blowing smoke to the four directions of the world, to those above, and to our mother (earth) my prayers would have more power.

"It must have been far away where I found that good old man, for my shadow did not return to my body until after sunrise. I awoke and saw it shining into the cave. My woman had rebuilt the fire, was cooking. 'Let that be for a time,' I said, 'and come and sit with me.' I told her all; where I had been, what the kind old man had said, and she was glad. Right there one-half of the arrows in my quiver, with the tongue of the elk I had killed, we hung up as a sacrifice, and then we went home, my woman carrying meat, as much as was possible for her to handle. I could carry but little.

"I had a North gun (Hudson's Bay Company's make),

but no powder and no balls; the one flint was bad.
From a friend I borrowed a trap and in a short time I
caught six beavers with it. Another friend going in to
Fort Benton to trade took them with him and brought
me what I needed, new flints and ammunition, and then
I began to hunt mountain lions. I had never hunted
mountain lions; neither had any of our people. Some
one occasionally came across one and killed it, and he
was thought to be a lucky man, for the skins of these
animals have always been medicine. They are made
into quiver and bow cases, or the owners use them for
saddle skins. Used in any way, they give one success in
hunting or in war. No, I had never hunted these animals
but now I was bound to get one. Again she there and
I went afoot into the mountains. I took both gun and
bow, the latter for killing meat. The silent arrow
alarms nothing; the boom of a gun arouses every living
thing; the sleeping ones awake, prick up their ears, sniff
the wind, and watch.

"We walked along the shore of the creek. Here, there,
plainly marked in the mud, and on damp sand were'footprints of those I sought, footprints, but nothing more.
We went into the deep timber; although many might
have passed there, they could make no sign, leave no
tracks on the dry, dead leaves. We went higher, up
through the timber, up where the rock is chief and trees
grow small and low. There we sat all through the day,
peering out through bushes surrounding the place, seeing
once a small black bear, once a fisher, but no other living
thing, except little birds, and eagles lazily flying around.
But near sunset came a band of bighorn feeding toward us,
following the wind. I fitted an arrow to my bow and
shot one, a little young one. It bleated and fell over,
and the rest, at first running away scared, came back

with its mother and looked at it curiously, looked all
around, trying to understand what had happened. I
then shot the mother. We left her lying, in hopes of
finding a mountain lion by it the next day, and taking the
young one we went away down the mountain and camped
for the night near a stream of water.

"We passed many days like that, many days. We
camped wherever night came upon us, going home only
when our lodge required meat, or when camp was to be
moved. Thus passed the summer, and in all that time
we saw not once that which I sought. Twice during that
time I died, and each time I was dead longer than before.
I became much discouraged; I did not doubt my dream's
words; no, I was sure that old man had spoken truth,
but I felt that I was going to die before I could do all
he had told me to do. From the Belt Mountains we
moved to Yellow River, from there across to Snowy
Mountains. Then came winter, and snow fell on the
high slopes, falling lower, still lower, until the mountains
were white clear to the plains. Nothing was now hidden
from me of the happenings of the night; wherever I
went the snow gave me the story as well as if some one
had looked on, had seen it all, and then related it. Here
walked, and fed, and played, and rested deer and elk;
here a bear prowled around, turning over logs and stones.
There were tracks of wolf, and coyote, and bobcat and
fox, each hunting in his own way for something with
which to fill his belly. Yes, and here, what is this heap
of brush and sticks and leaves, soiled snow and earth?
Up through it protrudes an antler. Over there is blood;
something has been dragged through the snow. Ah!
there, over there, is a trail of big, round footprints near
together. Here in the night a mountain lion sprang
upon a buck deer, killed it and ate his fill, dragged the

remains over to his place and covered them with all the loose things he could paw together. Thus I explained it to my woman. 'And,' I told her, 'he has not gone far; his belly is full; somewhere near he lies stretched out, asleep.'

"But what should I do? Hide somewhere nearby and wait for him to return? He might not come until far in the night when I could not see him. He might, when coming, get wind of me and turn, never to come back. No, I would trail him. I would go as carefully as he himself when he crept along, preparing to spring upon a deer. I would see him before he should awake and notice me, and I would kill him where he lay. Thus did I plan; thus did I explain to my woman telling how to follow me at a distance, just so near that she could see me once in a while, no nearer. She was pleased. 'You will surely kill him,' she said. I was glad, excited. After all these moons at last I had a trail to follow, and on the snow that was almost as good as seeing the animal far off and approaching him. Think then, friend, think of my despair when, almost within sight of the covered deer, I found where the animal had lain on a big log, had seen us talking, and bounded away into the dark woods with long leaps! It was too much. Again I got dizzy, staggered, and was dead before I dropped upon the snow.

"That time my woman got me home, going back for a horse for me to ride, and I lay in the lodge many days, weak in body, sick in heart, discouraged. But friends came in to cheer me. Their women brought choice meat, and tongues, dried berries, soups, anything good. So we fared well, and day by day my strength came back. At last, one evening, a friend who had been hunting came hurrying in. 'Kyi!' said he, 'I have good news for

you.   Up in a cañon where I trailed a wounded deer, I
came to a hole in the rocks.   A hard-beaten trail leads
from it out to the water, then parts into many smaller
trails.   A mountain lion lives there with her young.   I
did not scare them.   I did not even kill the deer I
followed to the place, but came at once to tell you.

"Once more I took courage, and as soon as it was
daylight I started for the place with my friend and my
woman.   We rode away to the south, then up a creek,
tied our horses and entered a walled cañon.   From
there it was not far to the cave.   Snow had fallen during
the night; the freshest tracks led into the cave; in there
was the mother, and three young, partly grown, and they
were somewhere back in the darkness, watching us
perhaps.

"I was scared; of course I was.   Men had been killed
by these animals when following them into their dens.
And this one had young; she would fight all the more
fiercely.   Yes, I was afraid, but for all that I must go
in; as well die there as in some other place, of the sickness from which I suffered.   I prepared to go in.   My
woman cried and begged me not to go.   My friend proposed that we sit and watch for the animals to come out.
I fixed the priming in my gun, took my knife in my
teeth, got down on my hands and knees and crawled in.
It was just a narrow, low hole in the wall, and my body
shut off most of the light, yet there was enough for me
to see ahead dimly, and after a little I saw before me
two green-red eyes, big, wide eyes of fire.   I stooped
lower, letting in more light, and could see the old one's
body, see her ears laid back tight on her head, see the
tip of her tail swishing this way, that way.   She growled
a little, a low, soft growl.   She lay on her belly and her
forefeet shifted back and forth, seeking the secure hold;

she was about to spring upon me. More dimly I saw her cubs behind her, but they did not matter. I slowly raised my gun, but before I could aim it, she sprang. I fired; the ball met her in the air; her body struck me and knocked the breath out of me, and once more I died.

"They pulled me out of the cave, and, while my woman cared for me, my friend went back in, shot the three young with his bow and arrows, and dragged them out with the body of the mother. My ball had struck her fair in the breast. So, now, at last, I had that which my dream had told me to get, and I prayed, I sang the songs as I had been told to do. It was not many nights after that, sitting on my couch, I said the prayers and sang the first one of the songs. I had just finished it when something gave way inside of me, and blood and foul matter streamed from my mouth. There was no pain. After a time the blood ceased running. I washed my mouth, got up and walked around. I no longer felt a tightness here in my side. I felt light on foot; as if I could run and jump, and I was hungry. I knew what had happened; even as the old man had foretold, the growth inside me had been clawed open. I was well. We made great sacrifice for this next day. I have been well ever since. Not only that, but my medicine has cured many sick ones. Kyi!"

That is one of the stories I heard that winter and jotted down in my note-book. Verily, there is nothing like faith and courage for the cure of ills, mental and physical, in savage and in the civilised alike.

For Nät-ah'-ki and for me this was a happy winter. It was for all of us except Berry, who chafed over the "endless days of cold and snow." I don't know how many times he went down on the flat and measured it. So many acres here for oats, so many there for potatoes, for turnips, for peas. We would buy a lot of sows, he said, and raise pigs as well as cattle. Spring came early. Toward the end of March the bulls were rounded up and yoked to the plows. Old Mrs. Berry and the Crow Woman prepared a little plot of ground in a bend of the creek, and sorted seeds they had obtained at some distant time from their people, the Mandans and Rees. I didn't know anything about ploughing and planting, nor did I wish to learn.

Nät-ah'-ki and I rode among the cattle—and found that the calves disappeared about as fast as they were born. Wolves were numerous. "Oh!" she would exclaim, as we rode slowly homeward from a day with the cattle. "Oh, isn't this happy and peaceful! Our strong, warm home there, our pretty room, the men planting things for us, the good meat we own feeding on these hills. Oh, it is much better than living in a camp and trailing from place to place across endless plains, ever expecting to hear the yells of the enemy and the whistle of bullets!"

"Oh! I don't know," I replied. "This is good enough. I like any place my little woman likes; but don't you remember what fun we had in camp, the dancing and feasting, the big hunts, the stories we heard of nights. That was great fun, Nät-ah'-ki."

"Shame on you!" she exclaimed. "I really believe you are an Indian, even if your skin is white. Now, I want to be white, to live like white people, and I'm just going to make you do so, too. Do you hear? You must quit these Indian ways."

In June more than a foot of snow fell upon our fields of growing things, and when it melted, there came a frost and froze everything. Berry cursed loud and frequently. In July and August we tried to put up some hay, but rain spoiled it as fast as it was cut. In the fall we had no grain to thresh, no potatoes nor turnips. not even cabbage to put into our big root house. After the fall branding, we found that we had an increase in our cattle of only 15 per cent. The wolves were accountable for the additional forty-five per cent. we should have had. "This here ranching and cattle raising," said Berry, "isn't what it's cracked up to be. Let's sell out and get back into the trade. There's more fun and excitement in that anyhow."

Of course I agreed to that, and he went into Fort Benton to find a buyer for the place. He found one, but the man would not make the deal until spring, so we put in another winter there, which was also a happy one for some of us—for Nät-ah'-ki and me, at least. Ah, me! why shouldn't we have been happy? We were young, we loved each other; nothing else mattered.

CHAPTER XXVIII

MAY found us again installed in the little abode in Fort Benton, but not for long. Berry was anxious to be doing something and, learning that Fort Conrad was for sale, we bought it. This place, as I have previously mentioned, was built at the upper end of a large bottom on the Marias River, where the Dry Fork joins the larger stream. It was not much of a fort, just two rows of connecting log cabins, with stables and a corral at the west end of them, the whole thing forming three sides of a square. It was a good location, however, for, besides the trade in robes we expected to get, it was on the trail between Fort Benton and Fort Macleod, and the travel and freighting over it was heavy in the summer time. The women were especially pleased with the purchase. They had regretted leaving our home on Back Fat Creek, but now they had another one, farther away from the mountains, where the summers were warmer and longer. "Here," said Crow Woman, "my beans and corn and squash will surely grow. I am glad."

"This is happiness," Nät-ah'-ki said, as we sat in the shade of a big cottonwood by the river's edge. "See the beautiful trees above there, and below, and the pretty island with its young timber. And on all sides the high, steep hills—protection from the winter winds."

"Yes," I said, "it is a pretty place. I like it better than I did the other one."

"Say this for me," she continued, leaning over and drawing me to her. "Say this: We will live here always; live here until we die, and they bury us out across there where the big trees grow."

I said it, and added thereto, "If it be possible for us to do so," watching the expectant, pleased expression of her eyes suddenly change to one of pain.

"Oh, why," she asked, "why did you spoil it all? Don't you know that you can do anything you wish to?"

"No, I don't," I replied. "No one can always do only that he wishes to do. But let us not worry; we will try to live here always."

"Yes," she sighed, "we will try; we will have courage. Oh, good Sun, kind Sun! Pity us! Let us live here in peace and happiness to great age."

Even then Berry and I had some idea of the changes that were to take place, but we did not dream that they were so near at hand. We looked for the old, free, careless times to last for fifteen or twenty years at least.

Unannounced, without having written a line of their intention to visit us, Ashton and Diana drove in from Fort Benton one evening, having arrived there by steamboat the day before. Nothing could have pleased us more than to welcome them back. Nät-ah'-ki actually cried from joy as she clasped her "daughter" in her arms. We noticed instantly a great change in Ashton. We could no longer call him Never Laughs, for he began joking and laughing before he got out of the wagon; there was a merry glint in his eyes; he ran around like a boy, throwing things out recklessly. The sad, solemn, silent, slow-moving Ashton had been, as it were, reincarnated; and it did us good to see the change in him; it made us joyous with him.

And Diana, ah! there was a woman, if you please!

Words fail me. I cannot describe her. Diana she was in features and figure, but the spirit within was that of the noble, human, loving, gentle woman—all pure, all good. Who could believe that this was the thin, frail, wild-eyed little thing Ashton had rescued and brought to our lodge not so many years since? Could this lovely, accomplished, refined woman have been born in a lodge and trailed with her people over the plains in pursuit of the moving herds? It seemed impossible.

What a happy evening we passed. How vivacious, and affectionate Diana was, sitting now with Nät-ah'-ki, again with the old woman, clasping them lovingly in her arms, inquiring into all the little incidents of their daily lives. Education, travel, a knowledge of the great world had not turned her head; the people of her blood were as dear to her as ever. She told me that it had been her daily practice to speak over in the quiet of her room so much Blackfoot, to translate a verse or two of English into it, lest she forget her mother's tongue.

I cast about in my mind for the cause of the change in Ashton. "Perhaps," I thought, "he has fallen in love with Diana; is going to marry her; he may already have married her." I looked at her hand; she wore neither engagement nor wedding ring. It was late when we separated, Diana going with the old woman to their room, Ashton to a spare one we had. When we were alone, Nät-ah'-ki came over, leaned against me, and sighed heavily. "What is it?" I asked. "Why are you sad?"

"Oh!" she exclaimed, "I am so disappointed. This long, long time I have been praying for it, yet it has not come to pass. Why doesn't he marry my daughter? Is it that he thinks she is not good enough

for him? That he does not love her? How can he help
loving one so handsome, so good, so true-hearted?"

"Little woman," I said, "don't be impatient. I
think everything will come right. Have you not noticed
how different he is—how he laughs, how bright his eyes
are? I am sure that he loves her; that if he has not
asked her to marry him, he will when he thinks that the
right time has come."

Little did we think as we sat and talked, how near
that time was, and what an unexpected and dramatic
event would lead up to it. 'Twas a few evenings later.
Ashton was lazily smoking, sitting by the table in my
room. There was a bit of fire on the hearth, occasionally flaring up and illuminating the rude walls, again
dying away, leaving everything shadowy and dim.
Diana and Nät-ah'-ki sat together on a couch; I lay
stretched out on the bed. We were all silent, each one
occupied with his thoughts. A team and wagon were
driven into the little square outside, and through the
open door we heard a silvery, anxious voice ask, "Can
you tell me, sir, if Mr. Ashton is stopping here?"

Ashton sprang from his chair, made one or two strides,
stopped, considering something for a moment, then
returned and resumed his seat.

"Yes, madam," Berry was saying, "he is here; you
will find him over in that room."

She did not notice us as she hurried in. The flame
leaped up, revealing Ashton's face, pale and stern. She
hurried over to him and placed a hand on his shoulder.
"Oh, my dear," she cried, "I've found you at last. I
wrote several times. Did you never get my letters?
Oh, I'm free; free, do you hear? I've got my divorce;
I've come to tell you that it was all a mistake; to beg
your forgiveness; to——"

"Diana, child, come here," said Ashton, quietly, interrupting her. The girl arose and walked over to him, placed her hand in the one he held out to her appealingly. The woman—and she was a tall, handsome one, too; fair-haired, blue-eyed—stood looking at them in astonishment, in fear, her hands clasped convulsively on her bosom.

"Diana, my dear," Ashton continued, looking lovingly down into her face, "will you marry me?"

"Yes, Chief," she replied, clearly, firmly. "Yes."

He arose, and put his arm around her, facing the other woman. "Sadie," he said, "I forgive you all that you have done to me—your broken promises, your unfaithfulness, the years of misery I passed in trying to forget. I have found peace and happiness at last, thanks to this dear one by my side. I bid you goodnight, and good-bye. No doubt you will be returning to town early in the morning."

With his arm still around her waist, he and Diana passed out of the room. The woman sank into the chair he had vacated, bent over on the table, burying her face in her arms, and sobbed heart-brokenly. Nät-ah'-ki and I arose, and also left the room, tiptoeing across the floor and out into the night. "Oh!" the little woman exclaimed, when we were well beyond the fort. "Oh!" and she shook me as hard as she could. "Why didn't you teach me your language? Tell me quick, who she is. What said they? What did he tell my daughter?"

I explained it all as clearly as I could, and then Nät-ah'-ki nearly went crazy with joy. She danced around me, and kissed me, and said that I was a good boy. I hoped I was. I couldn't see, though, that I had done anything to further this much-desired end of affairs between Ashton and Diana. We came upon them sitting on the shore end of our ferryboat. "Come here," said Ashton. Diana jumped up and embraced Nät-ah'-ki, and the two went back to the house.

"Old man," I said, "I congratulate you. You've found peace and happiness, as you well said a few moments ago. You can't help being happy with Diana."

"Ah!" he exclaimed, "isn't she—my boy, what she is to me, has long been, is beyond the telling. I feel that I am not worthy of her; yet she loves me devotedly, truly. She told me so here to-night."

"But about the other one?" I ventured. "What are we going to do with her?"

"She cannot go back to-night. Have Nät-ah'-ki give her something to eat and a bed. I presume her driver can look out for himself."

"That woman has been the curse of my life," he added. "I loved her deeply, devotedly. She promised to marry me. I believed in her goodness and faithfulness as one does in that of his mother. But she threw me over for a wealthier man. And now—now—well, enough of her; I'm going to find Diana and ask her to walk with me."

"There is some cold, boiled meat," said Nät-ah'-ki, "some bread and stewed sarvis berries. If she will come into the Indian country hunting my daughter's man, even that is too good for her. I will make her a bed of buffalo robes and blankets, although she doesn't deserve it."

But the woman would not eat. Nät-ah'-ki made a bed for her on the floor of the trade room, and there we left her to her thoughts—and they were no doubt bitter. In the morning she asked for Ashton, begged me tell him to come to her for a moment. I told her that he had gone hunting and would not return until evening. She chafed at the driver's delay in hitching up, refused anything but a cup of coffee which I carried in to her. At last the team was ready, and she got in and started away without once looking back, without even thanking us for her night's lodging. And thus she passed out of Ashton's life.

I had told her truly that Ashton had gone hunting; he and Diana had ridden away at sun-up, but I imagine they did not go far—waiting on some nearby hill to see the visitor depart. As soon as the conveyance had crossed the bottom and climbed the hill up on to the plain, they returned, as happy and high-spirited as two children, and we all had breakfast together.

"This is what we may call our wedding breakfast," said Ashton, as we all sat down.

"That so?" Berry asked. "Are you going in to the Fort to-day and be married? You can't make it with such a late start."

"No," he replied, hesitatingly. "No. Diana and I have talked the matter over, and we are agreed that a simple signed and witnessed marriage contract is just as valid as is a marriage before a justice of the peace or by a clergyman. We intend to make it out this morning. What think you, friends?"

"It strikes me all right," said Berry.

"And me, too," I replied.

"My parents married without any ceremony whatever," Diana remarked. "Anyhow, what pleases my Chief pleases me." She looked across at him, and there was a world of love and faith in her eyes.

Năt-ah'-ki, sitting by my side, gently pressed my knee, which was one of her ways of asking what was being said. I told her, but she made no comment,

remaining silent during the meal. The old woman and
Mrs. Berry were pleased with the idea. "Ai!" said the
Crow Woman. "Let him fix the paper. It is enough;
writing cannot lie. What matters a Black Robe saying
many words? People married and lived happily together all their lives before these talking men were ever
heard of. They can do so still."

But after breakfast Nät-ah'-ki called me aside. "Will
this way of writing things make her sure enough his
wife?" she asked. "A wife according to the white men's
laws?"

"Indeed it will," I replied. "It will be a marriage
that can no more be put aside than ours. As strong as
if a thousand Black Robes together had said the words."

"It is well then; I am glad; let them do it at once. I
want to see my daughter married and happy with this
good man."

Right there on the dining table, the breakfast things
having been cleared away, we drew up the paper, Ashton
and I. Omitting the date and signatures, it read:

"We, the undersigned, hereby agree to live together
as man and wife until death parts us."

Short, wasn't it? They signed it. So did Berry and
I, as witnesses, the women standing by and watching us
interestedly. Then Ashton took Diana in his arms and
kissed her gently before us all. There were tears in her
eyes.

You see how frank and open they were before us; not
at all ashamed to show their love, express their feelings.
It did us good. We felt that we were witnessing something very sacred, very ennobling. It made us think
good thoughts; gave us the desire to lead better lives
ourselves.

They went out, remounted their horses and passed the

day somewhere on the big plains which Diana loved so
well. In the evening we saw them returning, riding slowly
side by side. "The Sun is good," said Nät-ah'-ki. "He
has listened to my prayers and given them perfect
happiness. Tell me, do you love me as much as he
does my beautiful daughter?"

Never mind what my answer was. I think it was
satisfactory.

The marriage contract was sent in to Fort Benton
and recorded by the County Clerk. Unless it was burned
in the fire which destroyed the Court House some years
later, the curious may find the transcription there. The
contract itself stamped with the county seal, was duly
returned and given to Diana.

We now made ready for a hunt, long postponed. Nät-
ah'-ki sent for her mother, I for my good friends Weasel
Tail and Talks-with-the-buffalo, just three lodges of us.
They having arrived, we pulled out westward one lovely
July morning, en route to the Two Medicine Lakes.
Passing the Medicine Rock, Nät-ah'-ki seriously and
Diana mischievously laid upon it little sacrifices, the
former a bead necklace, the latter a bow of ribbon from
her hair. For some ten or twelve miles the trail led over
the high rolling plains, where we saw some antelope and
a few buffalo. Weasel Tail circled out and killed one of
the former, a fat, dry doe, which saved Ashton and me
from making any exertion toward supplying meat that
hot day. 'Twas more pleasant when we again rode down
into the valley of the Marias, where the trail wound
through cool groves of cottonwood, crossing and re-
crossing the river, over shallow, rippling fords, where
the animals drank as if they could never get enough.
Late in the afternoon we arrived at Willows Round, a

large, broad bottom, where good old Sorrel Horse had, as he said, ceased from wandering and built himself a home.   At that time this place, our Fort Conrad, and Mose Solomon's, at the mouth of the river, were the only ones located on the whole length of the Marias.   Now every last bottom on both sides of it, no matter how small, dry, and worthless it may be, is enclosed with someone's wire fence.

Our lodges were pitched near the new cabin of peeled, shining logs, and we strolled over to inspect it.   Sorrel Horse greeted Diana with marked embarrassment.   She seemed to him, with her dainty, gracious ways, dressed as she was in a wonderfully becoming out-door suit, to be a creature from a far and unknown world.   He addressed her as "Miss Ashton."   I corrected him. "Mrs. Ashton," he said, "excuse me, ma'm."

Diana walked over and placed a hand on his shoulder. "Dear friend," she said, "is that all the greeting you have for me—can't you wish me joy?"

His constrained manner disappeared instantly; he bent over and lightly kissed her.   "Bless your heart," he said.   "I wish you all the happiness in this world. Put it there; shake."

In the evening he brought over a bundle of fine beaver skins and threw them down by the doorway of our lodge. "Here's something," he told Diana, "for your wedding present.   They'll make you a warm cloak.   Somehow this ranchin' business don't hit me right; it's too lonesome, and I can't help but go out an' set my traps once in a while."

Bear Head was camping with Sorrel Horse, herding the cattle and making himself generally useful; but when we came along he threw up his job and ordered his wife to make preparations to accompany us.   The grim old mountains were calling him also. There were now four lodges of us. Bear Head's the greatest, for it sheltered a half dozen children of various ages. Their happy laughter and prattle enlivened our otherwise quiet camp.

In the morning an early start was made, and evening found us away up on the Medicine River, where the first pines grow. The next noon we went into camp on the shores of the lake, our lodges being pitched in a grassy little bit of prairie on the north side. Back of us rose the long, high pine and quaking aspen ridge, which divides the deep valley from the plains. In front, across the lake, was a long cliff-topped mountain of gray sandstone, its slope densely forested with pines. The grand view was to the west. First, but three or four miles distant, a huge, heart-shaped, snow-patched mountain, which I named Rising Wolf, in honour of the greatest plainsman of us all, my friend Hugh Monroe. Beyond that, hemming in a vast amphitheatre of lake and forest, rose more mountains, cliff-faced and needle-pointed, forming the divide of the great range. Rose and gold they were in the rising sun, jet black when silhouetted against the evening sky. We never tired of gazing at them, their shifting colours, the fleecy clouds of a morning banding their splendid heights.

The camp site selected, Ashton and I jointed the rods he had brought out from the East, set reels, strung lines, and attached the moistened leaders and flies. Then we walked down to the outlet of the lake, only a hundred yards or so distant, followed by every one in our camp, including the children. I had talked about the pleasures of fly-fishing. The Indians were anxious to see this, to them, new phase of the white man's arts. Ashton made the first cast, and his artificial flies were the first that ever lit upon the waters of the Two Medicine. The response was generous. The placid water heaved and swirled with the rush of unsophisticated trout, and one big fellow, leaping clear from the depths, took the dropper with him in his descent. The women screamed. "Ah-hah-hai'!" the men exclaimed, clapping hand to mouth, "Strange are the ways of the white men. Their shrewdness has no end; they can do everything."

The big trout made a good fight, as all good trout should do, and at last came to the surface floating on its side, exhausted. I slipped the landing net under it and lifted it out, and again there were exclamations of surprise from our audience, with many comments upon the success of it all, the taking of so large a fish with such delicate tackle. Trout we had in abundance, rolled in yellow corn meal and fried to that delicate brown colour, and unsurpassable flavour which all true fishermen appreciate.

The sandbars along the inlet to the lake were all cut up with tracks of elk and occasional moose. Once upon a time the beavers had constructed a huge dam clear across the valley and parallel with the shore of the lake, but the stream had broken through it, and the erstwhile bed of the great pond was now an almost impenetrable thicket of red willow, a favourite food of the moose. Ashton said that he wanted to kill one of the great animals, and requested us to let him have that especial part of the valley for his hunting ground. Thither he and Diana wended their way every afternoon to wait and watch for some unwary game to appear, often remaining so late that they had no little difficulty in finding their way home through the dark forest. Thus day after day was passed, but no shot was ever heard from their retreat, and each night they had to report that they hadn't seen a living thing larger than a passing mink or beaver.

"The newly married man," Bear Head remarked, "can only get meat by leaving his woman in the lodge and going away to hunt alone."

"Ai, that it true," Weasel Tail agreed. "They cannot sit quietly together. They have so much to say: 'Do you love me? Why do you love me? Will you always love me?' Such are the questions they ask each other, over and over again, and never tire of answering. I know all about it; we were that way ourselves once, hah, my girl?"

"Ai!" his wife replied, "that you were, and you still keep asking those questions. How silly you are!"

Of course, we all laughed at Weasel Tail, and in truth he looked rather sheepish over his wife's frank disclosure. He hurriedly changed the subject by saying that he would himself go with the hunters in the afternoon, and try to get them a shot at the desired game.

They returned quite early that evening, and asked Weasel Tail to eat supper with us. "Well, what luck had you?" I inquired.

Neither Diana nor Ashton seemed inclined to answer, bending over their plates after a quick glance at each other, and becoming very much interested in their food. I repeated the question in Blackfoot, and Weasel Tail laughed heartily. "It is as I suspected," he replied. "There are many tracks on the sandbars of elk, and moose, and deer, but they are very old; no game has been along there these many days. Out on the point of a sandbar lies a big log, from which one can see far up and down the river. There they have sat, and the game, coming to water, have seen them first, looking cautiously through the bushes before stepping out in the open. They have talked, too, very low they say, but a moose can hear even the fall of a distant leaf. Also, the winds have blown up and down and across the valley, and told of their presence, and one by one the animals have left, sneaking away with careful footfalls to distant places."

"Well, it doesn't matter," said Diana, in Blackfoot. "We have sat and looked at the grand old mountains, and the clear streams, the feeding trout and prowling minks, and our tramps have given us health and strength. After all, that is better than killing things. Isn't that true, Chief?" she asked, repeating to Ashton in English what she had said.

"We have certainly had a pleasant time, my dear," he replied, smilingly; "but we have not contributed our share; we must try some other place to-morrow, and bring home meat."

Nät-ah'-ki and I went with them the following morning, riding up the valley to the shore of the upper lake on the way. We stopped to view the falls, which are certainly interesting. The river disappears in a mass of large boulders a short distance below the lake, and a mile farther down gushes from a cañon in a high cliff into a lovely foam-flecked pool. The cliff itself is at least a hundred feet in height, and the fall is about a third of that. There are no trout above the pool.

Seen from a distance, the mountain I had named Rising Wolf was grand and imposing; from a nearer view, it proved to be a truly stupendous mass of red and black, and dark-gray slate. It rises steeply from the depths of the lake in a series of reefs and cliffs, cut by streams of talus, and tapers to a sharp, walled dome. High up on its eastern side, in a deep and timbered pocket, lies a field of perpetual snow and ice. There are grassy slopes, and groves of pine, thickets of sarvis and blueberry here and there, clear up to the foot of the dome.

"Mah-kwo'-i-pwo-ahts!   Mah-kwo'-i-pwo-ahts!" * said Nät-ah'-ki, softly. "Truly, his name will never die."

I know not what life there may be now upon the mountain's grassy slopes and beetling cliffs, but on that day the wild creatures were certainly in evidence. On the lower part several bands of ewe bighorn and their young; higher up, singly and two and three and four together, some old rams, lazily feeding or lying down, but always watchful of their surroundings. And then, up on the higher cliffs there were goats, numbers of them, the snow-white, uncouth, long-haired alpine creatures which the naturalists tell us are really antelope.

"Always Laughing," said Nät-ah'-ki to Ashton— she had given him a new and happier name, you perceive—"remember your words of yesterday! Across up there is plenty of fat meat; go and kill some, lest we starve."

"Oh," he said to Diana, "tell her that it would be a sin to kill the pretty things. We cannot starve, for there are always plenty of trout to be caught in the pool below our lodge."

"In other words," I remarked, "he is too lazy to climb. Well, I will not go. I have killed my share of the provisions, and we'll do without meat until he provides it."

Just then a big bull elk appeared on the farther shore of the outlet, and Ashton, crawling slowly back into the timber behind us, went after it. We sat as still as possible, anxiously watching the animal and our horses,

---

* Rising Wolf! Rising Wolf!

fearing that it would take fright at them. The women were so excited that they could scarcely contain themselves. "Oh," one would whisper, "why doesn't he hurry?" And then the other, "It is going away, he'll never get a shot at it. Isn't it too bad?"

The bull was in a happy mood. He drank standing belly-deep in the water, walked out and kicked up his heels, raced up and down the beach several times, sniffed and pawed the sand. And then a rifle cracked, and he fell limply, instantly, and never even kicked. We went over with the horses, and I cut up the animal, taking all the best of the fat and juicy meat.

Thus the days passed in peace and happiness. Before we left, the skins of bear and moose and elk, deer and goat and beaver adorned our camp, killed mostly by the Indians. Ashton hunted little. He preferred to sit and gaze into Diana's splendid love-lit eyes, and I—had I not Nät-ah'-ki, faithful, true, and tried companion? Her gay laughter and happy chatter is still echoing in my ears.

CHAPTER XXIX

A GAME OF FATE

WE RETURNED to the fort early in September, and shortly afterward Ashton and Diana went East. Nät-ah'-ki was for a time well nigh prostrated over the separation, for she fairly worshipped Diana. Indeed we all felt sorry to see them depart, for they were truly, both of them, very near and dear to us all.

During the summer we had put in a good stock of merchandise, expecting to have a fine winter trade at the fort, but now came the disquieting news that there were practically no buffalo to the north, the west, or the south of us. We could not believe it at first; it seemed impossible; somewhere away to the north we argued, the great herds still roamed, and in due time they would return. But theory soon gave way to fact. Save for a few hundred in the Great Slave Lake country, and a few more scattered about the Porcupine Hills, the buffalo had drifted southeastward from the plains of Northwestern Canada into Montana, and they never recrossed the line. This was the winter of 1878–79, it will be remembered. At the same time the herds which had ranged along the foot of the Rockies from Canada south to the Missouri River left that part of the country never to return. South of the Missouri to the Yellowstone and beyond, in all Montana, save on the headwaters of Milk River, the Marias, Teton, and along Sun River, and into western Dakota, the buffalo were,' however, apparently as plentiful as ever.

The Piegans had intended to winter in the vicinity of Fort Conrad and trade with us, but of course they were obliged to change their plans and go to buffalo, and we had to accompany them to get any trade at all. We left it to the women whether they would remain at home or accompany us, and all but Nät-ah'-ki elected to stay at the fort. Her prompt decision to accompany me was exceedingly pleasing, for I had felt that it would be well-nigh impossible to go alone, even for a few months; that the life would be unendurable. Yet for her own sake I demurred: "You love this place," I said to her. "You can be comfortable sitting here before the fire when Cold Maker comes down from the North. You had better remain."

"Is it because you love me no more," she asked, "that you tell me this?" And when I replied that I was thinking only of her comfort, she added: "I am no white woman, to be housed up, and waited on. It is my duty to go with you and do the cooking; keep the lodge warm; do all I can to make you comfortable."

"Oh!" I said, "if that is why you would go, just because you think you must, why, remain here. I'll live with Weasel Tail; his wife will take care of us."

"How you can use words!" she exclaimed. "Always, always you search around with them and make me say all that is in my mind. Know then, if you will, that I go because I must follow my heart; you have taken it."

"That is exactly what I hoped you would say; but why could you not have told me at first that you wanted to go because you cared for me?"

"Know this," she replied, "a woman does not like to be always telling her man that she loves him; she likes to think it and to keep it deep down in her heart, lest he tire of it. That would be terrible, to love and have your love cast aside."

Many and many a time I have thought of that talk by the evening fire, and I wonder, I wonder now, if all women are that way, chary of expressing their innermost thoughts. Women, I take it, are generally past men's understanding; but I believe that I knew Nät-ah'-ki. I believe I knew her.

We pulled out, Berry, Nät-ah'-ki and I, with a couple of four-horse team loads, leaving a man to look after the fort and the women. Travelling by way of Fort Benton, we were several days passing the mouth of the Marias. Just beyond that point the sight of buffalo on all sides gladdened our eyes, and we found the Piegan camp, pitched at the foot of the Bear Paws, red with meat, littered with drying hides. Nät-ah'-ki's mother was on hand as soon as we came to a stop, and the two women put up our lodge while Berry and I unharnessed and cared for the stock. We finally turned them over to a boy who was to herd for us.

Big Lake's shadow had some time since departed for the Sandhills. Little Dog, another great leader and friend of the whites, had been dead a still longer time. White Calf was now the head chief of the tribe, and after him, Running Crane, Fast Buffalo Horse, and Three Suns were the principal men. They were men. Bighearted, brave, kindly men, every one of them; ever ready to help the distressed by word and deed. Our lodge was no sooner set up and supper under way than they came in to smoke and feast with us, Nät-ah'-ki's mother having gone around to invite them. Also came Weasel Tail and Talks-with-the-buffalo and Bear Head and other friends. The talk was mainly about the disappearance of the buffalo in the North and West.

Some thought that they might have crossed the mountains; that the Nez Percés or some other tribe of the other side had found some means to drive or decoy them to the plains of the Columbia. Old Red Eagle, the great medicine-pipe man, declared that his dream had reliably informed him about the matter: "As it happened before in the long ago," he said, "so it is now. Some evil one has driven them into a great cave or natural corral in the mountains, and there holds them in his hate of us to whom they belong. They must be found and released, their captor killed. Were it not that I am blind, I would undertake to do it myself. Yes, I would start to-morrow and keep on, and on, and on, until I found them."

"It may be that your dream speaks truth," said Three Suns.

"Have patience; in summer our young men will go out to war, and they will search for the missing herds."

"Ai! Ai!" the old man grumbled. "Have patience! Wait! That is what they always say. It wasn't so in my day; was there something to do, we did it; now it is put off for fear of winter's cold or summer's heat."

White Calf closed the subject by saying that even if some one had cached the northern herds, there seemed to be a plenty left. "And they're on our own land, too," he added. "If any of the other side people come over here to hunt, we'll see that they never return; some of them at least."

We had been asked to trade, even before we unhitched our horses, but Berry said that nothing would be done in that line until evening. The feast over, and our guests departed, people began to flock in. One for a rifle; another for cartridges; others for tobacco, or sugar, coffee, and some, alas! for spirits. We had

nearly a wagon load of alcohol, which we diluted, four
to one, as occasion required. Before bedtime we sold
over five hundred dollars' worth of goods, wet and dry,
and it was easy to see that Berry would be kept pretty
constantly on the road all winter, hauling our furs to
Fort Benton and returning with fresh supplies of merchandise.

There was an unusual craze for gambling that winter.
By day, the men, when not hunting, played the wheel and
arrow game, rolling a small bead-spoked disk down a
beaten path and trying to throw, or cast an arrow into
it as it whizzed along. At night the camp resounded
with the solemn, weird, gambling chant from many
lodges. There the players sat, the two sides facing each
other, and played the "hide the bone game," striking
with small sticks the outer rail of the couches in time to
the song. Even the women gambled, and many were
the altercations over their bets.

In a lodge near us lived a young couple, Fisher and
his woman, The Lark. They were devoted to each
other, and were always together, even on the hunts.
People smiled and were pleased to see the untiring love
they had for each other. They seldom went visiting,
but were always making little feasts for their friends.
Fisher was a fine hunter and kept his lodge well supplied
with meats and skins, and he was a successful warrior,
too, as his large herd of horses testified. He was so devoted to his pretty little woman that he never went out
to gamble of an evening, nor invited parties to gamble
in his lodge; they played too long. Feasts were well
enough, for they were soon over, and he loved the quiet
evenings, just he and his woman chatting by the fire
after the guests had gone. Sometimes, when The Lark
was chipping a robe, and it was too cold to sit outside

and talk to her while he worked, Fisher strolled away to the nearest wheel game and played for a while. He was quite an expert at it and won more frequently than he lost. But one evil day he played against a young man named Glancing Arrow, and lost ten head of horses. I was busy trading in our lodge, but from time to time I got news of the game, and listened to the comments on it. Glancing Arrow, it seemed, had himself wanted to set up a lodge with The Lark. Her parents, for reasons unknown—he was a rich young man—had rejected his gift of horses and given her to the Fisher, who was not nearly so well off. This had pleased every one, for the Fisher was loved by every one, while Glancing Arrow was a surly, cross-grained, miserly sort of a fellow, and had not a single close friend. He had never married, and once had been heard to say that he would yet have The Lark for his woman.

"Fisher is crazy to gamble with him," said one of my customers. "To gamble with the best player in the camp, and the man who is his enemy. Yes, he is certainly crazy."

There was more news next morning. Sore over his loss, the Fisher had sought out Glancing Arrow, played the bone game with him nearly all night, and he had lost twelve more horses! In the course of the forenoon The Lark came over to visit Nät-ah'-ki, and I was called into the conference. The woman was crying and sorely distressed. "He is sleeping now," she said, "but when he awakes he is going to play with Glancing Arrow again. I have begged him not to, but for the first time he refuses to listen to me. All he will say is, 'I shall play; I shall win back my horses.' Just think, twenty-two horses are already lost, nearly half of our band, and to that dog, Glancing Arrow! Were it any one else who had

won them, I would not care so much; but to him! to
him!" And her sobs checked her words for a time.

"Go over and talk with him," she continued. "He
thinks much of you; will listen to your words; go and
talk him out of this madness."

I walked over to their lodge and found the Fisher still
in bed, lying propped up on one arm and staring moodily
at the fire. "You needn't say it," he began, before I
could open my mouth. "I know why you have come in;
she sent you to ask me to play no more, but I'm not
going to stop. I can't stop until I have won back all
that I have lost."

"But look here," I put in. "You may lose more if
you keep on, perhaps all you have, for I hear Glancing
Arrow is the most skilful of all the players. Just think
how much you are risking; what a shame it would be
were you to be set afoot, no horses with which to move
camp, not even one for your woman to ride."

"Oh! that could not happen," he said confidently.
"I could not lose them all. No, there is no use of your
talking. I must play again with him, and I'm sure that
I will win. I shall pray. I shall make a sacrifice. I
must win."

A howling southwest wind set in before noon, so there
was no gambling with the disk and arrows. The other
game could not be played in the daytime, according to
the ancient custom, lest bad luck befall the players. The
sun had not long set, however, before they began again,
the Fisher and Glancing Arrow, in the lodge of Heavy
Top. A big crowd gathered there to witness it, and to
encourage the Fisher, whom every one loved as much as
his opponent was despised. The Lark came over to our
lodge and sat with Nät-ah'-ki, who tried to cheer her
up with encouraging words, and stories that might direct

her thoughts from her trouble. But she was not to be amused and kept saying that she felt that something dreadful was going to happen. Time and again she went out and stood by the lodge in which the gambling was going on, listening and returning to tell us how the game progressed. "He has lost another horse," she would say; "they are going one by one." Once she reported that the Fisher had won one back. "But he'll lose it in the next game," she concluded despondently and began to cry.

"Oh! do go over there and put a stop to it," Nät-ah'-ki entreated me. "Do something, say something to end it."

I went, utterly at a loss what to do, quite sure that I was setting out on a useless errand, but still I went. The lodge was crowded, but room was made and I found a seat well to the back of it, and near the players. When the Fisher saw me, he frowned and shook his head, as much as to say: "Leave me alone." And, indeed, before that crowd I felt that I was powerless; that I could neither entreat nor advise him to stop playing and go home.

By the side of Glancing Arrow lay a little heap of small, red-painted, cylindrical sticks, used for markers, and each one represented a horse that he had won. I looked over in front of his opponent and counted seven more sticks. The Fisher had, then, but seven horses left. "We will play for two head this time," he said and threw two sticks out on the ground between them. The other placed a like number beside them, and the Fisher took the bones, one red-painted, the other with black bands. They began the song, the onlookers also joining in and beating time on the couch rail. Manipulating the little bones, the Fisher deftly passed them from one hand to the other, back and forth, back and forth, carried his hands within the robe folded across his lap, while he changed them there; then, at the conclusion of the song, he suddenly extended both fists toward his adversary, looking him steadily in the eyes. Raising his clenched right hand, forefinger extended, Glancing Arrow slapped it down into the palm of his left hand, the forefinger pointing at the left fist. The Fisher reluctantly opened it and exposed to view the black-banded bone. He had lost, and had now but five horses. He picked up the markers, counted and recounted them, divided them into parts of two and three, twos and one, and then bunching them, said: "These are the last. I will play you for the five head."

Glancing Arrow smiled; a cruel, sinister smile it was, and his evil little eyes sparkled. His eyes were set unusually close together in his hatchet-like face, and his large nose was very thin, and bowed owl-beak-like over his thin lips. His countenance always reminded me of the picture you see on tins of deviled ham. He made no comment on this raise of the stakes, but quickly laid out his five markers, and picked up the bones. Again the song began, and swelling out his bosom, he sang loudest of all, crossed his hands back and forth, up and down, forefingers crookedly extended. He rubbed them together, opened them and exposed the black-banded bone, now in one palm, now in the other, changing it so quickly that the observer was bewildered, or made certain that the bone still remained in the hand where he had last seen it, only to find that it had in some way been slipped into the other one. It was the latter ruse which deceived Fisher, for the instant the song ceased he pointed to the player's right hand, and the losing bone was tossed to him from it.

"Well," he said, "I have still a rifle, a lodge, a saddle, war-clothes, blankets, and robes. I will bet them all against ten head of horses."

"Ten it is," Glancing Arrow agreed, laying out ten markers, and again manipulating the bones as the song was renewed. But this time the song was not so strong. Some, perhaps from the acute interest they had in this last unusual stake, or because they wished to show their disapproval, did not sing at all, and those who did were half-hearted about it. And, as usual, Glancing Arrow won, won and laughed wickedly, loudly. The Fisher shivered as if from cold, drew his robe about him, preparing to leave. "Come over to-morrow," he said, "and I will turn it all over to you—the horses and everything else."

"Wait!" Glancing Arrow exclaimed, as he arose. "I will give you one more chance; I will give you the chance to get back everything you have lost; I will bet everything I have won from you against your woman."

Every one present clapped his hand to his mouth in surprise, and there was exclamations, deep and heart-felt, of horror and disapproval. "The dog!" one said. "Knock him on the head!" cried another. "Throw him out!" others exclaimed.

But Glancing Arrow did not heed them he sat non-chalantly bunching and counting his markers, the cruel smile still on his lips, the evil fire in his beady eyes. The Fisher shivered again, arose and passed around to the doorway. There he stopped and stood like one in a trance. Could it be, I wondered, that he was even con-sidering the offer? I arose, too, and went over to him. "Come home with me," I said. "Come to my lodge; your woman awaits you there."

"Yes, go, go!" said others. "Go home with him."

But he shook my hand from his shoulder and quickly returned to his seat. "Begin!" he cried to his adversary. "We will play. We will play for her"—and he added under his breath, "for her and another thing."

Perhaps Glancing Arrow did not hear the latter part of the sentence, or, if he did, he made no sign. He picked up the bones and began to sing, but no one joined in, not even the Fisher, and looking at the rows of sullen, scowling faces staring at him, he faltered, but kept on with it in a manner to the end, and extended his closed hands before him. There ensued a moment of tense silence. Breasts heaved and eyes flashed, and if wishes could have killed, Glancing Arrow had died where he sat. I myself, in spite of my raising, felt an almost uncontrollable desire to spring upon him, bury my fingers in his throat and choke him to death. Some, indeed, half rose from their seats, and I saw several hands firmly gripping a knife handle.

The Fisher looked him steadily in the eyes so long and with such an agonising expression, that the suspense became almost unbearable. Twice he raised his hand to denote his choice, and twice drew back. But at last he pointed to the left fist, and received—the unmarked bone!

Some of the onlookers sprang up; there were cries of "Kill him! Kill him!" Knives were drawn; Heavy Top reached for his carbine. But the Fisher motioned them back to their places, and there was that in his expression, something so quiet, and ominous, and determined, that they obeyed him. "Come to-morrow," he told the winner, "and you shall have all that you have won."

"No," said Glancing Arrow, doggedly, "not to-morrow. I will take the lodge and the robes and the blankets and the woman to-night; the horses to-morrow."

"Come on then, it shall be as you say."

And somehow we let them pass out into the darkness. No one followed, nor spoke. We all felt that something was going to happen. But some of those who had been standing outside listening, did follow, and there were several witnesses of the end of it all. The Lark had been standing behind the lodge, had heard herself put up for the last stake; heard the demand of the winner, and then she had fled homeward. A little later, almost as swiftly went thither the Fisher, followed by the man who had won his all. They went inside, a man or two entering in behind them.

"There she is!" the Fisher exclaimed, pointing to the couch where the woman lay completely covered with a buffalo robe. "There she is," he continued, "but you shall never touch her. I am going to kill you, to make a sacrifice of you here in her presence."

His words and the terrible expression of his face so paralysed Glancing Arrow that he did not try to defend himself, but sank to the ground, crying, "Have pity, pity me!" even before the Fisher sprang upon him and thrust a knife again and again, deep into his neck and bosom.

We sitting in the lodge awaiting we knew not what, heard the dying man's screams and rushed out, tearing the lodge skin loose from its pegs as we went. When I had reached the scene, it was all over. Glancing Arrow lay dead beside the fire and the Fisher stood over him looking down at his work, a pleased, childish expression on his face.

"Why, yes, of course," he said softly, dreamily, "I remember now, he wanted her; he has always wanted

her, my little woman. And I have killed him. See,
little woman, he is dead, completely dead; you need
fear no more to go to the river for water, or to the timber
for fuel. Get up and see for yourself; he is surely
dead."

But The Lark did not move, and, bending over, he
drew back her covering, and gave a heartrending, gasping
cry. She, too, was dead. Covering herself with her
robe, she had grasped a knife in both hands and pressed
it straight down into her heart. Her hands still firmly
held the hilt, and if ever a dead face expressed anguish
and horror, hers surely did. The sight seemed to bring
the Fisher to his senses—I doubt not that he had been
demented for several days. "It is my fault," he said.
"My fault, my fault! But you shall not go alone. I
am with you yet."

And before any of us could interfere, he plunged the
knife he still held into his own bosom, and fell over
beside her, the life-blood streaming from his mouth.
Oh! it was a terrible sight, one that often returns to me
in my dreams, and I awake, shivering and bathed in
perspiration. We men fled; there was nothing we could
do. Women came and prepared the bodies for burial,
and in the morning they were taken away and lashed in
their aerial sepulchres. Then we moved away from the
place, eastward to the next little creek. There was no
gambling thereafter for a very long time, the whole camp
went into mourning, as it were, for the two young lives
we missed. Fortunately, or unfortunately, as different
persons may view it, the Blackfoot language is exceedingly poor in words for cursing; but such as it contains
we used often to execrate the memory of Glancing
Arrow.

CHAPTER XXX

TRADE, HUNT, AND WAR PARTY

OUR trade flourished. Berry was almost constantly on the road, so I had few opportunities to do any hunting. There were days when I saw a band of buffalo 'loping swiftly over the distant plain pursued by the hunters, or when some friend came into our lodge and told of an exciting chase—I found camp life irksome at such times, and longed to be able to go and come as I pleased.

"To-morrow you shall be trader," I said to Nät-ah'-ki one evening, "and I will go hunting. I must have a ride. I am getting weak sitting here in the lodge day after day."

"You shall go," she said. "Why didn't you tell me long ago? I can trade as well as you can. I know just how much to give for everything. But I will *not* put my thumb in the cup when I measure out sugar or coffee or tea."

"The cup has no handle," I interposed.

"But there are other cups of the very same size with handles. You and Berry ought to be ashamed of yourselves, to so cheat these poor people. Now, here is the one"—picking up a new tin one that Berry had just brought from the Fort. "This is the one I shall use. See, it has a strong handle and—and"——she turned it over and over, examining inside and outside. "Why, what a strangely made cup; it has two bottoms; it will

348

hold only a little more than half as much as a real cup. Oh, what rascals you traders are!"

"Wait!" I exclaimed, "you do not understand. There is another trader in this camp. He gives four cups of sugar for a wolf skin; with this one we have had made we will give seven cupfuls of sugar, or four of coffee, or five of tea. The people will get just as much for a skin or robe as they did before, but the other trader has no false cup; he cannot give as many real cupfuls; we will drive him out of here and get all of the trade."

And that is just what we did. As I have remarked before, Berry was the man to get trade; no one could successfully compete with him.

I went hunting in the morning as I had planned. There were six of us, including Big Plume and his nephew, a very bright, handsome, likeable young man named Moccasin. There were eight or ten inches of snow on the ground and the weather was cold. Thick, low clouds drifting southward obscured the sun, and snow fell intermittently, at times so fast that we could not see objects a hundred yards away. We rode eastward for four or five miles, before we saw anything save a few scattering bulls, and then a lull in the storm permitted a temporary view of a large scope of country. A half dozen bands of buffalo were in sight, one of several hundred head not half a mile farther on and across a wide coulée, a branch of which extended to where we were. We sat very still on our horses until another flurry of snow came down and blotted out the landscape, when we rode into the side coulée, down it and across the large one, and climbed the hill on the other side. When we topped the rise we were right in the herd, and then it was every man for himself. It was all very misty and un-certain chasing the white-covered creatures in the snowstorm, and half-blinded by the stinging clouds of snow their sharp hoofs threw into our eyes. I trusted to luck to ride safely among the hidden prairie dog and badger holes, and to bring down the quarry when I fired. The muffled reports of my companions' rifles sounded very far off, my own seemed more like the discharge of a toy pistol than anything else, yet before I had emptied the magazine I saw three different victims stop, and stagger, and fall, and I felt that I had killed my share of the game, and brought my excited horse to a stop. The others did even better than I, and we were several hours skinning our kill and preparing the meat for packing. Not that we intended to do that; the hunters' women would come for it the next day, and Big Plume was to have my share taken in for one of the hides and part of the meat.

It was all of 2 o'clock when we started homeward, after tying to our saddles the tongues and other choice parts of the buffalo. The wind had veered to west northwest and was blowing harder, driving the snow in clouds before it. We had not progressed more than a mile, shielding our faces with our hands or blankets, and trusting to our horses to find the back trail, when some-one cried out: "A war party ahead! Look! See them run!" And sure enough, there they were, a couple of hundred yards distant, five men running as fast as they could for the shelter of a nearby coulée. Moccasin was ahead of us and he put the whip to his horse as soon as he sighted them, regardless of his uncle's cries to wait and be cautious. Long before we could overtake him he had charged after them, firing his carbine rapidly, and we saw one of them fall. They, too, fired at him, and we saw that they carried muzzle-loaders. He was now almost on top of the four fleeing men when the one who had fallen rose up as he was passing and discharged a pistol at him, and doubling over in the saddle he hung on for a moment, then fell limply to the ground, his horse turning and running wildly back to us.

Big Plume hurried over to where he lay and dismounting beside him, raised him up in his arms. The rest of us made short work of the war party. One or two of them succeeded in reloading their guns and firing at us, but they did no damage and fell one after another, riddled with bullets from our Henry and Winchester repeaters. They were Assiniboins, of course, sneaking around in the cold and snow of winter as usual, and they had met their just deserts. My Piegan companions were for once quiet over their success, not even letting out a single shout of victory. They felt too badly over the fall of Moccasin, and quickly scalping and taking the weapons of the dead, they gathered around him in mute sympathy. It was plain to be seen that he had made his last run, fired his last shot. Cold as it was, beads of perspiration gathered on his pale face, and he writhed in pain. He had been shot in the abdomen. His horse had been caught and stood with the others nearby. "Help me to get into the saddle," he said faintly. "I must get home. I want to see my woman and my little girl before I die. I must see them. Help me up."

Faithful old Big Plume was crying. He had raised the young man and been father to him. "I can do nothing," he sobbed, "nothing. Some of you lift him up. Someone ride ahead and tell them what has happened."

"No," the wounded man said, "no one shall go first; they will learn about it soon enough. I am badly hurt, I know, but I am going to live to reach my lodge."

We got him up into the saddle and one, mounting behind, supported his drooping form. Another led the horse, and thus we resumed our homeward way.

Twice he fainted, and we stopped in a sheltered coulée, spread blankets and laid him on them, bathed his brow with snow and fed him snow when he revived. He was thirsty, calling for water, water, continually. The way seemed terribly long and coming night added to the general gloom of our party. We had started out so happily, had been so successful, and then in an instant death had come among us, our swift home-going had been changed into a funeral trail, a life full of happiness and love and contentment was going out. That was the way of it on the plains; the unexpected was always happening.

We came to the edge of camp at dusk and filed in past the lodges. People gathered and inquired what had happened. We told them, and some ran on ahead spreading the news. Before we came, Moccasin's wife ran from her lodge to meet us, sobbing heart-brokenly, cautioning us to be careful and carry him in as easily as possible. We laid him on his couch, and she leaned over and held him to her bosom, kissed him fervently, and called on the Sun to let him live. I went out and to my own lodge. Nät-ah'-ki met me at the doorway. She, too, was crying, for Moccasin was a distant relative. She looked at me anxiously to see if there was any blood on my clothes, and there was plenty of it, buffalo blood.

"Oh," she gasped, "and they have shot you, too? Show me, quick, where is it? Let me call for help."

"It is nothing," I told her, "nothing but blood from my kill. I am as well as ever."

"But you might have been killed," she cried. "You might have been killed. You are not going hunting any more in this country of war parties. You have no business to hunt. You are a trader, and you are going to stay right here with me where it is safe to live."

Moccasin, poor fellow, died in less than an hour after we got him home, and the wailing of wife and relatives was heart-breaking to hear. It was a sad time for us all, and made us think of the uncertainty of life. Three of the kindliest and best loved ones in the whole tribe had gone from us in so short a time, in such an unlooked-for manner.

We did not get all of the robes that were tanned that winter; whisky traders occasionally visited the camp and by giving large quantities of very bad liquor, bartered for some of them. The Piegans also made frequent trips to Fort Benton to trade. But we did get 2,200 robes, to say nothing of deer, elk, beaver, and other pelts, and were well satisfied. About April 1 we were home again at Fort Conrad, and Berry began at once to tear up the big bottom with his bull teams. Of nights he used up many a sheet of paper figuring out the profit in raising oats, sixty bushels to the acre, and in the pork-raising industry, sixteen pigs to the sow twice a year—or maybe thrice, I forget which; anyhow, it all seemed very plain, and sure, on paper. More plows were bought, some Berkshire pigs were ordered from the States, a ditch was dug to tap the Dry Fork of the Marias. Yes, we were going to be farmers for sure.

Away down at the end of the bottom, where the Dry Fork and the Marias met, the women planted their little garden and erected a brush-roofed summer house, under which they would sit in the heat of the day and watch their corn and pumpkins grow, morning and evening faithfully irrigating them with buckets of water. I passed much time with them there, or with rude pole and line angled for catfish and goldeyes in the deep hole nearby, the while listening to their quaint songs and still quainter tales of the long ago. Time and again Nät-ah'-ki would say: "What happiness; what peace. Let us pray that it may last."

The Piegans drifted westward from the Bear's Paw country and most of them returned to their agency, which was now located on Badger Creek, a tributary of the Marias, about fifty miles above the Fort. Some, however, encamped across the river from us and hunted antelope and deer, killing an occasional buffalo bull. Reports from the Agency told of hard times up there. The agent was said to be starving the people, and they were already talking of moving back to the buffalo country.

CHAPTER XXXI

NÄT-AH'-KI'S RIDE

WEEK after week, the Piegans waited for the buffalo to reappear on the plains of their reservation. With the hot weather they thought that some of the herds to the eastward would stray up to the cooler altitude, and they still believed that somewhere in the unknown fastnesses of the Rockies hordes of the animals had been cached, and that in some way they would be able to return to the open country. In the meantime the hunters scoured the foothills in quest of deer and elk and antelope, finding some, it is true, but barely enough to keep their families from actual starvation.

In our ranching work we were no more successful than the hunters in the chase. There were no rains, with the result that the Dry Fork remained dry, and our irrigating ditch was useless. Also, the thoroughbred Berkshires we procured from the States brought with them, or contracted en route some disease, and all died except the boar. He finally succumbed, after feasting upon the month's-old carcass of a strychnined wolf. All this was very annoying to Berry, but I must confess that I did not feel very badly about it. I was never cut out for a tiller of the soil, and I hoped that this experience would prove to him that he was not, either. We had a few cattle. They roamed the bottoms and the nearby hills, waxed fat on the short grama-grass and increased. Who would plough, and sow, and reap, if it rained, in preference to sitting in the shade and watching a bunch of cattle grow? Not I.

We did sit in the shade, the women and I. True, there was cooking to be done, but it was a matter of a few moments to boil some meat, bake a pan of biscuit, and heat the contents of a couple of tins. We did not go in for those things which require hours of preparation, and make women red in the face from heat and loss of temper. Washing? We wore soft things and none too many of them. There wasn't an ounce of starch in the land, thank heaven! Long bull trains trekked down into the bottom, and I sold the dust-powdered bull-whackers beer, and buckskins, and tobacco. I bought deer and antelope skins from the Indians, but mostly I sat in the shade.

In June the river was bank-full from the melting snow of the Rockies, and our cable ferry was used by all travellers. One day I had to cross a bull train, and for the first trip seven yokes of bulls were driven on board, all the yokes attached to the long lead-chain with which they pulled the wagons. I took the wheel, the ropes were cast off, and we left the shore, the bull-whacker of the team standing beside me. He was a French creole, a voluble, excitable, nervous man, as are most of his kind. When midway in the stream, where the water was deepest and swiftest, the lead yoke of bulls backed into the next one, they into the one behind them, and so on until they were all huddled to the rear of the boat, and their great weight threw the bow and upper side of the craft clear above the surface of the stream. Water poured into the hold through the submerged deck, and the increasing weight of it tilted the bow higher and higher until the bulls could no longer retain their footing and they began to slide off.

"Oh, mon Dieu!" the bull-whacker cried, "it is that they will drown; that they will in the chain entangle. Return, m'sieur, return to the shore!"

But I could do nothing, the boat would neither go forward nor back, and kept settling deeper in the water, which gurgled ominously under us. The bulls, finally slid off en masse, and how they did roll and snort and paw, often entirely submerged, but, strange to say, they drifted down to a bar and waded safely out in spite of the dangerous chain to which their yokes were attached. Freed from their weight the ferry surged the other way, dived into the stream as it were, and the strong current bore it down.

"Oh, mon Dieu! Oh sacré!" the Frenchman cried. "Save me, m'sieur. I cannot swim."

And he ran toward me with outstretched arms. I sprang backward to avoid his threatened embrace and fell, and the water sweeping over the deck carried me with it. I didn't mind that much, for I knew that the current would take me to the bar where the bulls had landed. I looked back at the Frenchman. The boat was now deep under the water and he had perched on the centre hog-chain post, which was itself only a couple of feet above the surface. I can see him to this day, sitting there on top of the post, his eyes saucer-like with terror, the ends of his fierce moustache pointing to heaven, and I can still hear him, as he repeatedly crossed himself, alternately praying and cursing and calling on his comrades ashore to save him from the turbid flood. He was such a funny sight that I laughed so I could hardly keep my head above the water.

"Hang on, Frenchy!" cried the wagon boss and others. "Just hang on, you'll come out all right."

He shook his fist at them. "H' I am sink. H' I am

drown. You maudit whack eet de bull," he answered,
"an' you tell me hang on. Oh, sacré! Oh, misère!
Oh, mon Dieu!"

I doubt not that he might have let go and sunk had
the boat settled any deeper in the water, but just then
the cable parted and it rose so that the deck was
barely awash, and drifted along after me. Down jumped
Frenchy and pirouetted around on its slippery surface,
and shouted and laughed for joy, snapped his fingers at
the men who had jeered him, and cried: "Adieu, adieu,
messieurs, me, I am bound for St. Louis, an' my sweetheart." The boat drifted ashore not far below, and we
had no difficulty in towing it back and repairing the
cable. Frenchy, however, would not cross with his
bulls, but went over with a load of the wagons, and he
took a plank with him, to use as a float in case of accident.

In the hot summer nights Nät-ah'-ki and I slept out on
the edge of a high-cut bank near the river. Oh, those
white, moonlit, perfect nights! They were so perfect,
so peaceful, that the beauty and wonder of it all kept us
awake long after we should have been sleeping soundly.
An owl hooted. " 'Tis the ghost of some unfortunate
one," she would say. "For some wrong he did, his
shadow became an owl, and he must long suffer, afraid
of the Sun, mournfully crying of nights, before he can
at last join the other shadows of our people who have
gone on to the Sandhills."

A wolf howled. "Oh, brother, why so sad? It
seems as if they were always crying for something that
has been taken from them, or that they have lost. Will
they ever find it, I wonder?"

The river now moved and gurgled under the bank, and
roared hollow down the rapid in the bend below. A
beaver, or perchance a big fish, splashed its silvery sur-

face, and she would nestle closer, shiver perhaps. " 'Tis
the people of the deep waters," she would whisper.
"Why, I wonder, was it given them to live away down
in the deep, dark, cold places, instead of on the land and
in the bright sunlight? Do you think they are happy
and warm and content as we are?"

Such questions I answered to the best of my ability.
"The goat loves the high, cold, bare cliffs of the mountains," I said to her, "the antelope the warm, low, bare
plains. No doubt the people of the river love its depths,
or they would live on the land as we do."

One night, after listening to the hooting of a big owl
up on the island, she said; "Just think how unhappy
that shadow is, and even were it permitted to go on to
the Sandhills, still it would be unhappy. They are
all unhappy there, our people who have gone from us,
living their shadow, make-believe lives. That is why I
do not want to die. It is so cold and cheerless there,
and your shadow could not be with me. White men's
shadows cannot enter the home of the Blackfeet dead."

I said nothing, and after a little she continued: "Tell
me, can it really be true that which the Black Robes say
about the next life, that the good people, Indian and
white, will go away up in the sky then and live happily
with World Maker forever?"

What could I do but encourage her? "What they
say," I replied, "is written in their ancient book. They
believe it. Yes, they do believe it, and I do, too. I am
glad to believe it. Even the Indian may enter there;
we can still be together after this life is over."

Still I had no comment to make, but I thought of
those lines of the old tent-maker:

> "And many a knot unravelled by the way,
> But not the knot of human fate."

But what a beautiful thing it is to have faith. He who has it—that simple, unquestioning, unreasoning faith of our ancestors; why, his heaven has begun right here on earth.

As the summer wore on the question of food became a very serious one to the Piegans, and we heard that the more northern tribes of the Blackfeet were also suffering. The Piegan agent, in his annual report to the Department of the Interior, had deplored the barbarism of his charges, their heathenish worship of strange gods, but he told nothing of their physical needs. "I have nothing for you," he said to the chiefs. "Take your people to buffalo and follow the herds."

This was in August. They all moved down near our place, and while the hunters rode the plains after antelope, the chiefs conferred with Berry, planning for the winter. They finally decided to move to the Judith country, where the buffalo were thought to be still plentiful and where, of course, there were practically as many elk and deer, beaver and wolves as ever. In September we also trailed out, Berry, the Crow Woman, Nät-ah'-ki and I, and in a week or more went into camp on the Judith River, only a mile or two above the mouth of Warm Spring Creek. In Fort Benton we had engaged a couple of extra men, and with their help we soon threw up a row of log cabins and a couple of rude fireplaces. We were located in the heart of an extensive cottonwood grove, sheltered from the northern winds, and right beside us ran the river, then fairly alive with big, fat trout. According to agreement, the Piegans came and pitched their lodges near us, and a part of the Blood tribe moved down from the north and mixed with them. We certainly had enough hunters, and if the buffalo were rather scarce in our immediate vicinity there were great herds of them only a day's journey to the eastward. As for the deer and elk, the country swarmed with them, and antelope, too.

Up on Warm Spring Creek there was a cattle ranch which had been located the previous year. A man named Brooks was its manager, and it was owned by a great firm which had large mercantile interests in Helena and Fort Benton and Fort Macleod, and also the tradership at the Blackfeet Agency, which the Piegans had left in search of game. This was, I believe, the only cattle ranch at that time in all the vast country lying between the Highwood Mountains and the Yellowstone. Since then that once rich-grassed country has supported hundreds of such ranches. And then came the sheep and fed it off. It would make the old-time hunters weep to see those barren plains and hills as they are to-day. I don't wish ever to see them again. I prefer to remember them as I last saw them, before they were despoiled by the white men's herds and flocks. Just think how many centuries those rolling plains furnished sustenance to the countless herds of buffalo and antelope which roamed them, and how many more centuries they might have lasted but for the white man's greed. I believe with the Indian that the white man is a terrible destroyer. He leaves the grassy plains mere brown wastes; before him the forests disappear, and only blackened stumps mark where once stood their green and lovely aisles. Why, he even dries up the streams, and tears down the mountains. And with him are crime, and hunger, and want such as were never before known. Does it pay? Is it right that the many must pay for the greed of the few?

Once only, during the winter, did I find time for a hunt, as Berry was on the road much of the time.

Nät-ah'-ki and I went once after buffalo, camping with
Red Bird's Tail, a genial man of thirty-five or forty years.
There were few lodges of us, but many people, and we
travelled as light as possible. We found buffalo toward
the close of the first day out, but went on until noon of
the next one, and camped on the head of Armells Creek.
I had never seen the buffalo more plentiful than we found
them there. From a little butte nearby we could see
that the prairie was black with them clear to the breaks
of the Missouri, and to the eastward where the buttes
of Big Crooked Creek and the Musselshell loomed in the
distance. The Moccasin Mountains shut off the view
to the south, but westward, whence we had come, there
were also buffalo.

"Ha!" exclaimed Red Bird's Tail, who had ridden
up beside me. "Who says the buffalo are about gone?
Why, it is as it has always been; the land is dark with
them. Never have I seen them more plentiful."

"Remember that we have come far to find them,"
I told him; "that the plains to the west, and away in
the north, are barren of them."

"Ah, that is true, but it will not be for long; they
must have all moved eastward for a time, as our fathers
tell us once happened before. They will go back again.
Surely, the good Sun will not forget us."

I had not the heart to destroy his hopes, to tell him
of the vast regions away to the east and south of
us, where there were no longer any buffalo, where
the antelope, even, had been practically exterminated.

Red Bird's Tail was the leader of our party, and the
hunters were subject to his orders. We had ridden out
on to the butte very early, and after getting a view of the
country and the position of the herds, he decided that a

certain herd southwest of us should be chased, as they would run westward into the wind, and not disturb the larger ones grazing here and there in other directions. We returned then to camp for our morning meal, and to wait until everyone had saddled his favourite horse and was ready to start. It was a warm day, some snow on the ground, but a mild chinook wind blowing, so Nät-ah'-ki accompanied us, as well as most of the other women. The lay of the land was favourable and we succeeded in riding right into the edge of the herd before they became alarmed, and then they ran, as Red Bird's Tail had predicted, southwestward into the wind and up a long slope, an outlying ridge of the mountains. That gave us an advantage, as the buffalo were not swift runners on an up-grade. On a down-hill run, however, they could easily outstrip the swiftest horse. All their weight was forward; there was not enough strength in their small, low hindquarters to propel their abnormally deep chests, huge heads, and heavy hump with any noticeable speed when they went up hill.

Nät-ah'-ki was riding a little mare of gentle mien and more than quiet disposition, which had been loaned her by one of our Blood friends for the trip. All the way from the Judith she kept plying her quirt and calling it sundry reproachful names, in order to keep it beside my more lively and spirited mount. But the moment we came near the herd, and the hunters dashed into it, the animal's demeanour suddenly changed. It reared up under her restraining hand, pranced sideways with arching neck and twitching ears, and then, getting the bit firmly in its teeth, it sprang out into the chase as madly as any other of the trained runners. Indeed, that is what it was, a well-trained buffalo horse, but the owner had not thought to tell us so. It was even swifter

than mine, and I felt no little anxiety as I saw it carry
her into that sea of madly running, shaggy-backed,
gleaming-eyed animals. In vain I urged my horse; I
could not overtake her, and my warning shouts were
lost in the thunder and rattle of a thousand hoofs. I
soon saw that she was not trying to hold in the animal,
but was quirting it instead, and once she looked back
at me and laughed, her eyes shining with excitement.
On we went, up the slope for a mile or more, and then
the scattering herd drew away from us and went flying
down the other side of the ridge.

"What made you do it?" I asked as we checked up
our sweating, panting horses. "Why did you do it? I
was so afraid you would get a fall, perhaps be hooked by
some of the wounded."

"Well," she replied, "at first I was scared, too, but it
was such fun, riding after them. Just think of it, I
struck four of them with my quirt! I just wanted to
keep on, and on, and I never thought of badger holes, or
falling, or anything else. And once a great big cow
looked up at me and snorted so hard that I felt her
warm breath. Tell me, how many did you kill?"

"Not one," I replied. I hadn't fired a shot; I had
noticed nothing, seen nothing but her as she rode in the
thick of it all, and I was more than glad when the run
ended. We looked back down the slope and saw the
hunters and their women already at work on the carcasses
of their kill, which dotted the snow. But we—we were
meatless. It would never do for us to return to camp
without some, so we rode on for a mile or two in the
direction the herd had gone, and then turned off into the
mountains. Up among the pines there were deer, both
kinds, and here and there were groups of elk feeding or
lying down in the open parks. While Nät-ah'-ki held

my horse I approached some of the elk, and by good luck killed a fat, dry cow. We built a fire and roasted some of the liver and a piece of tripe, and, after a hasty meal, rode back to camp with all the meat our horses could conveniently pack.

CHAPTER XXXII

CURBING THE WANDERERS

WE MADE another run the next day. It was an auspicious morning. The sun shone bright and warm, there was a big herd of buffalo nearby, everyone rode out from camp in the best of spirits. I had changed horses with Nät-ah'-ki; while mine liked to run as well as hers, it had a tender mouth, and she could easily control it. Once into the herd, I paid no attention to anyone else, but did my best to single out the fat cows, overtake and kill them. I did not need the meat nor robes, but there were those with us who had poor mounts, and what I killed I intended to give them. So I urged the little mare on, even after she had begun to show fatigue, and managed to kill seven head. When I stopped at last, no one was near me; looking back I saw the people gathered in two groups, and from the largest and nearest one arose the distressing wailing of the women for the dead. I soon learned the cause of it all; Young Arrow Maker had been killed, his horse disembowelled; Two Bows had been thrown and his leg was broken. A huge old bull, wounded and mad with pain, had lunged into Arrow Maker's horse, tearing out its flank and knocking the rider off on to the backs of its close-pursuing mates whence he had fallen to the ground and been literally trampled to death by the frantic-running herd. Two Bows' horse had stepped into a badger hole and he had been hurled to the ground with such force that he lay senseless, his right leg broken above the knee. Some of

366

the women's horses were dragging travois, and we laid the dead and the injured on them and they were taken to camp by their relatives. We hurried to skin the dead buffalo, some of the hunters taking no more of the meat than the tongue and boss ribs, and then we also went back to the lodges, very silently and quietly you may be sure. There was no feasting and visiting and singing that night. Instead, women wailing, men sitting solemnly by the fire, smoking and thinking upon the uncertainties of life, occasionally speaking praises of their dead comrade and regretting his untimely end.

They buried Arrow Maker in the morning, placing the body in the forks of a big cottonwood, and then we prepared to move camp, which took all the rest of the day, as meat was cut and dried to reduce weight, and the many hides had to be trimmed, the frozen ones thawed and folded for packing. There was not a man in camp who knew anything about mending a broken leg, but we splinted and bound Two Bows' fracture as best we could. On the succeeding morning we broke camp early and started homeward, every one being fairly frantic to get away from the unlucky place, to end the unlucky hunt before more misfortune should happen. The injured man was made as comfortable as possible on a couch lashed to a travois.

In the afternoon a blizzard set in, a bitterly cold one, which drifted and whirled the fine snow in clouds around us. A few decided to make camp in the first patch of timber we should come to, but the rest declared that they would not stop, but would keep on through the night until they arrived home. They were afraid to stop; more afraid of some dread misfortune overtaking them than they were of Cold Maker's blinding snow and intense cold. Evil spirits, they reasoned, hovered near them, had already caused death and suffering, and none would be safe until the hunt was ended and sacrifices made to the gods. Red Bird's Tail was one of those who elected to keep on. We could have stopped and found shelter with some family which turned off into a timbered coulée to camp until the storm should be over; but Nät-ah'-ki declared that she wasn't in the least cold and was anxious to get back to our comfortable shack and warm fire-place. "We can make it by midnight," she said, "and just think how pleasant it will be to eat before our little fire, and then sleep in our big, soft, warm bed. Don't be afraid for me, I can stand it."

That was a terrible night. There was a moon, but most of the time it was hidden by the low flying snow-spitting clouds. We simply hung on to our saddles and gave our horses the reins, trusting them to keep in the trail which Red Bird's Tail broke for us. We could not have guided them had we wished to, for our hands became so numb we were obliged to fold them in the robes and blankets which enveloped us. I rode directly behind Nät-ah'-ki, she next after our leader, whose family followed us. Looking back I could see them sometimes, but more often they were hidden in the blinding snow. Red Bird's Tail and many of the other men frequently sprang from their horses and walked, even ran, in vain effort to keep warm, but the women remained in the saddle and shivered, and some froze hands and faces. While still some six or eight miles from home, Red Bird's Tail, walking ahead of his horse, dropped into a spring, over which the snow had drifted. The water was waist-deep and froze on his leggings the instant he climbed out of the hole; but he made no complaint, walking sturdily on through the deepening drifts until we finally arrived home. It was all I could do to dismount, I was so stiff

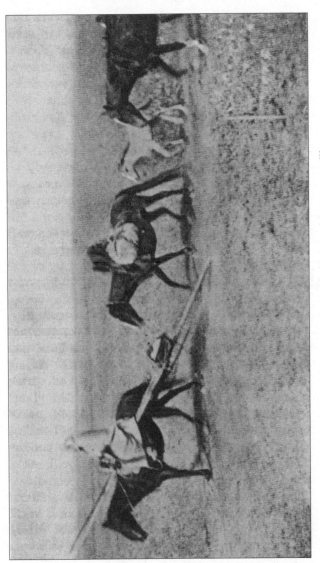

"We broke camp early and started homeward"

and cramped, and cold; and I had to lift Năt-ah'-ki
from her saddle and carry her inside. It was past one
o'clock, and we had been on the road something like
seventeen hours! I aroused one of the men to care for
our horses, and we crawled into bed, under a half-dozen
robes and blankets, shivering so hard that our teeth
chattered. But if you ever get really numb with cold, try
our way. You will get warm much sooner than by sitting
before the fire and swallowing hot drinks.

When we awoke in the morning it was nearly noon; and
we learned that a woman of our party was missing. Somehow, somewhere, in the fearful night she had dropped from
her horse and Cold Maker had claimed her for his own.
Her body was never found. I related the experiences
of the trip to Berry. "Well," he said, "I warned you
not to go. A man who can stay close to the fire in the
winter, but leaves it for a hunt out on the plains, is sure
locoed. Yes, sir, he's a blankety blank, plumb fool."

In September a man named Charles Walmsley, en
route from Fort Macleod to Fort Benton, was found
murdered on Cut Bank Creek, midway between the two
places. His wagon, harness, and other effects had been
partly burned and thrown into the stream. Suspicion
finally fell upon one, Turtle, and his companion, The
Rider, Blood Indians, who had spent several hundred
dollars Canadian money in Fort Benton for guns and
various things dear to the Indian's heart. They were
in the Blood section of camp, and learning their whereabouts, the sheriff of our county came out to arrest them,
bringing with him only the under-sheriff, Jeff Talbot.
There may have been braver men on the frontier than
Sheriff John J. Healy, but I never met them. He held
the office for I know not how many terms, and owned
the Fort Benton *Record*, the first newspaper to be

printed on the plains of Montana. Previous to this he had been an Indian trader, and was one of the leading men of Whoop Up and the northern trade; one of the "thieves, murderers, criminals of every stripe," as Miss Laut calls us.

He and Talbot drove in at our place about sundown one evening, and as soon as they had cared for their horses, he told why they had come.

Berry shook his head. "I wouldn't attempt to arrest them here if I were you," he said. "These Bloods are pretty mean, and Turtle has a whole lot of relatives and friends among them. I believe they'll fight. Old man, you'd better go back and get some of the soldiers at the fort to help you."

"I don't care a continental d—— if he has a thousand friends and relatives!" Healy exclaimed. "I've come out here after those Indians, and they're going back with me, dead or alive."

"Well," said Berry, "if you are bound to try it, of course we'll stay with you; but I don't like it a bit."

"No, sir," said Healy. "This is my funeral. On account of your trade you can't afford to mix up in it. They'd have it in for you and move away. Come on. Jeff."

They went, and we passed about fifteen minutes of pretty acute suspense. We armed our men and ourselves, and stood waiting to go to their aid, although we knew that if anything happened, we would be too late; and again, what could we few do against a big camp of angry Indians! But while we were talking, and you may be sure keeping a good watch on the camp, here came Healy and Talbot with their men, both securely handcuffed. One they chained to the centre post of our trade room, the other to a log wall of the kitchen.

"There!" Healy exclaimed, "that is done and I'm tired. Haven't you anything to give a hungry man? I'm just starving."

Healy spoke good Blackfoot. When he and Talbot went into the camp he inquired for Running Rabbit, the Blood chief, and they were shown into his lodge, where he quickly stated his business. The old chief said that he would send for them, and they could have a talk. "But," he concluded, "I can't be answerable for what may happen if you try to put your hands on them and take them away. My young men are wild. I can't control them."

The women sent to ask Turtle and The Rider to the chief's lodge had been cautioned to say nothing, to give no reason why they were wanted, and they came in and sat down quite unsuspicious, followed by a number of other men, curious to learn the cause of the white men's visit. Healy soon explained it.

"I don't know anything about it," said Turtle, "and I'm not going with you. I will not go; I'll fight; I've got lots of friends here who will help me."

He had no sooner spoken than Healy, who was a very powerful man, seized him and snapped a pair of handcuffs on his wrists, Talbot doing the same with The Rider. Both of the Indians were furious, and those sitting with them became greatly excited, some crying out, "You shall not take them." "We will not let them go." "Take off those iron things, or we will do you harm."

"Listen!" said Healy, holding up his hand warningly. "You all know me; I guess you know I am not afraid. I have got to take these two men with me. I am going to take them. If any of you interfere, I will not be the only one to die. You know how I can shoot—well, some of you will die before I do."

He had not pulled his gun; he stared them coldly in the eyes, and when he was aroused those eyes fairly made an evil-doer shiver.

"Come!" he said to Turtle, and, as if dazed, the Indian mechanically arose and followed him out, Talbot and the other following.

None of us slept much that night. Late in the evening a Piegan youth came in and told us that the Bloods were planning to rescue their friends, some proposing to attack the trading post, others saying that it would be better to waylay the officers on the trail next day. "You go back and tell them that I hope they'll try it," said Healy. "We've got some big Winchesters and six-shooters, and plenty of cartridges, and we'll have a real good time. Turtle and The Rider here will get our first two bullets."

The prisoners were taken safely to Helena, and when the trial came off, The Rider turned States evidence; Turtle had shot Walmsley in the back while he was cooking supper. He got imprisonment for life, and died two years later in the penitentiary in Detroit. No white man has since been killed by any Indians of the Blackfeet tribes.

The winter had been pretty hard, and the Indians did not kill so many buffalo as they would had the herds been nearer camp. Still, they were tanning a good number of robes, and had a large number of rawhides on hand, when, one evening, a detachment of soldiers under command of Lieutenant Crouse arrived from Fort Benton. It was pitiful to see the women and children run to hide in the brush, their eyes wide with fear. They had not forgotten the Baker massacre. The men said nothing, but they seized their weapons and stood about outside of their lodges, ready to fight if need be, until they saw the detachment halt and prepare to camp. It was not to be war then, they concluded, and called in their wives and little ones. But the soldiers' errand was only a degree or two less serious than would have been a battle. They had come to escort the Piegans back to their reservation, where there were no buffalo, nor game of any kind, and to fight them if they refused to go. A council was held. "Why, why," asked White Calf, his face ashen with suppressed anger, "is this to be done? By what right? We are on our own ground. It was always ours. Who shall say that we must leave it?"

Lieutenant Crouse told them that he was but an unwilling instrument, carrying out the order of his superiors, who in turn had been told by the Great Father himself that they must move the Piegans back to their Agency. Complaint had been made of them. The cattlemen claimed that they were killing their cattle and had requested that they be sent home. The Great Father had listened to their demand. The lieutenant was a gentle, kindly man, and did not like the mission on which he had been sent.

"Listen!" said White Calf. "Years ago there came some of the Great Father's men on a steamboat to the mouth of the Judith River, and there they made a treaty with our people. It was made on paper, which they and our chiefs put their names on. I was a young man then, but I had understanding and I well remember what was put on that paper in the white man's writing. It said that all the land lying north of the Musselshell River and the Missouri as far as the mouth of Milk River, up to the Canadian line, from the Rockies eastward to a line running north from the mouth of Milk River, all that country, it said, was ours. Since that time the whites have never bought any of it, nor even asked us for any. How then, can they say that we shall not hunt here?

"We are accused of killing cattle! We have not done so. Why should we when we have fat buffalo and deer and elk and other game, fat animals, all whose hides are useful! We do not wish to return to our Agency. The man there has nothing for us. There is no game in that region. If we go, we must starve. It is a dreadful thing to suffer for want of food. Pity our little children, our women, and our aged ones. Go you back to your fort and leave us in peace."

Others arose and talked, and their pleas to be allowed to remain in the game country were truly pathetic. I believe they brought moisture to the eyes of many of us. I am sure that there was a catch in the lieutenant's voice when he replied that he was powerless to do as they wished, and he asked them not to make it any harder for him by refusing to go. He then arose and left the council, asking to be informed soon what they concluded to do.

It did not take long to decide. "Of course," said White Calf, "we could kill the soldiers here, but others, many more, would replace them. They would kill off our women and children, even the new-born babies, as they did before on the Marias. No, we cannot fight them. Let us go back to the Agency and try in some way to procure food."

A couple of days later the lodges came down, we packed our robes and various impedimenta into wagons and abandoned the camp, and all took the trail for the north, escorted by the soldiers. This was in March, and the Indians' stock was so worn and poor that they could travel only twelve or fifteen miles a day, and hundreds of horses died along the trail. Heavily loaded as were our wagons, we made even better time than they, and arrived in Fort Benton ahead of them. Our total trade amounted to eight hundred robes, three thousand deer, elk, and antelope hides, and I forget how many beaver and wolf skins.

From Fort Benton the Indians journeyed slowly out to our place, Fort Conrad, and thence straggled on up to their Agency, where the women tanned their raw hides, and from the sale of the robes they kept from actual starvation for a time.

And now, here is the true explanation of this unjust and cruel treatment of the Piegans: As before stated, the owners of that lone cattle ranch on Big Spring Creek also owned the traders' post at the Agency, and they wanted to have the Indians back there, well knowing that they would get some hundreds of robes from them. So they trumped up the charge that the Piegans were slaughtering their cattle, and having powerful influence in Washington, their complaint was listened to, and believed. They got the robes all right, and, seeing the successful trade they were doing, they induced an innocent pilgrim to purchase the tradership from them. He got an empty bag, for by mid-summer the Piegans hadn't a single robe to sell, nor anything else with which to purchase a pound of tea.

By right that vast tract of country lying between the Missouri and Musselshell rivers and from the Missouri to the Marias still belongs to the Blackfeet. The treaty of 1855 guaranteed it to them, but it was taken away by two executive orders of July 2, 1873, and August 19, 1874. If some good lawyer would take up the case, he could undoubtedly get redress for them, and a very handsome fee for himself.

CHAPTER XXXIII

HOME again at Fort Conrad. Somehow Nät-ah'-ki and I liked that place better than any we had lived in. The river, murmuring and gurgling by our window, the lovely green groves in the grassy bottoms, the sloping rise of the valley, the rude room itself built of massive logs, cool in summer, warm in winter and alight with the blaze in the hearth, seemed to us all that we could desire. "Let us never leave here again," she said; "let us stay right here in peace and comfort."

But I told her, as I had before, that we could not always do as we wished; that in a few weeks, or months, we might be obliged to take the trail to buffalo again.

Berry made a flying trip through the buffalo country in May, and upon his return we made preparations to establish a trading post on the Missouri at a place named Carrol, something like a hundred and fifty miles below Fort Benton. Steele and Broadwater, partners in the "Diamond R." outfit, which was a great transportation company, had started the place some years before with the view of hauling freight from the steamboats there directly to Helena, but for various reasons this plan had failed, and their buildings had long since fallen into the ever-encroaching river. We chose the location because it lay south of the Little Rocky Mountains, north of the Snowies, had good wagon roads leading out of it, and above all because it seemed to be in the very centre of the remaining buffalo country. We sent a trusty Indian north into Canada to notify the Blackfeet and Bloods of our intention, and they agreed to move down there as soon as possible. So did our near neighbours, the Piegans. We counted on having a big trade, and as it turned out, we were not mistaken.

It was about the first of July (1880) that we embarked on the Red Cloud at Fort Benton, Berry, the Crow Woman, Nät-ah'-ki, and I. There went with us also a French half-breed, named Eli Gardipie, the best rifle-shot, the best buffalo runner, and all-around hunter I ever knew. He was six feet two in height, rather slender, and I never saw any one who could keep up with him walking or running, for he had the wind and the muscle to endure. At the mouth of the Judith we came to the buffalo, the bottoms covered with them, the river black with them swimming across, some north, some south. And we saw herds of deer and elk and antelope, and on the bare cliffs and buttes many a flock of bighorn. The sight of all the game gladdened our eyes, and astonished the "tenderfeet" passengers. They made a rush for their rifles and shotguns and toy pistols, but the captain of the boat forbade any shooting. He told Gardipie, however, that he would like to eat some roast bighorn saddle, and gave him permission to kill one. Soon afterward we saw a fine big ram standing near the top of a butte watching us. It was at least three hundred yards away, but a moment after Gardipie's rifle cracked it toppled over and rolled and bounded down into the river with a mighty splash. The captain reversed the big stern wheel, and waited for it to float alongside, when the roustabouts drew it on deck. That was about as difficult a shot as I ever saw made. The tenderfeet gathered around Gardipie, and stared at him in open-mouthed wonder.

We arrived at Carrol late in the afternoon. We had tons and tons of trade goods aboard, and it was wonderful to see how quickly the deckhands put the stuff ashore. Berry's bull train had preceded us, overland, and the men had already put up a commodious two-room cabin, which was to be our kitchen and dining room. We took possession of it at once, and the women cooked us a good meal.

By the middle of September we were in good shape for the winter, having built a large log store and warehouse 40 x 125 feet, a smoke-house for curing buffalo tongues, and a row of sleeping quarters. True to their promise, the Blackfeet and Bloods came down from the north, and a little later came about two thousand Canadian Crees, under Chief Big Bear. There also trailed in a large number of Red River French and English halfbreeds with their awkward, creaking, ironless, two-wheel carts. Surely, we were not going to lack for customers. An opposition trader had started a small store about two hundred yards above us. He had never been in the Indian trade, but boasted of his commercial successes in the States, and said that he would soon put us out of business, even if he did not have such a large stock of goods. When the Blackfeet appeared on the opposite side of the river, he went across and invited the chiefs to feast with him. They all got into his boat and came over, but the moment they stepped ashore a bee-line was made for our place, and the welcome they well knew awaited them. The trader was about the most chagrined man you can imagine. We made things interesting for him before the winter was over.

The North Blackfeet were friendly with the Crees; had intermarried with them to some extent. The two tribes camped side by side in the bottoms near us all winter. The Bloods, however, were not so friendly to them, and hunted out south of the river, along the foot of the Snowies. The chiefs of the two tribes made a sort of armistice, agreeing that for the winter, at least, there should be no trouble between them. But the Piegans would not meet their long-time enemy, and hunted in the country to the west of us, occasionally sending out a war party to kill a few of the Crees and drive off their stock. We got none of their trade.

Nät-ah'-ki and the Crow Woman were highly indignant when they saw the Crees pull in from the north. "By what right," asked the latter, "are they here? The soldiers ought to drive them back to their brush swamps. It is wrong to allow them to kill the buffalo and other game belonging to our people."

"They are dog-eating dogs!" Nät-ah'-ki exclaimed. "If you are going to ask their chiefs in here to feast, you can find someone to do the cooking, for I will not." And she kept her word. Seeing how she felt about it, I found an English halfbreed family to take charge of the mess. Nät-ah'-ki had lost a brother and an uncle in war with the Crees, and I could not blame her for feeling as she did toward them. The Piegans, however, had always beaten the Crees, as they were braver, better armed, and better horsemen. Where the town of Lethbridge, Alberta, now stands, they once had a battle with them in which two hundred and forty of the Crees were killed, and many more drowned while attempting to escape by swimming the river.

I cannot explain why I also had a deep dislike for the Crees unless it was that Nät-ah'-ki's enemies were naturally mine, too. I am ashamed to say that I did hate and despise them, their looks, manners, and even their language. I soon learned their words for the different articles of trade, but would never use them, pretending that I did not understand, and obliging them to tell me what they wanted either in Blackfoot, which most of them spoke, or by means of the sign language. Their chief, Big Bear, was a short, broad, heavy-featured, small-eyed man, with a head of hair which seemed never to have known the comb. Why he was a chief I could never learn. He did not seem to have even ordinary intelligence, and his war record did not compare with that of the average Blackfoot.

Even more than the Crees, I disliked their half brothers, the French-Cree Red River breeds. They were not dark, but actually black-skinned, like the negro, and they dressed in black, both women and men, the latter wearing a bit of colour, a bright red sash around the waist. The women's kerchiefs even were black. And then the men had such a despicable way of wearing their hair, cut straight off just above the shoulders, and standing out around the head like a huge mop. But it was not for their looks that I disliked them so much as it was their habits and customs. They ate dogs, for one thing; they pretended to be faithful and zealous members of the Church, but were the worst set of liars and thieves that ever travelled across the plains; they hated the Americans as much as they did the English, and in their vile bastard French cursed us until, one day, I could stand it no longer. I jumped over the counter and struck one of them, a fellow named Amiott, a stinging blow in the cheek which sent him sprawling to the floor, and it was all I could do to keep from kicking him when he was down. "That is for your low-down cursing of us," I told him. "I will not hear any more of it in this place. If you don't like it, you and the others here go and heel yourselves and come back."

Strange to say, we did not lose any trade by this. The very ones I had called down remained our customers, and quiet ones they were, too.

Louis Riel! How well and yet how little I knew him, he who led the halfbreed rebellion of 1885 in Canada, you remember. He was a fine-looking man, even if his bright black eyes were a bit shifty and uncertain in their gaze; and he had such courtly manners. When still thirty or forty yards away he would remove his wide sombrero with a grand sweep and approach you bowing and smiling, and filling the air with high-flown compliments. He had a fine education; the Jesuits having trained him for the priesthood; but certain lapses had prevented his ordination. It was his education, I believe, which caused his downfall, for he overestimated himself and his power. Still, I was never able to determine whether he really believed in his cause and his power to right what he called the wrongs of his oppressed and defrauded people, or whether he got up the row, expecting to be bought off by the Canadian Government and to live in wealth ever afterward. Also, it may be that in his estimate of himself, his people, and his position, he was mentally unbalanced. He came to us with his people from the plains of the north and soon got into Berry's good graces, for he was an exceedingly smooth and persuasive talker. He wanted some goods on credit with which to trade in his camp, and got them. We kept an open account with him for nearly two years. It is still open, for he left, vanished between sun and sun, owing a balance of seven hundred dollars.

"Well," said Berry, "I don't know but what we are about even. He must have bowed to us about seven hundred times, and I reckon that such grand and low bows as those are worth about a dollar apiece."

"Do you know," Riel once told me, "these people of mine are just as were the children of Israel, a persecuted race deprived of their heritage. But I will redress their wrongs; I will wrest justice for them from the tyrant. I will be unto them a second David. Yes, I can compare myself to the great leader of the Jews. I, too, am writing psalms. Riding at the head of our column I think them out, and by the evening fire, in the stillness of the night, put them on paper. Some day I shall have them printed."

None of the Red River halfbreeds, save Riel, had the slightest conception of the power of the Canadian, and back of that, the English people. But he knew, for he had been eastward to Ottawa, Montreal, and Quebec, and from his reading had acquired an all-round knowledge of the world in general. Yet there at our place he held meeting after meeting and wrought his people up to the highest pitch of enthusiasm, telling them that the Canadian-English were few and inexperienced, and that in a very few weeks they could subdue them by force of arms. Asked for our opinion, we told them that they had no earthly chance to win, and so did a Catholic priest, Father Scullin, who lived with us. The Bishop of Edmonton had sent him there to look after the spiritual welfare of the different tribes. He spoke Cree, and Blackfoot, and the Canadian French fluently. Had the buffalo lasted, I doubt if Riel would have succeeded in getting the Red Rivers to revolt. But when they could no longer live by the chase, and began to starve, they became desperate and broke out. That was four years after the matter was first debated there on the Missouri. The whole body of them, Crees and Red Rivers, did not put up as good a fight as a handful of Blackfeet would have made, and Riel was tried, condemned, and hanged for treason.

Far different from the French were the English and
Scotch Red River breeds, who came down to us. They
were neither negro-hued nor black-hearted and it was a
pleasure to trade and associate with them. The women
were mostly fair-haired, blue-eyed, rosy-cheeked dames,
and the men great muscular, sturdy specimens of manhood,
good to look upon. But hold! I must not utterly con-
demn the French breed women. I remember that some
of them were exceedingly lovely, even in the sombre
and outlandish garb they wore. There was a certain
Amelie X., for instance, whose husband, a Frenchman,
was killed in a buffalo chase. Every young French
breed in camp was courting her, but she told them to go
about their business and leave her alone. "I don't
want no more French mans," she told us. "I don't
want no H'Injun, no H'Euglis mans. I want Americane
mans, me."

Long John Pape and Mike Duval fought over her, and
the former was badly whipped. Mike thought then
that he had her sure, and was begging her to name the
day, when, lo! one morning Billy Burns walked into her
cabin, picked her up in his arms without a word, and
carrying her over to our place he set her on her feet
before the astonished priest. "Just hitch us up," he
said, "and be quick about it."

"I won't!" Amelie screamed, giving him a resounding
slap in the face. "I won't! Go way from me, you bad
mans! Let me alone!"

"Oh, well," said Billy, "if you won't of course you
won't. I thought you kind o' liked me."

He turned away abruptly and started for the door,
but Amelie ran after him and grasped his arm.
"Come back, you big fools!" she commanded, with a
stamp of her pretty, moccasined foot. "Come back!

Me, h'I'm only make it joke; course I marry you; you got blue h'eyes."

They stood again before the father; "It's a go, then?" he asked them. It was, and he married them then and there.

Such a blowout as there was that night! The dancing and drinking were something to be remembered! Long John and Duval not only made friends, but when Nät-ah'-ki and I looked in for a moment, they were weeping on each other's shoulders. Billy and Amelie had fled. Having provided the cabin, the musicians, the solid and liquid refreshments for the party, they hitched a horse to a halfbreed sled and sped away down the river to the camp of a friend.

The buffalo remained in our vicinity and their numbers did not seem to diminish, although a daily horde of hunters rode out to slay them. I went once, with a number of the Red River breeds. We sighted a herd soon after passing the rim of the valley and, screened from their sight by a sharp rise of ground, my companions dismounted, removed their hats, fell upon their knees, crossed themselves, and one old patriarch offered up a long prayer, asking for successful chase and that no harm befall them or their horses in the run. Then they sprang up into the saddles and were off, quirting their horses madly and cursing them with the most terrible oaths at their command. Some, who found not sufficient of them in their own tongues, swore also in broken English.

"Paul," I said to one of them after the run, "had you been killed in the chase, where would your soul have gone?"

"Why, to the good God, most certainement."

"But after you prayed you cursed your horse; you used terrible oaths."

"Ah! but that was in the excitement; to speed the ill-born brute. The good God knows I meant no disrespect; most certainement. My—what you call him—soul would have gone to the pleasant place."

To accommodate the Bloods, and a large camp of Red Rivers, late in the fall we established a branch post on Flat Willow Creek, a tributary of the Musselshell. I rode over there several times during the winter, through great herds of buffalo, and antelope, and once I saw a band of wild horses, wilder by far than the game with which they mingled. Along the foot of the Snowy Mountains, in which the Flat Willow has its source, there were immense herds of elk and deer, and we bought large numbers of their skins.

I think that the Crees and Red Rivers loved liquor more than any other people I met on the plains. The Blackfeet liked it, but not well enough to impoverish themselves for it. The former, however, would sell anything they had to obtain it, even their women, and it was rare for a family to have more than half a dozen horses. Many of the Crees were obliged to walk when moving camp, packing their few effects on dogs. They were not lazy, however, and killed and tanned a great many robes which they exchanged for liquor, tea, and tobacco, seldom buying any finery. There were nights when at least a thousand of them would be drunk together, dancing and singing around little fires built down in the timber, some crying foolishly, some making love, others going through all sorts of strange and uncouth antics. There was very little quarrelling among them, not half a dozen being killed in the whole winter. More than that number froze to death, falling on their way in the night and being unable to rise and go on.

CHAPTER XXXIV

WHEN spring came the Blackfeet and Bloods moved back into Canada in order to get their treaty money from the Government. They intended to return in the fall, but now crossed the line again. The Crees and Red Rivers remained with us. Our trade for the season footed up four thousand buffalo robes and about an equal number of deer, elk, and antelope skins. For the robes we received $28,000, for the skins, some beaver and wolf pelts about $5,000 more. That was our banner season, and the biggest one Berry had ever experienced. It was remarkable in that it occurred when the buffalo were so near extermination.

We were looking forward to a quiet summer, as usual, when orders came from the Sioux Agency Indian traders of Dakota, and from firms in the Northwest Territory of Canada for pemmican and dried meat. The letters all had the same story to tell, "The buffalo are gone," they said. "Send us as many tons of the stuff as you can for our trade." The Crees and their half brothers were happy when we told them that we would buy all they could bring us, and they lost no time in beginning to hunt. Everything went that was meat— poor cows, old bulls, and perhaps crippled horses. The meat was dried in wide, thin, flat sheets, and done up in rawhide-thonged bales. Pemmican was made by pounding the dried meat into fragments and mixing it with tallow and grease extracted from the animals' bones.

386

It was packed into green hide, flat, oblong bags, and the covering shrunk so tightly over the mass as it dried that a package of it had the solidity and weight of a rock. I do not remember how much of the stuff we got during the summer, literally cords and cords of the dried meat and hundreds of bags of pemmican, all of which we sold at a good profit.

There came to our place one day in midsummer a tall, slender man, who from his face and the black, sharp-ended, up-curling moustache he wore, reminded one of pictures of the old-time Spanish cavaliers. He spoke English, pure English, much better, indeed, than that of any white man around, better than many West Point graduates of the army. He introduced himself as William Jackson. The name seemed familiar, but I could not place him until he said that he was sometimes called Sik-si-ka'-kwan—Blackfoot Man. Then I knew. How often I had heard old man Monroe mention him, his favourite grandson; his bravery and kindness of heart. I couldn't help shaking hands with him and saying, "I have long hoped to meet you, Sik-si-ka'-kwan; your grandfather has told me much about you." Well, we became lasting friends; friends to the day of his death, and I hope that together we accomplished some measure of good in penance for our many sins.

No one can make me believe that there is nothing in heredity. There was Jackson, for instance. On his mother's side, he came from the Monroes, a notedly brave family of Scotch Highlanders, and from the La Roches, a noble French family, some of whom early emigrated to America. His father, Thomas Jackson, had taken part in the Seminole and other Indian wars of 1832; his great grandfathers on both sides had fought in the Revolution. No wonder, then, that he took to

war as a profession, enlisting at an early age as scout in
the United States army.

The summer previous to his enlistment he made a
name for himself by killing three Sioux. He and his
mother went berrying in the breaks of the river north
of Fort Union, and when four or five miles away they
saw five Sioux sneaking down on them, following a deep
coulée running parallel with the ridge upon which they
were riding. The Sioux were just entering a big thicket
and imagined that they and their horses had not been
seen. Jackson kept on a little way, gradually riding off
to the west side of the ridge and out of sight of the
enemy. Then he told his mother what he had seen,
made her take his horse, which was the stronger and
swifter of the two, and told her to ride back to the Fort
for help as swiftly as she could. She cried and objected,
saying that if he was to be killed she wanted to die with
him. But he finally assured her that he could take care
of himself for a time and she started back as fast as the
horse could run. Jackson at once went up to the top
of the ridge, peering over it very carefully. In a moment
the Sioux mounted and burst out of the brush full tilt
after his mother. There was his chance, and kneeling
to get a more steady aim, he fired his Henry rifle a number of times, dropping two of the enemy. But that did
not stop the others, who came swiftly up the ridge, so
he mounted his horse and took the back trail. One
of the horses the Sioux rode proved to be a better animal
than his, the other two not so swift. The rider of the
former kept gaining on him, firing his muzzle-loader as
fast as he could, and Jackson kept shooting back at
short intervals, failing also to hit his foe. Finally,
when the Sioux had lessened the gap between them to
about a hundred yards, Jackson stopped his horse, and

jumping off, knelt down and took a careful aim at his
pursuer. He must have been a very brave Sioux, as
he never stopped, but whipped his horse harder than
ever. Jackson fired twice at him; the second shot hit
him fairly in the breast and he instantly rolled off to the
ground, where he lay perfectly still. Then Jackson
remounted and rode on, the remaining two Sioux pursuing him for a half-mile or so, when they stopped,
seemed to talk together for a moment, and turned back
to take care of their dead.

Jackson was a favourite with the army officers,
especially Generals Custer and Miles. On the morning
of the battle of the Little Big Horn, June 25, 1876, he,
with the other scouts, was detailed to accompany
Major Reno. Had they accompanied Custer, they
would have undoubtedly shared his fate. As it was,
they did what they could—at the expense of the lives
of most of them—to save Reno and his command from
utter annihilation, for when the Sioux charged, they
held their ground for a time, to give the soldiers a chance
to retreat across the river and up on the hill, where they
were nearly overcome several times by the enemy.
Jackson was finally cut off from the command with
Lieutenant DeRudio, Interpreter Girard, and a soldier.
They lay in the thick brush all that day and the next,
and then when evening came Jackson ventured out,
took sufficient leggings and blankets from the enemy
lying about, and when they had dressed themselves in
the leggings and moccasins, and wrapped blankets
about themselves, he led them right through the watch-
fires of the Sioux to their comrades up on the
hill. Only once were they accosted. "Who goes
there?" asked someone sitting by a small fire roasting meat.

Jackson, who spoke Sioux perfectly, replied, "It is only us, we're going over here a little way."

"Well, go where you're going," said their questioner. "I'm going to sit right here and eat some meat."

At the time he came to the store at Carrol, Jackson was trading with the Indians out near the Judith Mountains. I was sorry to part with him. I hardly expected to meet him again, but I did some years afterward on the reservation where all the "squaw men," as we were called, were driven by the tenderfeet, the "pilgrims," with their five-cent ways of doing business.

Winter came again, and the Crees and Red River breeds were still with us, but the buffalo were not so plentiful as they had been the previous winter. Their range was also smaller, extending from the mouth of Judith River eastward to the Round Butte, on the north side of the Missouri, a distance of one hundred and twenty-five miles, and back from the river not more than forty miles. They were far more plentiful on the south side, between the Missouri and the Yellowstone, but so were the hunters. They were hemmed in on the east by the Assiniboins and Yanktonai Sioux, on the south by the Crows, and a horde of white skin-hunters that the Northern Pacific, then being constructed along the Yellowstone, had brought into the country. In the midst of the herds were our Crees and Red Rivers. The white hunters were the most destructive of all, and piled up more than one hundred thousand buffalo hides along the Yellowstone that winter, which they sold for about two dollars each to Eastern tannery buyers. We got twenty-seven hundred robes, about a thousand deer, antelope, and elk skins, and the rest of the traders along the river, all told, had about as many more. Most of the robes we got were killed in the early part of the

winter.   As the season advanced the hunters had to ride
farther and farther to find the game.   There was no
doubt but that the end of the trade was near.

In February we ran short of trade blankets, and I
went to a trading post up at the mouth of the Judith
after more, taking Nät-ah'-ki with me.   The river was
solidly frozen, so we took that route, each driving a pony
hitched to a Red River sled.   It was pleasant, travelling
up the familiar river over the smooth ice.   The weather
was not too cold, and it neither blew nor snowed.   We
travelled the first day to the foot of the Dauphin Rapids,
and camped in the cabin of some "woodhawks," temporarily absent.   They had left the latch-string out and
a notice on the rude table which read: "Make yourself
to hum, stranger, an' shet the door when you leeve."

We did make ourselves "to hum."   Nät-ah'-ki
cooked a good meal in the hearth, and then we sat long
before the pleasant fire in the most comfortable of chairs.
They were merely green buffalo hides stretched over a
pole frame work, but they had been used as the skins
dried and fitted perfectly; every part of the body had
just the proper support.

The next day we reached our destination, and on the
following one started homeward with our loads of blankets.   It was about four in the afternoon that we saw
some buffalo scurrying southward across the river, and
heard some firing back in the breaks.   A little later
we saw a large camp of Indians file down into a bottom
below us.   I was not a little uneasy at first, for I feared
that they might be Assiniboins, and they had recently
killed a woodhawk, and committed other depredations
along the river.   I stopped my horse and asked Nät-ah'-
ki what we had best do, drive on as rapidly as possible
or stop and camp with them.   She gazed at them

intently for a moment; they were already pitching their lodges, and a painted lodge-skin was just then elevated and spread around the poles. "Oh!" she cried, with a happy catch of the breath which was almost a sob, "Oh, they are our people. See! that is the buffalo medicine lodge they have put up. Hurry! let us go over to them."

They were indeed some of the Piegans under Red Bird's Tail, with whom we camped that night. They were as pleased to meet us as we were them, and it was far into the night when we reluctantly went to bed, the supply of lodge fuel having given out. "We are near the end of it," Red Bird's Tail said to me. "We have hunted far this winter, along Milk River, in the Wolf Mountains (Little Rockies), and now over here on the Big River, and we have just about had meat enough to eat. Friend, I fear that this is our last buffalo hunt."

I told him of the conditions south and east of us, that there were no buffalo anywhere, except the few between us and the Yellowstone, and even there no herds of more than a hundred or so, "Are you sure," he said; "sure that the white men have seen all the land which they say lies between the two salt waters? Haven't they overlooked some big part of the country where our buffalo have congregated and from whence they may return?"

"There is no place in the whole land," I replied, "north, south, east, or west, that the white men have not travelled, are not travelling right now, and none of them can find buffalo. Do not believe, as many of your people do, that they have driven them away in order to deprive you of your living. White men are just as anxious to kill buffalo for their hides and meat as you are."

Erecting the Medicine Lodge

The Medicine Lodge

"Then, that being the case," he said with a deep sigh, "misery and death are at hand for me and mine. We are going to starve."

On our way homeward the next morning, I saw a lone buffalo calf—almost a yearling then—standing dejectedly, forlornly, in a clump of rye grass near the river. I killed it, and took off the hide, horns, hoofs, and all. The Crow Woman tanned it for me later and decorated the flesh side with gaudy porcupine quill work. That was my last buffalo. Along in the afternoon we startled something like seventy-five head which had come to the frozen stream in search of water. They scampered wildly across the bottom and up the slope of the valley to the plains. That was the last herd of them that Nät-ah'-ki and I ever saw.

The little woman and I had been homesick for some time. While we loved the great river, its lovely valley and fantastic "bad lands," we did not like the people temporarily there. We were ever talking and dreaming of our home on the Marias, and so one May morning, we embarked on the first boat of the season for Fort Benton, and thence to Fort Conrad. And thus we bade good-bye forever to the old plains' life and the buffalo and the Indian trade.

Berry soon followed us, leaving a man in charge of our place, which we ran—at a loss—for another year, getting only three hundred, mostly bull robes, the last winter, 1882–3.

CHAPTER XXXV

THE "WINTER OF DEATH"

THE summer days slipped by happily for all of us. Berry's mother and the Crow Woman made themselves a little garden, where the Marias and its Dry Fork join, irrigating it with water carried from the river. Their corn and pumpkins and beans, all of the stock which the natives had cultivated long before Columbus saw America, grew apace. The old women erected a shelter hard by their thriving plants, a roof of brush supported by four posts; and there Nät-ah'-ki and I spent many a pleasant afternoon with them, listening to their quaint tales, and the still more quaint songs which they occasionally sung. Early in the spring, Berry had again torn up the earth with his bulls and plows, and sown it with oats and wheat. Strange to say—for it was again a dry year—they grew and ripened, and were harvested and stacked, but never marketed. The pigs undermined the stacks, cattle and horses broke through the corral and trampled them, and all went to waste. We were no farmers whatever.

All summer we had Piegans with us from time to time, and they told harrowing tales of hard times up at their Agency. The weekly rations, they said, lasted but one day. There was no game of any kind to be found; their Agent would give them nothing. Those with us and scattered along the river, by hard hunting found deer and antelope enough to keep themselves alive, but those remaining at the Agency actually suffered for want of food. They were the ones who could not get away. They had lost their horses through a skin disease which had spread among the herds, or had sold them to the trader for provisions.

In September Nät-ah'-ki and I went up to the Agency to see for ourselves what was the condition of affairs. Arriving at the main camp, just below the Agency stockade, at dusk, we stopped with old Lodge-pole Chief for the night. "Leave our food sacks with the saddles," I said to Nät-ah'-ki, "we will see what they have to eat."

The old man and his wives welcomed us cordially. "Hurry," he commanded the women, "cook a meal for our friends. They must be hungry after their long ride." He spoke as if the lodge was filled with provisions. He smiled happily and rubbed his hands together as he talked. But his wives did not smile, nor hurry. From a parfleche they brought forth three small potatoes and set them to boil, and from another one, two quarter-pound trout, which they also boiled. After a time they set them before us. " 'Tis all we have," said one of the women, pathetically, brushing the tears from her eyes. " 'Tis all we have. We are very poor."

At that poor old Lodge-pole Chief broke down. "It is the truth," he said, haltingly. "We have nothing. There are no more buffalo, the Great Father sends us but a little food—gone in a day. We are very hungry. There are fish to be sure, forbidden by the gods, unclean. We eat them, however, but they do not give us any strength, and I doubt not that we will be punished for eating them. It seems as if our gods had forsaken us."

Nät-ah'-ki went out and brought back one of our food sacks and handed to the women three or four tins of beans, corned beef and corn, some sugar, coffee, and flour. To the old man she gave a piece of tobacco. Ah! how their faces brightened! How they talked and laughed as they cooked and ate a good meal. It was a pleasure to watch them.

The next day we rode to the various camps and found the same conditions in each. Not what one could call actual starvation, but something very near it; so near it that the most vigorous of the men and women showed the want of food. They appealed to me for help, and I gave freely what I had; but that of course was a mere nothing, as compared to their needs. Nät-ah'-ki's mother had been long in one of the camps, caring for a sick relative, now dead. We rescued her from the place of famine and made our way back to the Fort.

After a talk with Berry, I determined to write a full account of what I had seen on the Reservation, and this I did, sending it to a certain New York paper for publication. I wanted the American people to know how their helpless wards were being used. I knew that some good people somewhere, would take the matter up and see that sufficient food was sent them to keep soul and body together. My contribution was never printed. I was a subscriber to the paper, and scanned its columns for weeks and months after I had sent in my registered manuscript. Alas! I did not then know how much politics affected even such an ordinary position as Indian Agent, and especially at that time, when the "Indian Office" was in the hands of a "ring." I had sent my story to the paper which was the mainstay of the Administration. Of course, they would not print it, and I gave up. Both Berry and I advised the Indians to kill their Agent, and see if that would not awaken people to their necessities; but they were afraid to do it; they remembered the Baker massacre. I know now where I could have sent that story, whence it would have been scattered broadcast throughout the land; but I was young, and easily discouraged, and so matters drifted and drifted along from bad to worse. Not many of the people died during the winter from actual want.

Summer came. The Agent gave out a few potatoes to the Indians to plant. Some actually did plant them; others were so hungry that they ate what was given them. Also, in the early spring they scraped the inner bark of pine and cottonwood, and dug "pomme blanche," a tuberous growth something like a turnip, for food. Then came fishing time, and they caught trout. Somehow they got through the summer, and then came winter again, the starvation winter, the winter of death, as it was called, and from which ever afterward everything was dated. In his annual report of the summer, the Agent had written at great length about the heathenish rites of his people, but had said little of their needs. He told of the many hundred acres they had planted with potatoes and turnips—they may have planted five acres all told. In fact, he gave no hint of the approaching calamity. For years in his annual report he had recorded a constant increase in the tribe's resources; he would not now, it seemed, take back his words and make himself out a liar. It had been through his own single, strenuous efforts that the Blackfeet had risen to their present stage of civilisation, "but their heathenish rites were most deplorable."

Early in the fall, about fifty lodges of people came down and remained with us. There were still a few antelope, but when they failed to make a successful hunt, we gave them from what we had. None of them perished. But up at the Agency, as January and February passed, the situation was terrible. Old Almost-a-dog, day after day, by ones and twos and threes, checked off the deaths of the starved ones. Women crowded around the windows of the Agent's office, held up their skinny children to his gaze, and asked for a cup of flour or rice or beans or corn—anything, in fact, that would appease hunger. He waved them away! "Go," he would say surlily "Go away! Go away! I have nothing for you." Of course he hadn't. The $30,000 appropriated for the Blackfeet had disappeared—somewhere, I suppose. The Indian ring got a part, and the rest, from which must be subtracted a freight tariff of 5 cents per pound, was used to buy many unnecessary things. Beef and flour were what the people needed, and did not get. In one part of the stockade the Agent kept about fifty chickens, a couple of tame wild geese and some ducks, which were daily fed an abundance of corn, freighted all the way from Sioux City up to Fort Benton by steamboat, and then more than a hundred miles overland, for the use of the Indians. The corn was Government property, which, by law, the Agent could neither buy nor in any way convert to his own use. Nevertheless, he fed it liberally to his hens, and the Indian mothers stood around mournfully watching, and furtively picking up a kernel of the grain here and there. And day by day the people died. There were several thousand pounds of this grain, but the chickens needed it.

The news of all this did not reach us until February, when Wolf Head came in one day riding the sorriest looking horse I ever saw. It had a little hair in places, the skin along the back was wrinkled, and here and there had been deeply frozen. "There are not many of them up there that look better," said Wolf Head, sadly. "Most of our herds are dead." And then he went on to

tell of the starving and dying people. Long before he
had finished, Nät-ah'-ki began to cry, and so did the
Crow Woman, who was the only one of the others present.
But while they cried, they were quickly heating some
food and coffee, which they placed on the table before
Wolf Head and told him to eat. Never in my life did
I see food disappear so quickly, in such huge portions. I
arose after a little and took the different things away.
"You shall have them later," I said. The women protested until I convinced them that starving people sometimes die when given much food after their long fast. In
the evening our place was well filled with the Indians from
camp, and Wolf Head repeated what he had told us of
the suffering and dying people. He named some of the
dead, and one by one some of the listeners stole away to
mourn for relatives they had lost. Here, there, sitting
on the frozen ground or bank of the river they wailed,
calling over and over the loved one's name. The sound
of it was so distressing, so nerve-racking, that I felt like
going out and asking them to desist and go home. But
I could not do it. It was their way, their ancient way,
of expressing their sorrow. What right had I to interfere; of what account were my nerves beside their sor-
rows?

When Wolf Head ended his harrowing tale, for a time
all the men sat very still, not even smoking, and then
they began, one by one, to heap such curses on their
Agent and white men in general as their language permitted. Berry and I listened in silence; we knew they
did not mean us—we knew that they regarded us as
members of their tribe, their very own people. But we
were nevertheless ashamed before them, sore that the
cupidity and carelessness and lust for land of the white
race had brought them and theirs to this pass. After

talk had somewhat drifted into half silences, Berry said
what he could in the way of condolence, adding, "We
told you months ago to kill that Agent of yours. Had
you done that, there would have been a great excitement
where the white people live, and men would have been
sent here to look into the matter. They would have
learned that you were without food, and a plenty would
have been sent to you."

I said nothing. A thought had suddenly struck me
which I at once put into execution. I sat down and
wrote a letter to a New York gentleman with whom I had
had some correspondence, but had never met, explaining
fully the sad plight the Blackfeet were in. I can't say why I
wrote to him, but I believe that fate directed me, for my
story in due time reached a sympathetic hand, and I was
told to go on up to the Agency and write an account of
what I saw there. Unknown to me this gentleman had
ridden several trails in the West, and had formed a
different opinion of Indians from what most white men
have. In time he became what may be called an honor-
ary member of the Blackfeet, the Pawnees, the Chey-
ennes, and other Northern tribes. The Fisher Cap, as
the Blackfeet call him, has done more for them than all
the different "Indian Rights," "Indian Aid" societies
put together. He has rid them of thieving agents;
helped them to get good ones; to get full value for the
lands they have been obliged to sell; accompanied their
delegations to Washington, and stood by them in their
petitions to the Indian Office.

Well, I saddled a horse and rode up to the Agency.
Not exactly to it, for I did not wish to get my friends into
trouble. The Indian Police had been ordered by the
Agent to arrest every white man they found on the
Reservation. If I rode right into the stockade, the

Police would have to arrest me or resign, and I wished none of them to leave the service, for the Agent gave them plenty of food for themselves and families. Therefore, I rode from one camp to another for a day, and what I saw was heart-rending. I entered and sat down in the lodges of friends with whom I had feasted not so long since on boiled buffalo tongues and ribs, on rich pemmican and other good things of the plains. Their women were mostly sitting gazing hopelessly at the fire, and upon seeing me drew their old, thin robes about them, to hide their rent and worn-out dresses. And the men! There was no hearty, full-voiced "Ok'-yi!" from them. They spoke the word of welcome of course, but in a low key, and their eyes could not meet mine, for they were ashamed. There was nothing in the lodge to eat, and the greatest of humiliations to a Blackfoot is to be unable to set out a little feast for his visitors. But when I began to speak about their predicament, they roused up quickly enough and spoke of their suffering children and wives, and of the deaths, and sometimes as they talked a woman would begin to sob and go out; one who had, perhaps, lost a child of her own. It was all very sad.

Leaving the camps in the vicinity of the Agency, I rode over to Birch Creek, the southern boundary of the Reservation, where there was a small camp. I found the people there slightly better off. A few range cattle were wintering in the vicinity, and the hunters occasionally went out in the night and killed one, so thoroughly covering up or removing all traces of blood and offal that had one ridden by the next day he would never have suspected what had been done there but a few hours before. It has always been a heinous offence to kill, rebrand, or maverick cattle in the range country, and the Indians knew it, hence their caution. The cattlemen knew of course that their herds were growing smaller, but they could prove nothing, so they merely damned the Indians and talked about "wiping them off the face of the earth." Even that last remnant of the Blackfeet's once vast territory, their Reservation, was coveted by the great cattle kings for many years, and, as you shall learn later, they eventually got the run of it, after surreptitiously fattening upon it, in connivance with various agents, thousands of beeves for the Chicago market.

CHAPTER XXXVI

THE "BLACK ROBE'S" HELP

DURING my visits to the various camps, I had heard much of a certain Black Robe or priest, whom the people called Stahk'-tsi kye-wak-sin—Eats-in-the-middle-of-the-day. "He is a man," the people told me, "a real kind-hearted man. Twice the Agent has ordered him off of the reservation, but he returns to talk with us, and help us as he can."

I learned that he had built a Nät-o-wap'-o-yis, or sacred house, on the non-reservation side of Birch Creek, and thither I went after visiting the last of the camps. I found the Rev. P. P. Prando, S. J., at home in his rude shed-like room, attached to the little log chapel, and there we two struck up a fine friendship, which was never broken. I am not a religious man—far from it; that is as to a belief in a revealed religion and some certain creed. But how I do admire these Jesuits. They have always been at the front here in America; have suffered hardships, cold and heat, hunger and thirst, and gone through such dangers as the representatives of no other creed have done. Nothing has daunted them in their zeal to propagate their faith in wild and savage lands. There was Father De Smet, for instance, who ascended the Missouri in 1840, and established a mission among the Flathead Indians. You should read his story. He crossed the Rockies, of course, to reach the Flathead country, and then he made a trip with my old friend, Hugh Monroe, among the Blackfeet on the east side of the Rockies, during which they had several narrow escapes from Assiniboin and Yanktonai war parties. But the Father found conditions unfavourable for founding a mission among the Blackfeet, for they were forever roaming over their vast hunting ground, one winter on the Saskatchewan, for instance, and the next far to the south on the tributaries of the Missouri or the Yellowstone.

Father Prando made me welcome; made me know that I was welcome, and I stopped with him for the night. We had supper; some yeast-powder biscuits, rancid bacon, some vile tea, no sugar. "It is all I have," he said, deprecatingly, "but what would you? I have given a little here, and a little there, and this is all that remains."

Even that was better than I had found for several days, and I ate a number of the biscuits. We began to talk about the starving Indians, and I learned with surprise and pleasure, that the good Father had been trying for some time to obtain relief for them. He had written to the authorities in Washington, without result. Then he had corresponded with the army officers at Fort Shaw, especially with Colonel—now General—Edward A. Maule, and they had accomplished something. Reporting to the War Department the condition of the Blackfeet, there had been a lively scene between the officials of that and the Indian Department, with the result that an inspector was to be sent out. He was supposed even then to be on his way. "And now," the good Father concluded, "it all depends upon the inspector. If he be honest, all will be well; if dishonest, then————" his voice trembled, and he could say no more.

It seemed that there was nothing more for me to do, so

I started homeward by way of the Agency. When
nearing the stockade, I met a policeman, and his face
was one big broad smile. "Yesterday," he told me,
"came a man from the home of the Great Father, and
we are saved. I carry this letter from him to the soldiers; they are to bring us food;" and with that he
hurried on.

Down at the trader's store (it contained about a
wagon load of goods) I at last got the details of all that
had happened. I am sure that never before, nor since,
has the Indian service had a more efficient man
than was Inspector, or Special Agent, G. Arrived at
the stockade, he had the driver stop just within the
gates. "Where is that chicken house?" he yelled,
jumping from the wagon and staring at the gaunt forms
of the Indians, standing apathetically around. The
driver pointed it out to him, and he ran and kicked open
the door, shoved the chickens out and piled out after
them several sacks of corn. "Here, you," he called to
the astonished spectators, "take these; take the chickens
and go and eat something."

If the Indians did not understand the words, they at
least understood his actions—and what a scramble
there was for grain and fleeing, squawking hens. The
Inspector hurried on across to the office, kicked open the
door and came face to face with the Agent, who had
arisen, and was staring at him in astonishment. "You
———— ———— canting old hypocrite," he cried, "I've
just given your Indians those chickens, and some Government corn. What do you mean by denying that your
charges are starving? Hey? What do you mean, sir?"

"They are not starving," the Agent replied. "I will
admit that they haven't a large ration, but they are not
starving by any means. Not starving by any means,

sir. But who are you, sir? What right have you, breaking in here and questioning me?"

"Here is my card," the Inspector replied "and I'll just add that I suspend you right now. Your goose is cooked."

The agent read the card and sank back into his chair, speechless.

The Inspector drew on the Fort Shaw commissary for what supplies could be spared, and bought more at Helena, but they were a long, long time in coming. Owing to the melting spring snow, the roads were almost impassable, so, still for a few weeks, Almost-a-dog kept cutting notches in his willow mortuary record, and at the end, after a bountiful supply of food had arrived and a new and kind and honest Agent was looking out for their welfare, the total numbered five hundred and fifty-five! Nearly one-fourth of the tribe had passed away. The living, weakened by their long privation, became an easy prey to tuberculosis in its various forms. To-day there are but thirteen hundred full-blooded Blackfeet, seven hundred less than there were in 1884. They are going fast; they might as well, for there is no place left for them to abide in even comparative prosperity and peace. Since 1884, they have sold three million dollars' worth of land, and the money has mostly been used to purchase for them food, farm machinery, and cattle. Under the few good Agents they have had they did remarkably well. For instance, under one Agent who served two terms, their cattle increased to something like twenty-four thousand head, for he allowed them to sell only steers and old dry cows. Under a succeeding Agent, however, their fine herd practically disappeared. Cows, calves, yearlings, were bought by the trader, rebranded and driven to his range in the vicinity of the Bear's Paw Mountains.   Also, the Reservation was always, except during the short administration of an army officer, over-run with the stock of the great cattle kings.   Their round-ups drove away many of the Indian stock, the vast number of steers they kept shoving upon the reserve caused the grass to become more and more sparse.   To-day, I am told, the range is about gone, and the Indians are about to receive their allotments of land.   When that happens and the surplus land is opened to settlement, the sheepmen will drive their flocks upon it, and thereafter the Blackfeet will be unable to raise either horses or cattle. In a very few years, those once richly grassed hills will become as bare of verdure as is the middle of a country road.

I could not help but go back to tell the good Father that his efforts to aid the Indians had proved more than successful, and thus I stayed another night with him. He told me of his work with the Crows, among whom he had been for several years, long enough, in fact, to learn their language.   Like most of those frontier Jesuits, he could do things: He had a good knowledge of medicine and surgery.   He could build a log cabin; repair a broken wagon wheel; survey and construct an irrigating ditch; and he was a successful fisherman and good shot.   I came across him one afternoon away down on Milk River.   He had been visiting some distant parishioners, and had tethered out his horses for a short rest.   He was broiling something over a small fire, and looking up, invited me to alight and eat with him. "It is a badger," he said, "that I have just killed."

"But," I expostulated, "they are not good to eat. I never heard of anyone eating badgers, did you?"

"My son," he replied, deliberately turning the meat over the glowing coals, "everything that God has made, has some use, if we could only discern it. This badger now, He made it; I am very hungry; therefore, I broil its meat—I killed it and it is mine—and I shall satisfy my hunger."

"But see here!" I went on, dismounting and sitting down by his fire, "When you are travelling around this way, why don't you have a well-filled 'grub' box in your wagon?"

"I had; there is the box, you see; but save for a little salt and pepper, it is now empty. The people I visited were very poor, and I gave them all."

There you have it in a word. They gave them *all*, those Jesuits of the frontier. All their strength and endurance, bodily and mental; gave even the necessities of life, in their zeal to "gather the heathen into the shelter of the Cross." This same man, at the age of sixty, have I not known him more than once to start out at dusk and drive all night through a forty-degrees-below blizzard, to reach the bedside of some dying Indian who had sent for him to administer the last sacrament!

"Mistaken zeal," "folly," many of us may say. Well, granting that, yet must we still regard with reverence and something akin to awe, the men who dare all things, endure all things, for the faith that is in their hearts.

But to continue my story: Arrived home, I stabled my horse, and went to my room to hang up my shaps and spurs. I found Nät-ah'-ki in bed, her eyes swollen with weeping; and when she saw me, she sprang up and clung to me crying: "They are dead, both dead! My daughter, my handsome daughter, Always Laughs; they two who loved each other so much, both are dead! Both drowned in the everywheres water." *

* *Mo-to-yi-awk-hi*—The Ocean

And then she told me, little by little, as she could between her fits of sobbing, of what Berry had read in the newspaper received that morning.   Ashton's boat had foundered in a great storm, and all on board were lost.   I sought out Berry, and he handed me the paper in silence. It was all too true.   We were never again to see Ashton and Diana.   Their yacht, and all it held, lay at the bottom of the Gulf of Mexico.

That was a sad time for us all.   Berry and his wife went to their room.   Old Mrs. Berry and the Crow Woman were mourning and crying, away down by the river.   I went back to comfort Nät-ah'-ki if I could, and the men cooked their supper.   I talked long, far into the night with the little woman, saying all I could, everything I could think of, to allay her grief—and my own too; but in the end, it was she who solved the problem, in a way.   I had thrown another chunk or two on the fire, and leaned back in my chair.   She had been silent some little time.   "Come here," she finally said. So I went over and sat down beside her, and she grasped my hand with her own trembling one.

"I have been thinking this," she began, falteringly; but her voice became firmer as she went on, "This: They died together, didn't they?   Yes.   I think that when they saw that they must drown, they clung to one another, and said a few words, if they had time, and even kissed each other, no matter if there were other people there.   That is what we would have done, is it not?"

"Yes."

"Well then," she concluded, "it isn't so bad as it might have been, for one was not left to mourn for the other.   We must all die sometime, but I think the Sun and the white man's God favour those whom—

loving each other as they did—they permit to die that way."

She got up, and removing from wall and shelf various little gifts Diana had given her, packed them carefully away in the bottom of a trunk. "I cannot bear to look at them now," she said sadly, "but some day, when I am more used to it, I will take them out and set them in their places."

She went back to bed and fell asleep, while I sat long after by the waning fire, thinking much upon her words. More and more, as the years went by, I realised that Nät-ah'-ki was—well, I'll not say what I thought. Perhaps some of you, of sympathetic nature, can fill in the blank.

It was several years before Diana's gifts again took their place in our abode to delight the eye and the mind of the dwellers therein. But many a time did I see Nät-ah'-ki quietly take a picture of her daughter from the trunk, and, after gazing at it lovingly, go away by herself to mourn.

CHAPTER XXXVII

THE very last of the buffalo herds disappeared in 1883. In the spring of 1884 a large flotilla of steamboats was tied up at the Fort Benton levee; among them the "Black Hills" and "Dacotah," boats of great size and carrying capacity. The latter came up but once in a season—when the Missouri was bank full from the melting snow in the mountains—and this was their last trip for all time to come. Not only was it the last trip for them, but for all the smaller boats. The railroad was coming. It had already crossed Dakota, and was creeping rapidly across the Montana plains. Tying up at night, using enormous quantities of wood fuel in order to overcome the swift current of the Missouri, the steamboats could not compete with the freight carrier of the rails.

When the railroad did finally enter the Rocky Mountain country, a branch running to Fort Benton, Great Falls, Helena, and Butte, the main line crossing the divide through the Two Medicine Pass, it brought in its coaches many immigrants from the "States," at whom the old-timers laughed. "What are they coming here for?" they asked. "What are they going to do—these hard-hatted men and delicate looking women?"

They soon found out. The new-comers settled here and there in the valleys, and took up the available water rights; they opened stores in the towns and crossroads places and reduced prices to a five-cent basis; they even gave exact change in pennies. Heretofore a spool of

411

thread, even a lamp-wick, had been sold for two bits. The old storekeepers and traders, with their easy, liberal ways, could not hold their own in this new order of things; they could not change their life-long habits, and one by one they went to the wall.

The men married to Indian women—squawmen, as they were contemptuously called—suffered most, and, strange to say, the wives of the new-comers, not the men, were their bitterest enemies. They forbade their children to associate with the half-breed children, and at school the position of the latter was unbearable. The white ones beat them and called them opprobrious names. This hatred of the squawman was even carried into politics. One of them, as clean-minded, genial, fearless, and honest a man as I ever knew, was nominated for sheriff of the county upon the party ticket which always carried the day; but at that election he and he alone of all the candidates of his party was not elected. He was actually snowed under. The white women had so badgered their husbands and brothers, had so vehemently protested against the election of a squawman to any office, that they succeeded in accomplishing his defeat. And so, one by one, these men moved to the only place where they could live in peace, where there was not an enemy within a hundred and more miles of them, the Reservation; and there they settled to pass their remaining days. There were forty-two of them at one time; few are left.

Let me correct the general impression of the squawmen, at least as to those I have known, the men who married Blackfeet women. In the days of the Indians' dire extremity, they gave them all they could, and were content so long as there remained a little bacon and flour for their families; and some days there was not even that in the houses of some of them for they had given their all. With the Indian they starved for a time, perchance. Scattered here and there upon the Reservation, they built for themselves neat homes and corrals, and fenced their hay lands, all of which was an object lesson to the Indian. But they did more than that. They helped to build their red neighbours' cabins and stables; surveyed their irrigating ditches; taught them how to plough, and to manage a mowing machine. All this without thought of pay or profit. If you enter the home of a Blackfoot, you nearly always find the floor clean, the windows spotless, everything about in perfect order, the sewing machine and table covered with pretty cloths; the bed with clean, bright-hued blankets; the cooking utensils and tableware spotless and bright. No Government field-matrons have taught them to do this, for they have had none. This they learned by observing the ways of the squawmen's wives. I have seen hundreds of white homes—there are numbers of them in any city—so exceedingly dirty, their inmates so slovenly, that one turns from them in absolute disgust; but I have seen nothing like that among the Blackfeet.

In their opulent days, under a good agent, and when they had numbers of steers to sell, they bought much furniture, even good carpets. There came to me one day at that time a friend, and we smoked together. "You have a book with pictures of furniture," he said, "show me the best bedstead it tells about."

I complied. "There it is," pointing to the cut. "All brass, best of springs; price $80."

"Send for it," he said, "I want it. It costs only two steers, and what is that?"

"There are others," I went on, "just as good looking, part iron, part brass, which cost much less."

"Huh!" he exclaimed. "Old Tail-feathers-coming-over-the-hill has one that cost fifty dollars. I'm going to have the best."

Without the squawman, I do not know what the Blackfeet would have done in the making of their treaties with the Government; in getting rid of agents, of whom the less said the better—for the squawman fought their battles and bore the brunt of all the trouble. I have known an agent to order his police to kill a certain squawman on sight, because the man had reported to Washington his thievery; and others to order squawmen to leave the Reservation, separating them from their families, because they had spoken too openly regarding certain underhand doings. But at intervals there **were** good, honest, capable men in charge, under whom **the** Indians regained in a measure the prosperity they had lost. But such men did not last; with a change of administration they were always dismissed by the powers that be.

One thing the squawmen never succeeded in doing— they were never able to rid the Reservation of the great cattle kings' stock. The big men had an "understanding" with some agents, and at other times with certain politicians of great influence. So their stock remained and increased and fed down the rich grasses. Most of the Indians and most of the squawmen carefully tended their little herds in some favourable locality as near as possible to their homes; but always, once in the spring, once in the fall, the great round-up of the cattle kings swept like wild fire across the Reservation. Thirty or forty swift riders would swoop down on one of these little herds. Some of their cattle would be mixed in with them; but they did not stop to cut them out; there wasn't time; and they drove them all to some distant point or branding corral, and the owner of the little herd lost forever more or less of them. At last, so I am told, the Indians prevailed upon the Department to fence the south and east sides of the Reservation in order to keep the foreign stock out, and their own inside. There was no need of fencing the west and north sides, for the Rocky Mountains form the western boundary, and the Canadian line the northern. It cost $30,000 to build that fence, and then the cattle kings obtained permission to pasture 30,000 head of cattle within it. But perhaps it is as well. It is only hastening the end a bit, for the Blackfeet, as I have said before, are to have their lands allotted. Then will come the sheepmen, desolation in their wake, and then the end. It has been nearly the end for them this past winter. The Department decreed that no able-bodied person should receive rations. In that bleak country there is no chance of obtaining work, for the white men's ranches are few and far between. Even if a man obtained three months' work in summer time—something almost impossible—his wages could not by any means support his family for a year. A friend wrote me in January: "I was over on the Reservation to-day and visited many old friends. In most of the homes there was little, generally no food, and the people were sitting sadly around the stove, drinking wild tea."

In the hegira of the old-timers to the Reservation, Berry and I took part. Fort Conrad had been sold. Berry bought out the Reservation trader, goodwill and goods, for three hundred dollars.

I got an insane idea in my head that I wanted to be a sheepman, and locating some fine springs and hay ground about twelve miles above Fort Conrad, I built some good sheds, and a house, and put up great stacks of hay. The cattlemen burned me out. I guess they did right, for I had located the only water for miles around.

I left the blackened ruins and followed Berry.   I am glad
that they did burn me out, for I thus can truthfully say
that I had no part in the devastation of Montana's once
lovely plains.

We built us a home, Nät-ah'-ki and I, in a lovely
valley where the grass grew green and tall.   We were
a long time building it.   Up in the mountains where I cut
the logs, our camp under the towering pines was so
pleasant that we could hardly leave it for a couple of
days to haul home a wagon-load of material.   And there
were so many pleasant diversions that the axe leaned up
against a stump during long dreamy days, while we went
trout fishing, or trailed a deer or bear, or just remained
in camp listening to the wind in the pine tops, watching
the squirrels steal the remains of our breakfast, or an
occasional grouse strutting by.

"How peaceful it all is here," Nät-ah'-ki once said,
"How beautiful the pines, how lovely and fragile the
things that grow in the damp and shadowy places.   And
yet, there is something fearsome about these great
forests.   My people seldom venture into them alone.
The hunters always go in couples or three or four together,
the women in large numbers when they come to cut
lodge poles, and their men always with them."

"But why are they afraid?" I asked.   "I don't see
why they should be."

"There are many reasons," she replied.   "Here an
enemy can easily lie in wait for one and kill without risk
to himself.   And then—and then they say that ghosts
live in these long, wide, dark woods; that they follow a
hunter, or steal along by his side or in front of him; that
one knows they are about, for they sometimes step on a
stick which snaps, or rustle some loose leaves with their
feet.   Some men, it is said, have even seen these ghosts

peering at them from behind a distant tree. They had terrible, big, wide faces, and big, wicked eyes. Sometimes I even have thought that I was being followed by them. But, though I was terribly afraid, I have just kept on going, away down there to the spring for water. It is when you are away off there chopping and the blows of your axe cease, that I am most afraid. I stop and listen; if you begin to chop again soon, then all is well, and I go on with my work. But if there is a long silence then I begin to fear, I know not what; everything; the dim shadowy places away out around; the wind in the tree-tops which seems to be saying something I cannot understand. Oh, I become afraid, and I steal out to see if you are still there—if anything has happened to you——"

"Why—how is that?" I interposed, "I never saw you."

"No, you didn't see me. I went very quietly, very cautiously, just like one of those ghosts they talk about; but I always saw you. You would be sitting on a log, or lying on the ground, smoking, always smoking, and then I would be satisfied, and go back as quietly as I came."

"But when you came out that way, why didn't you come further and sit down and talk with me?" I asked.

"Had I done so," she replied, "you would have sat still longer idle, smoked more, and talked of those things you are ever dreaming and thinking about. Don't you know that the summer is nearly gone? And I do so much want to see that house built. I want to have a home of my own."

Thereupon I would for a time wield the axe with more vigour, and then again there would be a reaction—more days of idleness, or of wandering by the stream, or on the grim mountain slopes. But before snow came we had our modest home built and furnished, and were content.

It was the following spring that Nät-ah'-ki's mother died, after a very short illness. After the body had been wrapped with many a blanket and robe and securely bound with rawhide thongs, I was told to prepare a coffin for it. There was no lumber for sale within a hundred and fifty miles, but the good Jesuits, who had built a mission nearby, generously gave me the necessary boards and I made a long, wide box more than three feet in height. Then I asked where the grave should be dug. Nät-ah'-ki and the mourning relatives were horrified. "What," the former cried "bury mother in a hole in the dark, heavy, cold ground?

"No! our Agent has forbidden burials in trees, but he has said nothing about putting our dead in coffins on the top of the ground. Take the box up on the side of the hill where lie the remains of Red Eagle, of other relatives, and we will follow with all the rest in the other wagon."

I did as I was told, driving up the valley a half-mile or so, then turning up on the slope where lay half a dozen rude coffins side by side on a small level place. Removing the box from the wagon, I placed it at some little distance from the others and with pick and spade made an absolutely level place for it. Then came the others, a number of friends and relatives, even three men, also relatives of the good woman. Never before nor since have I known men to attend a funeral. They always remained in their lodges and mourned; so this was even greater proof of the love and esteem in which Nät-ah'-ki's mother had been held.

Nät-ah'-ki, from the moment her mother had died, had neither slept nor partaken of food, crying, crying

all the time. And now she insisted that none but she
and I should perform the last ceremonies. We carried
the tightly wrapped body and laid it in the big box, very
carefully and tenderly you may be sure, and then placed
at the sides and feet of it various little buckskin sacks,
small parfleche pouches, containing needles, awls,
thread and all the various implements and trinkets
which she had kept and guarded so carefully. I raised
and placed in position the two boards forming the cover.
Everyone was now crying, even the men. I held a nail
in position, and drove it partly down. How dreadfully
they sounded, the hammer blows hollowly, loudly rever-
berating from the big, half-empty box. I had kept up
thus far pretty well, but the cold, harsh, desecrating
hammering unnerved me. I tossed the implement
away, sat down, and in spite of all my efforts to control
myself, I cried with the rest. "I cannot do it," I said,
over and over, "I cannot drive those nails."

Nät-ah'-ki came and sat down, leaned on my shoulder
and reached out her trembling hands for mine.

"Our mother!" she said, "Our mother! just think;
we shall never, never see her again. Oh, why must she
have died while she had not even begun to grow old?"

One of the men stepped forward, "Go you two home,"
he said, "I will nail the boards."

So, in the gathering dusk, Nät-ah'-ki and I drove
home, unhitched the horses and turned them loose;
and then entering the silent house we went to bed. The
Crow Woman, always faithful and kind, came later, and
I heard her build a fire in the kitchen stove. Presently
she brought in a lamp, then some tea and a few slices of
bread and meat. Nät-ah'-ki was asleep; bending over
me she whispered; "Be more than ever kind to her now,
my son. Such a good mother as she had! There was

not one quite so good in all the earth; she will miss her so much. You must now be to her both her man and mother."

"I will," I replied, taking her hand. "You know that I will," whereupon she passed as silently out of the room and out of the house as she had come. It was a long, long time though before Nät-ah'-ki recovered her naturally high spirits, and even years afterward she would awake me in the night, crying, to talk about her mother.

.   .   .   .

Since the rails of the great road had crossed the land which Big Lake had said should never be desecrated by fire-wagons, I thought that we might as well ride upon them, but it was some time before I could persuade Nät-ah'-ki to do so. But at last she fell grievously ill, and I prevailed on her to see a famous physician who lived in a not far distant city, a man who had done much for me, and of whose wonderful surgical work I never tired telling, So, one morning we took seats in the rear Pullman of a train and started, Nät-ah'-ki sitting by the open window. Presently we came to a bridge spanning an exceedingly deep cañon, and looking down she gave a little cry of surprise, and terror, dropped to the floor and covered her face with her hands. I got her back on the seat, but it was some time before she recovered her composure. "It looked so awfully far down there," she said, "and supposing the bridge had broken, we would all have been killed."

I assured her that the bridges could not break, that the men who built them knew just how much they could hold up, and that was more than could be loaded on a train. Thenceforth she had no fear and loved the swift glide of a train, her favourite place in suitable weather being a seat out on the rear platform of the last Pullman.

We hadn't been on the train fifteen minutes when I suddenly realised something that I had never thought of before. Glancing at the women seated here and there, all of them dressed in neat and rich fabrics, some of them wearing gorgeous hats, I saw that Nät-ah'-ki was not in their class so far as wearing apparel was concerned. She wore a plain gingham dress, and carried a shawl and a sun-bonnet, all of which were considered very "swell" up on the Reservation, and had been so regarded in the days of the buffalo traders at Fort Benton. To my surprise, some of these ladies in the car came to talk with Nät-ah'-ki, and said many kind things to her. And the little woman was highly pleased, even excited by their visits. "Why," she said to me in surprise, "I did not think that white women would speak to me. I thought they all hated an Indian woman."

"Many do," I answered, "but they are not women of this class. There are women, and women. My mother is like these you have spoken to. Did you notice their dresses?" I added. "Well, so you must dress. I am glad that we arrive in the city at night. You shall be dressed like them before we go to the hospital."

Our train pulled into the city on time, and I hurried Nät-ah'-ki into a cab, and thence to the side entrance of a hotel, thence upstairs to a room which I had telegraphed for. It was a Saturday night and the stores were still open. I found a saleswoman in a department store to accompany me to the hotel and take Nät-ah'-ki's measure. In a little while we had her fitted out with waists and skirts, and a neat travelling coat. How pleased she was with them, and how proud I was of her. There was nothing, I thought, good enough to clothe that true and tried little body, whose candour, and gentleness, and innate refinement of mind were mirrored in her eyes.

We had dinner in our room. I suddenly remembered that I had not thought of one article of costume, a hat, and out I went to get it. In the lobby of the hotel I met an artist friend, and besought his aid in selecting the important gear. We looked at about five hundred, I thought, and at last decided upon a brown velvet thing with a black feather. We took it up to the room and Nät-ah'-ki tried it on. " 'Twas too small," we all declared, so back we went after another one. There didn't seem to be any larger ones, and we were discouraged. "They don't fit down," I told the woman, "can't be made to fit like this," raising my hat and jamming it down in place. The woman looked at me in astonishment. "Why, my dear sir!" she exclaimed, "Women do not wear their hats that way. They place them lightly on the top of the head, and secure them there with large pins, hat pins, running through the hair."

"Oh, I see," I said. "That's the way, is it? Well, give us back the hat and some pins, and we'll be fixed this time, sure."

But we weren't. Nät-ah'-ki wore her hair in two long braids, tied together and hanging down her back. There was no way of skewering that hat on, unless she wore her hair pompadour, or whatever you call it, bunched up on top of the head, you know, and of course she wouldn't do that. Nor did I wish her to; I liked to see those great heavy braids falling down, away down below the waist.

"I have it," said my friend, who had ridden some himself—in fact, had been a noted cowpuncher—"we'll just get a piece of rubber elastic sewed on, like the string on a sombrero. That will go under the braids, close to the skin, and there you are."

The store was just closing when I finally got the elastic, some thread and needles, and Nät-ah'-ki sewed it on. The hat stayed. One could hardly knock it off. Tired and thirsty, the artist and I withdrew in search of a long, fizzing drink, and Nät-ah'-ki went to bed. I found her wide awake when I returned. "Isn't this splendid!" she exclaimed, "everything as one could wish it. You merely push a little black thing and someone comes up to wait on you, to bring you your dinner, or water, or whatever you want. You turn faucets, and there is your water. With one turn you make the lightning-lamps burn, or go out. It is wonderful, wonderful. I could live here very happily."

"Is it better than the neat lodge we had, when we travelled about, when we camped right here where this city stands and hunted buffalo?"

"Oh, no, no," she cried, "it is not like those dear, dead, past times. But they are gone. Since we must travel the white man's road, as the chiefs say, let us take the best we can find along the way, and this is very nice."

In the morning we drove to the hospital, and took the elevator to the floor and room assigned to us. Nät-ah'-ki was put to bed by the Sisters, with whom she immediately became infatuated. Then came the doctor. "It is he," I told her, "the one who saved me."

She rose up in bed and grasped one of his hands in both her own. "Tell him," she said, "that I will be good and patient. That no matter how bad his medicines taste, I will take them, that no matter how much he hurts me, I will not cry out. Tell him I wish to get well quickly, so I can walk around, and do my work, and be happy and healthy once more."

"It is nothing organic," said the doctor. "It does not even need the knife. A week in bed, some medicine, and she can go home as well as ever."

This was pleasing news to Nät-ah'-ki, when she came to her senses. The chloroform did not even make her ill, and she was as cheerful as a lark from morning until night. The Sisters and nurses were always coming in to talk and joke with her, and when I was not on hand to interpret, they still seemed to understand one another, Nät-ah'-ki in some way making her thoughts known. One could hear her cheery laughter ringing out of the room and down the hall at almost any hour of day.

"Never in my life," said the Sister Superior, "have I known such another cheerful, innocent, happy woman. You are a lucky man, sir, to have such a wife."

Then came the happy day when we could set out for home again. We went, and for a long time Nät-ah'-ki talked of the wonderful things she had seen. Her faith in the Blackfoot men and women doctors was shattered, and she did not hesitate to say so. She told of the wonderful way in which her doctor had cut patients in the hospital and made them well; of his wonderful lightning-lamp (X-ray), with which one's bones, the whole skeleton, could be seen through the flesh. The whole tribe became interested and came from far and near to listen. After that, many a suffering one went to the great hospital and to her doctor, no matter what their ailment, in full faith that they would be cured.

On our homeward way, I remember, we saw a man and two women loading a hay wagon, the man on top of the load, the women sturdily pitching up great forkfuls of hay to him, regardless of the extreme heat of the day. The little woman was astonished, shocked. "I did not think," she said, "that white men would so abuse their women. A Blackfoot would not be so cruel. I begin to think that white women have a much harder time than we do."

"You are right," I told her, "most poor white women are slaves; they have to get up at three or four o'clock in the morning, cook three meals a day, make, mend, and wash their children's clothes, scrub floors, work in the garden, and when night comes they have hardly strength left to crawl to bed. Do you think you could do all that?"

"No," she replied, "I could not. I wonder if that is not why some white women so dislike us, because they have to work so dreadfully hard, while we have so much time to rest, or go visiting, or ride around here and there on the beautiful plains. Surely our life is happier than theirs, and you, oh, lucky was the day when you chose me to be your little woman."

.   .   .   .

The years passed happily for Năt-ah'-ki and me. We had a growing bunch of cattle which were rounded-up with the other Reservation stock twice a year. I built two small irrigating ditches and raised some hay. There was little work to do, and we made a trip somewhere every autumn, up into the Rockies with friends, or took a jaunt by rail to some distant point. Sometimes we would take a skiff and idly drift and camp along the Missouri for three or four hundred miles below Fort Benton, returning home by rail. I think that we enjoyed the water trips the best. The shifting, boiling flood, the weird cliffs, the beautifully timbered, silent valley had a peculiar fascination for us such as no place in the great mountains possessed. It was during one of these river trips that Năt-ah'-ki began to complain of sharp pain in the tips of her right hand fingers. "It is nothing but rheumatism," I said, "and will soon pass away."

But I was wrong. The pain grew worse, and abandoning our boat at the mouth of Milk River, we took the first train for the city where our doctor lived, and once more found ourselves in the hospital, in the very same room; the same good Sisters and nurses surrounding Nät-ah'-ki and trying to relieve her of the pain, which was now excruciating. The doctor came, felt her pulse, got out his stethoscope and moved it from place to place until, at last, it stopped at a point at the right side of the neck, close to the collar bone. There he listened long, and I began to feel alarmed. "It is not rheumatism," I said to myself. "Something is wrong with her heart."

The doctor gave some directions to the nurse; then turning to Nät-ah'-ki he said, "Take courage, little friend, we'll pull you through all right."

Nät-ah'-ki smiled. Then she grew drowsy under the influence of an opiate; and we left the room.

"Well, old man," said the doctor, "this time I can do little. She may live a year, but I doubt it."

For eleven months we all did what we could, and then one day, my faithful, loving, tender-hearted little woman passed away, and left me. By day I think about her, at night I dream of her. I wish that I had that faith which teaches us that we will meet again on the other shore. But all looks very dark to me.